ENCOURAGEMENT
FOR TODAY'S
PASTORS

ENCOURAGEMENT FOR TODAY'S PASTORS

Help from the Puritans

Joel R. Beeke
and
Terry Slachter

Reformation Heritage Books
Grand Rapids, Michigan

Reformation Heritage Books
2965 Leonard St. NE
Grand Rapids, MI 49525
616-977-0889 / Fax 616-285-3246
orders@heritagebooks.org
www.heritagebooks.org

Printed in the United States of America
13 14 15 16 17 18/10 9 8 7 6 5 4 3 2 1

The authors wish to thank Annette Gysen, Rev. Ray Lanning, Rev. Paul Smalley, Phyllis TenElshof, and Irene VandenBerg for their valuable assistance on this book.

Library of Congress Cataloging-in-Publication Data

Beeke, Joel R., 1952-
  Encouragement for today's pastors : help from the Puritans / Joel R. Beeke and Terry Slachter.
     pages cm
  Includes bibliographical references.
  ISBN 978-1-60178-220-5 (pbk. : alk. paper) 1. Clergy—Psychology.
2. Clergy—Religious life. 3. Puritans—History. 4. Clergy—Counseling of.
5. Clergy—Job stress. I. Title.
  BV4398.B44 2013
  253'.2—dc23
                              2012048363

For additional Reformed literature, request a free book list from Reformation Heritage Books at the above regular or e-mail address.

In memory of six wise ruling elders
who have been great friends
and Puritan-like sources of encouragement
for me in my pastoral ministry:

Bert Harskamp
Gordon Deur
Henry Langerak
Peter Vander Jagt
Peter Van Kempen
Uncle Richard Westrate

I count it one of life's greatest honors and joys
to have served Christ's church with these godly
"Barnabases" (consolers or encouragers),
who have often cheered and upheld my weary soul
as faithful "Aarons" and "Hurs" (Exodus 17:12).

—JRB

* * *

To the congregation of

East Leonard Church
Grand Rapids, Michigan

who have encouraged me in ministry
for the past ten years
through their practical support,
patient love,
and persistent intercession.

—TS

Contents

Introduction 1

Part One: Piety

1. Zeal for the Ministry of the Word..................... 17
2. "In Sweet Communion, Lord, with Thee" 25
3. Encouraged by God's Promises........................ 38

Part Two: Sovereignty

4. God Gives the Increase............................... 51
5. Submission to God's Will............................. 65

Part Three: Clarity

6. Taking Heed to Doctrine 79
7. Practicing What Is Preached 93
8. The Calling of the Shepherd.......................... 107

Part Four: Creativity and Community

9. History and Science 121
10. The Communion of Saints 132
11. A Cloud of Witnesses 141

Part Five: Dignity

12. "One among a Thousand" 153

13. Doing the Work of Angels 162

14. The Urgency and Importance of Preaching the Word...... 171

Part Six: Eternity

15. The Reward of Grace................................. 187

16. The Glories of Heaven............................... 197

Epilogue..209

Introduction

In the United States today, fifteen hundred pastors leave their churches each month due to conflict, burnout, or moral failure, according to ChristianityToday.com. Of the pastors serving churches, 23 percent have previously been fired or forced out of a pulpit, and 34 percent currently serve a congregation that forced its previous pastor to leave.[1] The problem seems to cut across all denominations. Some studies suggest that the average tenure of a pastor in a church in the United States is about three or four years.[2]

Another study, done by the Lutheran Church-Missouri Synod, found that 80 percent of its pastors who left churches did so because of behavioral problems in the church. Alan and Cheryl Klaas, who investigated the problem in the Lutheran Church, began their study with the expectation of finding that the problem lay in the training of the pastors: "We wondered if students got good services, if seminaries were recruiting the right people." However, they said in conclusion, "The fundamental finding is that people beating on each other is the main issue."

---

1. Ken Sande, "Strike the Shepherd: Losing Pastors in the Church," *Peacemaker Ministries,* http://www.peacemaker.net/site/apps/nlnet/content3.aspx?c=aqKFLTOBIp H&b=1084263&ct=1245867#4 (accessed January 9, 2012); John C. LaRue Jr. "Forced Exits: A Too-Common Ministry Hazard," *ChristianityToday.com* (February 14, 2009), http://www.christianitytoday.com/cbg/more/specialreport/6y2072.html (accessed January 9, 2012).

2. Rob Green, "Passing the Baton: A Theological and Practical Look at Pastoral Turnover," *Journal of Ministry and Theology* 10, no. 1 (Spring 2006): 54.

In the 1950s and 1960s, the Klaases said, 40 percent of Lutheran seminarians came from pastors' families. Today one Lutheran seminary reported that only 5 percent of its students come from pastors' families, and other seminaries said only 17 percent of their students come from pastors' families.[3]

The problem of pastors burning out, dropping out, or being driven out is also evident in other countries. In Australia, for example, four books were published in five years about clergy problems. The titles are telling: *The Plight of the Australian Clergy, High Calling, High Stress, Battle Guide for Christian Leaders—An Endangered Species,* and *Conflict and Decline.*[4]

So what is going on? Why are so many pastors leaving churches or even the ministry itself? Kevin Miller lists five typical cries of discouraged pastors:

1. "I cannot see any progress in my work."
2. "I cannot do what I'm truly gifted to do."
3. "Some difficult members are causing me pain."
4. "I don't get affirmation for what I do."
5. "I don't get enough rest and relaxation."[5]

Causes of Pastoral Discouragement

Archibald Hart suggests that several factors contribute to pastoral depression and burnout. First, the ministry is a people-oriented calling to lead a group of volunteers. A pastor cannot avoid problems such as troublesome personalities, interpersonal conflicts, and resulting frustrations in meeting his goals. Second, a minister's work

---

3. Alan C. Klaas and Cheryl D. Klaas, *Quiet Conversations: Concrete Help for Weary Ministry Leaders* (Kansas City, Mo.: Mission Growth Publications, 2000).

4. Norman W. H. Blaikie, *Plight of the Australian Clergy: To Convert, Care or Challenge?* (St. Lucia: University of Queensland Press, 1979); Robin J. Pryor, *High Calling, High Stress* (Bedford Park, S. Aust.: Uniting Church of Australia, Synod of Victoria, 1982); Cedric Taylor and Graeme Goldsworthy, *Battle Guide for Christian Leaders: An Endangered Species* (Cudgen, N.S.W.: Wellcare Publications, 1981); Kenneth Dempsey, *Conflict and Decline: Ministers and Laymen in an Australian Country Town* (North Ryde: Methuen, Australia, 1983).

5. Kevin A. Miller, *Secrets of Staying Power: Overcoming the Discouragements of Ministry* (Carol Stream: Ill.: Christianity Today, 1988), 48–49.

does not have clear boundaries. Feeling they can never complete any one task creates a lot of stress for pastors. Third, pastoral ministry lacks criteria for measuring success, yet most ministers (disclaimers aside) long to see tangible results of their work. Yet setting numerical goals in ministry is like grasping at the wind. Fourth, congregational expectations for a pastor are often unrealistically high. This not only sets up a minister for failure in meeting everyone's expectations but also tends to make him a people-pleaser.

Fifth, problems in a pastor's character, such as perfectionism, laziness, authoritarianism, or a victim mentality may exacerbate difficulties in church leadership. Sixth, many ministers come to a church with extremely idealistic anticipations. The idealism of youth combined with high spiritual aspirations can lead to grave disappointments if adjustments are not made in the first years of ministry. Seventh, many pastors feel guilty about their limitations, emotional ups and downs, and weaknesses.[6]

Some churches can be very hard on pastors. Matthew Henry (1662–1714) preached a funeral sermon for a young pastor who hadn't been at his church very long. Learning this was the second pastor within a short time to die while serving this congregation, Henry was moved to warn the people in the pews:

> God has a controversy with you [in] this place, of this congregation, from the head of which two such eminently useful men have been removed in so short a time, in both of whom you thought you had goods laid up for many years. He has a controversy with us who are ministers: for whereby our hands are very much weakened, and our glory is waxen thin.... The putting out of our candles is a bad omen of the removal of our candlestick; it is, at least, a call to us, to remember whence we are fallen, and repent, lest it be removed.[7]

6. Archibald D. Hart, *Coping with Depression in the Ministry and Other Helping Professions* (Waco, Tex.: Word Books, 1984), 115–25.

7. Matthew Henry, "A Sermon Preached at the Funeral of the Dr. Samuel Benion," in *The Complete Works of Matthew Henry* (1855; repr., Grand Rapids: Baker, 1979), 1:569.

Pastors must also realize that the world at large is no friend to gospel ministry. A century ago Christianity was well respected in our country. Even then, however, the world saved its broadest smiles for a nominal Christianity that did not threaten its idols or interfere with its pleasures. Today, in an increasingly secular, re-paganized, and, some say, post-Christian culture, ministers soon realize that the world's standards of success do not apply to the ministry. Pastors whose self-esteem is based upon meeting specific goals, such as increasing the number of people on membership rolls or attracting large numbers of people to worship services; garnering respect and attaining social prominence based on their position in a certain church; or peddling Christian novelties and pandering to Christian fads soon find that gospel ministry does not fulfill their ambitions. In addition, pastors who seek popularity especially among young people by being chic ("hipper than thou") and culturally accommodating will soon find that such recognition is hollow as well as fleeting. Still more tragic is the plight of those who reduce the Christian faith to a money-making racket. Matthew Henry warned ministers of his day about setting such false goals:

> They who deal in secular business, think they succeed well and gain their point, if they raise an estate, and advance their families, and make to themselves a name among the great ones of the earth; they rejoice because their wealth is great, and their hand has gotten much, and say, "Soul, take thine ease." But the ministry, though it is the best calling, is the worst trade, in the world; that is, it will prove so to those who make a mere trade of it, looking no further than to get money by it, and to enrich themselves.[8]

"Hold Fast"

There are also several factors in our current spiritual environment that drain a pastor's vital zeal for ministry. We must oppose these forces with the grace of our Lord. Hebrews 4:14 says, "Seeing then that we have a great high priest, that is passed into the heavens, Jesus the Son of God, let us hold fast our profession."

---

8. Matthew Henry, "A Sermon Concerning the Work and Success of the Ministry," in *Works*, 1:471.

What are these pressures? Some of us find ourselves in denominations where the standards of doctrine are being downgraded. We find ourselves in situations in which we must decide when and where to make a stand. The counsel of God's Holy Word is to hold fast to the solid truths of the Word of God. God's Word is truth, be it the written Word we know as the Bible, or the incarnate Word, Jesus Christ.

Some of us face opposition, perhaps from peers within our own denomination or from members in the pew who want us to join them in abandoning the historic doctrines of Reformation Christianity or to downplay the necessity to experience those doctrines in a personal and spiritual way. Brothers, we are called to "hold fast our profession" and the profession of our forefathers. A Christianity that is only a vague theory about the nature of things or a program for personal improvement and/or the amelioration of social evils is really no threat to the world or anything like "the power of God unto salvation."

Some of us are confronted with a cult of man-made traditions or a demand for trendy innovations in church life and worship. Such man-made imperatives bear down upon us, clinging to stagnation or calling for change. We are commanded to resist such ungodly demands as part of holding fast our profession of faith in the God who has commanded us to worship Him in the way appointed in His Word.

Some of us labor in situations where little growth is evident, numerical or spiritual. We are confronted with a painful lack of practical godliness and hunger for communion with God. We are confronted daily with unbelief, with apathy, with ignorance, with spiritual deadness, or with man-centered worldliness. Such signs of spiritual declension are enough to crush the soul of any servant of God and bring us to tears of sorrow and grief. Yet the call comes to us to "hold fast our profession," even in an evil day. Though we have to labor in churches in which very few members "pray their pastors full so that they may preach them full" (as some old Dutch pastors used to say), we are called to "hold fast our profession."

We are called to labor in the midst of the moral climate of a nation in which humanism is dominant, in which there is little regard for the holiness of God's name, the authority of His Word, or the demands of His law. Many are such fools as to say that there is no God

(Ps. 14:1); there is no fear of God before their eyes (Ps. 36:1), and God is not in all their thoughts (Ps. 10:4). God's kingdom does not come as we would have it. His revealed will is contradicted without shame or embarrassment, even among professing Christians. When we are discouraged and ask with Isaiah, "Who hath believed our report? and to whom is the arm of the LORD revealed?" (Isa. 53:1), we are called to "hold fast our profession."

When these discouragements take an inward turn, we must redouble our efforts to persevere. Perhaps we are burdened with overwork. We labor under the endless demands of pastoral counseling, church administration, and sermon preparation. We may work through the week but come to the Lord's Day still feeling woefully unprepared to preach the Word and find ourselves exhausted at the end of the "day of rest." Here too we are called to "hold fast our profession." We may find our souls in agony and yearn to see broken human beings brought to faith and restored after the image of Christ. When we say with Moses that our hands grow heavy in intercession (Ex. 17:12) and confess with the apostle Paul, "I travail in birth again until Christ be formed in you" (Gal. 4:19), we are called to "hold fast our profession."

Some of us are crippled by debilitating loneliness—perhaps having no congenial or like-minded colleagues in our locality. Maybe we feel deprived of kindred spirits who share our longing for the vital, experiential reality of the doctrines of grace we proclaim. Then too we are called "to hold fast our profession." To be a minister of the gospel in our day is often to tread a lonely path. In 1989 a hundred different occupations were surveyed and rated in terms of loneliness, and the second-loneliest job on the list was that of minister of the Word. Number one was a night watchman. Doesn't that tell us something? We are performing a lonely task, as men who watch for the souls of others, but even then the call comes: "Hold fast." Our Great High Priest, Jesus Christ, went alone to tread the winepress of the wrath of God on our behalf.

Some of us labor in the midst of strife and disunity within our own flocks. A minority of vocal members spreads foolish accusations and slanderous gossip that wound our fellow Christians, divide our churches, and grieve our souls. The group of critics perhaps is small as a percentage of the congregation, but the damage they do is disproportionately large. James Sparks wrote a book about such people and the evil they do, titled *Potshots at the Preacher.*[9]

Isn't that what goes on many times? You feel that there are people in the church who are angling to get you. They cause you great grief. They provoke a tendency to defensiveness in you. They engender bitterness within your soul. They force you into situations sometimes where it seems whatever you say or do will land you in trouble. And again, the advice is draw near to the throne of grace to obtain mercy and find grace to help you in your time of need, and hold fast your profession.

Then again, some of us are discouraged because we feel the withdrawing of the presence of God in our soul's consciousness for no apparent reason. Or perhaps after tackling important assignments or just before we have to preach under difficult circumstances, we may be assailed with temptations to doubt and distrust or by thoughts of our inadequacies and failures. When wave after wave of providential affliction breaks on our heads, even then the apostle says, "Hold fast your profession."

Perhaps more than anything else, some of us are discouraged on account of our own weak spiritual condition. Deep within we know that we resist having to deny ourselves, take up our cross, and follow Christ. We don't wrestle as we should against our own inward corruption. We are too comfortable with our natural self-centeredness. We tell ourselves that we deserve better treatment. In 1651, some Scottish ministers spoke for all of us when they confessed their "exceeding great selfishness in all that we do; acting from ourselves, for ourselves, and to ourselves."[10]

We are too unacquainted with ourselves, and so we are estranged from God. We study more to learn the right words to say than to experience spiritual realities as we should. We drink too much from human cisterns rather than draw water from the divine well. We are prone to wander from our Shepherd; we are prone to rest too little in God. Filled with ourselves, distracted by the cares of this life, or

---

9. James A. Sparks, *Potshots at the Preacher* (Nashville: Abingdon, 1977).
10. Horatius Bonar, *Words to the Winners of Souls* (Boston: American Tract Society, n.d.), 47.

enticed by the deceitfulness of riches, we have little hunger or thirst for the living God.

Our private lives sometimes contradict our ministerial lives; we are more holy in the pulpit than we are in private. This inconsistency wears away at our spiritual sensitivities, and deep within we are discouraged by ourselves and with ourselves. We know that we have abandoned the simplicity of faith. We have abandoned the godly concern we ought to have for the welfare of our flock, for the glory of the name of God. When the tide of unbelief sweeps in, we begin to excuse our unbelief more as an affliction to be pitied than a crime to be condemned and a sin to be repented of. We turn our unbelief into an excuse for self-indulgence, and before we know it, our ministries revolve around ourselves rather than God. We are our own greatest discouragements, our own greatest obstacles.

Under such conditions, where do servants of the Lord look for strength? Most fundamentally, you will find your strength in God's Word, "which is able to build you up," even in the midst of dissension in the church (Acts 20:32). Here in the Word we hear our Great High Priest speaking the words of eternal life (Heb. 4:14–16). Grace has been poured into His lips (Ps. 45:2). At the same time, His arrows are sharp when aimed at the target of the sins that live in our hearts (Ps. 45:5).

Here in Christ we find the intercessor who is fully competent to meet our every need. As William Symington observed, Christ is a skillful intercessor who knows God and us perfectly and thus can plead for us in accordance with both God's law and our needs. His intercession is marked by moral purity and absolute righteousness, pleasing in every way to the Judge of all the earth. Christ is a compassionate intercessor, "able to enter into their feelings, and to make their case his own." His intercession is prompt and timely, obtaining grace just at the point in the crisis when we most need it. He is an earnest intercessor, who presents His petitions for us with warmth and fervor. Christ intercedes with authority, as once licensed and authorized by God to obtain mercy for His own. He is unique as the Mediator who alone atones for sin and obtains all the graces of the covenant. Christ is a prevailing intercessor whose Father always hears Him. And He is a constant intercessor who never ceases to watch over us with His full energy.[11] Jesus Christ, who is "the same yesterday, and to day, and for ever" (Heb. 13:8), will be your anchor when you begin to slip away, your friend when you are have to stand alone, and your helper when your situation appears helpless. Therefore, go to the throne of grace.

The Scriptures advise us to learn from examples of faithful ministers (Heb. 13:7). The Puritans of seventeenth-century Britain are a body of such ministers, whose teaching and living can be particularly encouraging to troubled and discouraged pastors today. They were steadfast in adhering to Scripture as the Word of God, in confessing the great truths of the Reformed faith, and in applying sound doctrine to the problems of life in an age and culture with many parallels to our own.

Why the Puritans?

Some may object to using the Puritans as models, saying, "Those pastors didn't have to deal with the demanding people of today! They knew nothing about constantly being on call in a 24/7 culture. They had no Internet, iPods, or cell phones to interrupt their sermon preparation, family time, or private devotions." Others argue that the Puritans were negative killjoys who found sin in everything and everyone, constantly harping on the depravity of man. Still others will insist that people today wouldn't tolerate listening to hour-long Puritan sermons or endure a series on a book of the Bible that took years to complete.

Perhaps an abbreviated course on "Puritanism 101" is needed before we move on. *Puritan* was originally a pejorative term. It was used to compare conscientious Christians who sought to bring all of life under the Word of God to the heretical, ascetic medieval sect known as the *Cathari* ("pure ones"). In other words, the term was meant as an accusation that these Christians were too zealous for purity and too precise in their religion. It also implied they were fanatical and could never have fun. *Puritan* was first used in Britain in the 1560s for people who sought to press the reformation of the church's doctrine, worship, and government farther than Queen

---

11. William Symington, *On the Atonement and Intercession of Jesus Christ* (New York: Robert Carter, 1847), 284–96.

Elizabeth I, who reigned from 1558 to 1603, deemed necessary. The name stuck and came to denote a host of faithful ministers and lay-people who, in the face of opposition and persecution, stood for the Christianity of the Bible for many generations. Though caricatures of the Puritans persist today, in reality they were humble Christians who loved Christ and sought to glorify God by obeying His Word in all areas of life: personal, domestic, social, vocational, ecclesiastical, and national.

Puritanism continued under the reigns of James I (1603–1625) and Charles I (1625–1649). The Puritans rose to power in the era of the Commonwealth and Protectorate (1649–1660) and persisted during the reigns of Charles II (1660–1685), James II (1685–1688), and William of Orange (1688–1702). They suffered persecution, however, particularly under Charles I and Charles II, who arrested, imprisoned, fined, maimed, hanged, or exiled them for their convictions. Persecution under Charles I motivated many Puritans to colonize New England. Charles II ejected two thousand Puritan ministers from the Church of England for refusing to submit to the Act of Uniformity (1662). Later writers such as Jonathan Edwards (1703–1758) were Puritan at heart but are not usually included by scholars in the historical Puritan movement of the late sixteenth and seventeenth centuries. It should also be noted that the Puritans had many like-minded brethren in other countries, such as Scotland and the Netherlands.

Though it is difficult to define Puritanism, we may outline its main traits and emphases. In 1628 Scottish historian David Calderwood (1575–1650) described Puritanism as a movement characterized by (1) opposition to unbiblical hierarchy in the authority structures of the church; (2) advocacy of the Reformed doctrines of God's sovereign grace; (3) refusal to conform to any requirement in worship not commanded in Scripture; (4) the cherishing of personal, experiential religion of the heart and not merely outward religiosity; and (5) separation from popular sins with an insistence on walking according to God's laws in every area of life.[12]

---

12. David Calderwood, *The Pastor and the Prelate* (1628; repr., Philadelphia: Samuel Agnew, 1844), 64.

In 1646 Englishman John Geree (c. 1601–1649) described the ideal "Old English Puritan" as a person who "honored God above all, and under God gave every one his due." He believed Scripture alone should direct worship. He devoted himself to prayer in private, in family worship, and in public worship. The ideal Puritan valued reading Scripture in private and public, but he also esteemed the preaching of the Word as one of God's most powerful instruments. Specifically, he recommended preaching that avoided "vain flourishes of wit" while plainly and clearly declaring the contents of Scripture and applying them to people's consciences. He set apart the Lord's Day for rest, worship, and private devotion. He cherished baptism and the Lord's Supper but rejected any notion that they automatically conveyed grace. He said religion called us to obedience in every sphere: "The best Christians should be the best husbands, best wives, best parents, best children, best magistrates, best subjects, that the doctrine of God might be adorned, not blasphemed."[13]

Doctrinally, Puritanism embraced a broad, vigorous, and confessional Reformed orthodoxy; experientially, it was warm and devoted to communion with God; ecclesiastically, it was committed to honoring the Scriptures alone as God's rule for the faith and life of the church; politically, it honored earthly rulers but was bound in conscience to honor God above the king; evangelistically, it was aggressive yet tender in presenting the free offer of the gospel and calling sinners to Christ; pastorally, it fostered the pursuit of practical holiness and spiritual growth.

Puritan pastors faced many trials, including opposition, persecution, imprisonment, expulsion from their congregations, financial hardships, physical harm, and even death. They also had to deal with other ills of life in the seventeenth century, such as these:

1. A very high mortality rate. Estimates vary, but between a quarter and a third of English children died before reaching puberty. Many adults did not live past their thirties, and people in their late

---

13. John Geree, "Character of an Old English Puritane," in *Images of English Puritanism: A Collection of Contemporary Sources 1589–1646*, ed. Lawrence A. Sasek (Baton Rouge: Louisiana State University Press, 1989), 207–12.

fifties and early sixties were said to have reached "old age" (though some people did live into their eighties and beyond).[14]

2. Self-imposed exile in Europe, especially the Netherlands, which meant departing in haste, traveling in disguise, and dealing with the stresses of relocating to a foreign culture.

3. Transatlantic travel to New England, where they faced the hardships of pioneering, including famine, disease, and attacks from the French, Spanish, and Native Americans.

4. Political upheaval and civil war in England (1642–1651), as well as wars between England, Scotland, and Ireland.

5. Sickness and death from the plague in London and other population centers that swept thousands of people into eternity almost overnight.

6. The horrors of the Great Fire of London in early September 1666, which destroyed thirteen thousand homes and eighty-seven church buildings and was so hot that it melted iron bars.

7. The surge of religious sects in the mid-seventeenth century promoting all kinds of strange new teachings, reviving old heresies, and militating against the true faith.

8. Growing lack of respect for the Word of God and the office of minister. This was especially true in New England as society became more secularized, pluralistic, and skeptical of orthodoxy and institutional religion.[15]

9. A profound awareness of the spiritual battles that pastors face when dealing with the pressures of the world, the temptations of the flesh, and the assaults of the devil. John Flavel (1628–1691) wrote these sobering words about a pastor's calling and work:

> The labours of the ministry will exhaust the very marrow from your bones, hasten old age and death. They are fitly compared to the toil of men in harvest, to the labours of a woman in travail, and to the agonies of soldiers in the extremity of a battle. We must watch when others sleep. And indeed it is not so much

---

14. For a collation of statistics, see Marsha Urban, *Seventeenth-Century Mother's Advice Books* (New York: Palgrave Macmillan, 2006), 10–11.

15. Allen Carden, *Puritan Christianity in America: Religion and Life in Seventeenth-Century Massachusetts* (Grand Rapids: Baker, 1989), 113.

the expense of our labours, as the loss of them, that kills us. It is not with us, as with other labourers: They find their work as they leave it, so do not we. Sin and Satan unravel almost all we do, the impressions we make on our people's souls in one sermon, vanish before the next.... Yea, we must fight in defense of the truths we preach, as well as study them to paleness, and preach them unto faintness: but well-spent head, lungs, and all; welcome pained breasts, aching backs, and trembling legs; if we can by all but approve ourselves Christ's faithful servants, and hear that joyful voice from his mouth, "Well done, good and faithful servants."[16]

It should be acknowledged that a few Puritans fell into extremes, giving credence to the unattractive caricature that has attached itself to the movement as a whole. Here as elsewhere, the reader is urged to "prove all things; hold fast that which is good" (1 Thess. 5:21). The goal is adaptation, not imitation. It is not necessary to imitate Puritans in order to profit from their faith, their example, and their writings.

It also must be remembered that in their own day, the Puritans suffered many setbacks and defeats and failed to achieve some of their most important aims with regard to the reformation of the Church of England. Despite difficulties, discouragements, and apparent defeat, the Puritans had an enormous impact on the spiritual life of the English-speaking world. This impact was seen and felt well into the nineteenth century, when J. C. Ryle wrote, "The Puritans, as a body, have done more to elevate the national character than any class of Englishmen that ever lived."[17] Nor is anyone prepared to deny that traces of the influence of the Puritans in Britain, the Netherlands, and North America persist to this day.

The diligent study of the Scriptures strengthened Puritan pastors in the seventeenth century and enabled them to keep going in ministry, even in the worst of times. God encouraged them so they might encourage others (2 Cor. 1:4). Reading the Puritans has

---

16. John Flavel, "The Character of a True Evangelical Pastor," in *The Works of John Flavel* (Edinburgh: Banner of Truth, 1968), 6:568–69.

17. J. C. Ryle, introduction to *The Complete Works of Thomas Manton* (London: James Nisbet, 1871), 2:xi.

encouraged us immensely. It is our conviction that the Puritans have much to say to pastors today. Though this book is intended to strengthen the mind, it aims primarily at ways in which the Puritans can strengthen the heart.[18]

May our God and Father use this book to strengthen pastors by His Spirit so that Christ will dwell in their hearts through faith, fill them with the fullness of God's glorious love, and equip them for every good work, in the pursuit of their calling.

---

18. For a treatment of Puritan teachings on most major doctrines of systematic theology, see Joel R. Beeke and Mark Jones, *A Puritan Theology: Doctrine for Life* (Grand Rapids: Reformation Heritage Books, 2012).

PART ONE

Piety

It is our calling, as the Bridegroom's Friends, to woo and win souls to Christ, to set him forth to the people as crucified among them (Gal. 3:1), to present him in all his attractive excellencies, that all hearts may be ravished with his beauty, and charmed into his arms by love.

—JOHN FLAVEL

CHAPTER 1

❦

Zeal for the Ministry of the Word

A weary and discouraged pastor who sees the title of this chapter might be tempted to stop reading, thinking, "I was zealous once. But now I'm ill-tempered and just plain tired! Zeal means trouble. Zeal causes pastors to be burned out, cussed out, or thrown out by the sheep or goats that pasture with them."

Puritan pastors were familiar with burn-out and other challenges that pastors face today. Yet they cherished Word-based zeal and sought to fan it into flame. William Fenner (1600–1640) wrote, "Zeal is the fire of the soul…. Every man and woman in the world is set on fire of hell or of heaven…. Zeal is the running of the soul. If thou be not zealous for God, thou runnest away after the things of this world."[1]

The Puritans not only wrote about zeal, but they also walked in it. John Flavel was a zealous pastor. After he was ejected from the ministry in the Church of England in 1662, he continued to meet in secret with his parishioners. He preached in the woods, in the dark night, and even on island rocks near the shore before the tide submerged his makeshift pulpit. On one occasion he dressed in women's clothing to reach a secret place for worship. On another occasion, Flavel had to ditch his horse in the sea before swimming through rocky shoals to reach a safe port.

---

1. William Fenner, *A Treatise of the Affections* (London: A. M. for J. Rothwell, 1650), 132–33.

When was the last time a mob came to your house and burned you in effigy? Flavel experienced this and more. What kept him going? What kept him zealous in ministry even when it cost him so much? The simple answer is that it was the same passion that burned in the hearts of most of the Puritans—a desire to glorify God. Solomon Stoddard (1643–1729), grandfather of Jonathan Edwards, summarized the heart of a zealous pastor this way:

> The Spirit gives them a zeal for God's glory and the salvation of souls. When the Spirit of God is upon them, they will be much concerned for God's glory. So it was with Elijah in 1 Kings 19:10.... They will not be indifferent whether God's kingdom flourishes or not; their hearts will not be upon the world, but their hearts will be engaged for God's honor, and for the salvation of men's souls.[2]

At the center of zeal for the Lord is the Spirit who rules and energizes the heart. Samuel Ward (1577–1640) wrote, "In plain English, zeal is nothing but heat.... It is a spiritual heat wrought in the heart of man by the Holy Ghost, improving the good affections of love, joy, hope, etc., for the best service and furtherance of God's glory."[3] Oliver Bowles (d. 1674) said zeal "is a holy ardor kindled by the Holy Spirit of God in the affections, improving a man to the utmost for God's glory, and the church's good."[4]

The prerequisite for zeal in ministry is a heart that is in love with and on fire for the Lord Jesus. At issue for every Christian, and certainly for every pastor, is Christ's question to Peter, "Lovest thou me?" (John 21:15–17). Biblical zeal is not a violent outburst of pride but a steady flame of love for God that radiates warmth toward others. Jonathan Edwards said, "Christian zeal [is] indeed a flame, but a sweet one;

---

2. Solomon Stoddard, "The Importance of Gospel Preachers," in *The Puritan Pulpit: Solomon Stoddard* (Orlando: Soli Deo Gloria, 2005), 208.

3. Samuel Ward, *Sermons and Treatises* (1636; repr., Edinburgh: Banner of Truth, 1996), 72.

4. Oliver Bowles, *Zeal for God's House Quickened* (London: Richard Bishop for Samuel Gellibrand, 1643), 5.

or rather it is the heat and fervor of a sweet flame. For the flame of which it is the heat, is no other than that of divine love."[5]

How Does the Spirit Create Zeal in Pastors?

A Puritan pastor would answer this question by first asking, "Are you a saved, Spirit-led believer?" Richard Baxter (1615–1691) pulled no punches in *The Reformed Pastor*. He asked:

> Can any reasonable man imagine, that God should save men for offering salvation to others while they refused it themselves; and for telling others truths which they themselves neglected and abused? Many a tailor goes in rags that maketh costly clothes for others; and many a cook scarcely satisfies his hunger, when he hath dressed for others the most costly dishes. Believe it, brethren, God never saved any man for being a preacher, nor because he was an able preacher; but because he was a justified, sanctified man, and consequently faithful in his Master's work.[6]

Baxter experienced firsthand what a defective ministry was when he was asked to assist the parish minister at Kidderminster as a guest lecturer. Baxter found the man to be "utterly insufficient for ministry, presented by a papist, unlearned, but preached once a quarter which was so weakly, as exposed him to laughter...[who] frequented alehouses and had sometimes been drunk."[7] Baxter went on to say that the man's wife would often walk out of church because she couldn't stand to hear him preach.

The Puritans had little sympathy for pastors who were mere professionals offering a gospel to which they were strangers. Thomas Watson (c. 1620–1686) said about such ministers:

> How sad it is for a minister to preach that to others which he never felt in his own soul; to exhort others to holiness and

5. Jonathan Edwards, *The Works of Jonathan Edwards, Volume 2, Religious Affections*, ed. John E. Smith (New Haven: Yale University Press, 1959), 352.

6. Richard Baxter, *The Reformed Pastor* (New York: American Tract Society, 1829), 90.

7. Richard Baxter, *The Autobiography of Richard Baxter* (Mobile, Ala.: R. E. Pub., n.d.), 24.

himself a stranger to it. Oh, that this were not too often so. How many blow the Lord's trumpet with foul breath!... The life of a minister should be a walking Bible.... They who live in contradiction to what they preach disgrace this excellent calling. They turn their books into cups. And though they are angels by office, yet they are devils in their lives.[8]

Once the issue of salvation was settled, a Puritan spiritual diagnostician would proceed to the next question: "Is the old man of flesh dying within you?" Many Puritans had diagnostic tools for themselves and other pastors to determine whether the governing principle or motivation for their ministry was based upon true zeal for the Lord. In their writings we find at least seven tests for ministers to determine if they were "dying to self."

1. *Am I industrious and busy in the work of the Lord?* Thomas Brooks (1608–1680) said, "The zealous soul is continually saying to himself, 'What shall I render to the Lord?'"[9] Thomas Watson wrote,

The minister must not be idle. Sloth is as inexcusable as sleeping in a sentry. John the Baptist was a "voice crying" (Matt. 3:3). A dumb minister is of no more use than a dead physician. A man of God must work in the Lord's vineyard. It was Augustine's wish that Christ might find him at his coming either praying or preaching.[10]

2. *Is there a distinct difference in the way I live in the world as a Christian? Do members of my congregation see the difference?* William Perkins (1558–1602) offered this sad commentary on the spiritual landscape of his time:

In many parts of our land there is by God's blessing much teaching, yet there is little reformation in the lives of most.... What is the cause? It cannot lie in the gospel; nor in our doctrine, nor in the teaching of it. One principal cause is that many ministers come into God's presence unsanctified, and in their sins, little concerned about how loosely they live before their people....

---

8. Thomas Watson, *The Godly Man's Picture* (Edinburgh: Banner of Truth, 1992), 155.

9. Thomas Brooks, "The Unsearchable Riches of Christ," in *The Works of Thomas Brooks* (1861–1867; repr., Edinburgh: Banner of Truth, 2001), 3:58–59. Cf. Ps. 116:12.

10. Watson, *The Godly Man's Picture*, 154.

If ministers are to see any fruit from their ministry, they must first sanctify themselves and cleanse their hearts by repentance before they presume to stand up to rebuke sin in others.[11]

3. Am I truly grieved when church members voice an unhealthy dependence upon my leadership or when they shower me with praise and excessive honor? Thomas Foxcroft (1697–1769) raised this issue in his inaugural sermon at First Congregational Church in Boston:

Dependence upon ministers is a derogation from the Lord of glory, whose appropriate and sole prerogative is to give strength unto His people.... Unto Christ is due the glory of efficiency, but to them the honor of instrumentality.[12]

4. Do I do good works or serve even in sacrificial ways so that people will sing my praises? The modern term for this problem is having a *hidden agenda.* Thomas Shepard (1605–1649) confessed this sin of the heart in a journal entry, saying:

On Sabbath when I came home I saw the hypocrisy of my heart that in my ministry I sought to comfort others and quicken others that the glory might reflect on me as well as on God. Here upon I considered how ill the Lord took this and how adverse he was from this self-seeking, by the sight of which I labored to be averse from it myself and purposed to carry it in my mind as one strong means to help against it for time to come.[13]

Stoddard issued a similar warning:

When you are zealous, there is no occasion to say, "Behold his zeal for the Lord." A man may become a zealous man; he may have a spirit to promote ordinances; he may go to any expense rather than live without them. He may have a zeal against the pride and drunkenness of the land. He may hope that men take notice of it, and call it zeal for the Lord (2 Kings 10:16). But

---

11. William Perkins, *The Art of Prophesying* (Edinburgh: Banner of Truth, 2002), 150–51.

12. Thomas Foxcroft, *The Gospel Ministry* (Grand Rapids: Soli Deo Gloria, 2008), 74.

13. Thomas Shepard, *The Works of Thomas Shepard* (New York: AMS Press, 1967), 3:411.

there is no occasion for God to say so. God takes notice that there is another spirit in him…. Some men take great pains in preaching, praying, and reading. Some men say that they weary themselves for God. But God says, "There is no love for me in their services." God slights the service and says, "That man takes great pains so that men may observe and commend him."[14]

Stoddard's comments are especially poignant because of what he as pastor of First Church of Northampton, Massachusetts, had experienced. Before Stoddard was ordained—or even converted—his wife and some women from town sensed Stoddard's true spiritual condition and began praying for him. Stoddard was finally brought to a personal experience of Christ's grace while he was administering the Lord's Supper.[15]

5. *Is my aim in ministry to promote my own reputation or to enrich myself financially?* Promoting self through ministry is the sin of crass professionalism. Pastors guilty of this are only hirelings, not true shepherds. Richard Sibbes (1577–1635) wrote,

And especially ministers, their aim it should not be for the fleece, it should not be to gain respect, or any advantage to themselves to bestow some spiritual good thing. As the apostles saith, "To bestow some good things upon you" (Rom. 1:11), some grace, as he calls it. This should be their aim, not to receive good from them, so much as to do them good. Ministers are fathers, they should have that tender disposition.[16]

6. *Am I envious of the success of other pastors and their ministries?* In a funeral sermon for his friend and colleague Richard Fairclough (1621–1682), John Howe (1630–1705) issued a warning to all preachers of the gospel when contemplating the success of their colleagues:

How horrid would it be, should we behold with envy what we are to suppose [is] done out of love and good-will! They are great admirers of themselves, and lovers of some interest of

---

14. Solomon Stoddard, "Natural Men Are Under the Government of Self-Love," in *Puritan Pulpit*, 66.

15. Ralph J. Coffman, *Solomon Stoddard* (Boston: Twayne Pub., 1978), 60.

16. Richard Sibbes, "Commentary on II Corinthians," in *The Works of Richard Sibbes* (Edinburgh: James Nichol, 1860), 330.

their own more than his, that cannot endure to see his work done by other hands than theirs; or that have nothing of that disposition in them which those words express, "Let him increase, and me decrease."[17]

7. Do I look beyond the felt needs of people and the day-to-day activities of ministry toward a higher purpose? When writing about the Christian's labor and reward, William Gurnall (1616–1679) argued that pastors should always be mindful of their chief end in life:

> If I aim at the comfort and relief of a poor man's necessity in my alms (which I may and ought to do), yet if this is the highest I look, and my eye does not pass beyond this to the glory of God, it becomes unacceptable. A man may lose the prize by shooting short as well as wide of the mark. Now how hard is it to keep our eye fixed on this ultimate end? Truly, even as hard as to keep our eye fixed on a single object through an optic glass, held by trembling hand.[18]

Gurnall's observation is painfully accurate. Given our weakness and infirmity as mere men, it is difficult for us to keep our eye fixed on the ultimate purpose of our lives and ministries: the glory of God. We keep our eyes fixed on the glory of God only with the aid of "an optic glass, held by trembling hands." Think of the chaotic result of a novice videographer who can't keep his camera steady! The next two chapters will show us how the Holy Spirit clarified the vision and steadied the grip of the Puritans.

Ask the Spirit for the Fire of Love

As ministers of the gospel, we have a high calling to fulfill and only a short time to do it. We cannot afford to waste precious time in idleness or unproductive activity. The glory of God and the welfare of immortal souls hang in the balance every hour. John Reynolds (1667–1727) wrote, "O what a world of good may we all do, if we had the true zeal of God! How many occasions and opportunities are

---

17. John Howe, "A Funeral Sermon for Mr. Richard Fairclough," in *The Works of John Howe* (Ligonier, Pa.: Soli Deo Gloria, 1990), 3:394.

18. William Gurnall, *The Christian's Labor and Reward* (Morgan, Pa.: Soli Deo Gloria, 2004), 11.

put into our hands every day (in what condition and circumstances soever we are) which, if we were acted by this principle, would render us great benefactors to mankind, by discouraging vice and impiety, and promoting virtue and goodness in the world?" He concluded, "Let us ardently love the Lord Jesus, and the affairs of His redemption and glory! Let us be serious and diligent in all the offices of a truly sacred zeal![19]

Before reading any further, we recommend that you pause for prayer. John Preston (1587–1628) wrote, "The love of God is peculiarly the work of the Holy Ghost.... Therefore the way to get it is earnestly to pray.... We are no more able to love the Lord than cold water is able to heat itself...so the Holy Ghost must breed that fire of love in us, it must be kindled from heaven, or else we shall never have it."[20]

Stop right where you are, and call upon the Lord to inflame your heart with love for Him and zeal for His glory. Christ assures us that the Father will give the Holy Spirit to His children if they ask (Luke 11:13). So in the name of the Son (John 16:23, 24), ask the Father to fill you with joy and peace in believing so that you may bound in hope, through the power of the Holy Ghost (Rom. 15:13); specifically, to shed His love abroad in your heart through the Spirit (Rom. 5:5), to strengthen you by His Spirit in the inner man (Eph. 3:16), and to make your life and ministry bear much fruit, that He may be glorified in you (John 15:8).

---

19. John Reynolds, *Zeal a Virtue: or, A Discourse Concerning Sacred Zeal* (London: John Clark, 1716), 184–85.

20. John Preston, *The Breastplate of Faith and Love*, 2 vols. in one (1634; facsimile repr., Edinburgh: Banner of Truth, 1979), 2:50.

CHAPTER 2

"In Sweet Communion, Lord, with Thee"

In Psalm 73, Asaph says his faith would be overwhelmed by circumstances unless he took time to draw near to God. He wrote:

> In sweet communion, Lord, with Thee,
> I constantly abide;
> My hand Thou holdest in Thy own
> To keep me near Thy side.
>
> To live apart from God is death,
> 'Tis good His face to seek;
> My refuge is the living God,
> His praise I long to speak.[1]

Jonathan Edwards would have heartily agreed with Asaph. Edwards was part of the last generation of Puritan pastors in New England. As a scholar, a student of Christian experience, and a preacher of the gospel, Edwards rivaled or surpassed many of his seventeenth-century predecessors. As the offspring and heir of the Puritans, he also mobilized the great spiritual disciplines handed down from his spiritual forebears. Edwards recorded his personal experience of the glory of Christ in this passage from his "Personal Narrative":

> Once, as I rode out into the woods for my health, in 1737, having alighted from my horse in a retired place, as my manner commonly has been, to walk for divine contemplation and prayer, I had a view, that for me was extraordinary of the glory of the Son

---

1. *The Psalter* (1912), no. 203, stanzas 1, 5.

of God, as Mediator between God and man, and his wonderful, great, full, pure and sweet grace and love, and meek and gentle condescension. This grace that appeared so calm and sweet, appeared also great above the heavens. The person of Christ appeared ineffably excellent, with an excellency great enough to swallow up all thought and conception...which continued, as near as I can judge, about an hour; which kept me the greater part of the time in a flood of tears, and weeping aloud.[2]

In this chapter we will explore how Puritan pastors kept their eyes focused on the glory of the Lord through the spiritual disciplines of prayer, meditation, and journaling. What we will discover about their devotional lives and how they may challenge us today should encourage twenty-first-century pastors to cultivate these spiritual disciplines more effectively.

The Priority of Prayer

One of the first things that might surprise today's pastors is the amount of time Puritan pastors devoted to prayer.[3] Many of them engaged in family and personal worship three times a day. John Norton (1606–1663), a colleague of John Cotton (1584–1652), described Cotton's typical Sabbath schedule while at home:

He began his Sabbath [the previous] evening; [he] then performed family-duty after supper, being larger than ordinary in exposition, after which he catechized his children and servants, then returned to his study. The morning following, family-worship being ended, he retired into his study, until the bell called him away. Upon his return from meeting, he returned again into his study (the place of his labour and prayer) unto his private devotions; where (having a small repast carried him up for his dinner) he continued till the tolling of the bell. The public service being over, he withdrew for a space to his prementioned oratory for his sacred address unto God, as in the forenoon; then came down,

---

2. Jonathan Edwards, "Personal Narrative," in *The Works of Jonathan Edwards,* ed. Sereno E. Dwight (London: Henry G. Bohn, 1865), 1:lxxxix.

3. For more on the Puritans and prayer, see Joel R. Beeke and Brian G. Najapfour, eds., *Taking Hold of God: Reformed and Puritan Perspectives on Prayer* (Grand Rapids: Reformation Heritage Books, 2011).

repeated the sermon in the family, prayed, after supper sang a psalm, and towards bed-time betaking himself again to his study, he closed the day with prayer. Thus he spent the Sabbath continually.[4]

It wasn't unusual for Puritan pastors to rise early in the morning so they could spend hours in personal devotions. John Howe eulogized Richard Fairclough as a man who would, "every day, for many years together, be up by three in the morning or sooner, and to be with God (which was his dear delight) when others slept."[5] Why did the Puritans devote themselves to prayer with such discipline and fervency?

The first reason was to cast their burdens on God. Puritan pastors unloaded their guilt and shame before the Lord but also anything else that troubled their hearts. Prayer was a means of catharsis for them. Samuel Rutherford (1600–1661) wrote to Marion M'Naught in a letter dating around 1630, "I have many a grieved heart daily in my calling. I would be undone if I had not access to the King's chamber of presence, to show him all the business. The devil rages, and is mad to see the water drawn from his own mill; but would to God we could be the Lord's instruments to build the Son of God's house."[6]

Richard Baxter said in *The Reformed Pastor* that when his heart grew cold, his congregants could feel the difference:

> I confess I must speak it by lamentable experience, that I publish to my flock the distempers of my own soul. When I let my heart grow cold, my preaching is cold; and when it is confused, my preaching is confused: and so I can often observe also in the best of my hearers, that when I have grown cold in preaching they have grown cold too; and the next prayers which I have heard from them have been too like my preaching.[7]

A second reason for these times of sustained prayer was to allow pastors to focus on supplication for their families and for their

---

4. John Norton, *Abel Being Dead, Yet Speaketh* (New York: Scholars' Facsimiles and Reprints, 1978), 27.

5. John Howe, "A Funeral Service for Mr. Richard Fairclough," in *Works*, 3:408.

6. Samuel Rutherford, *Letters of Samuel Rutherford* (Edinburgh: Banner of Truth, 2006), 17.

7. Baxter, *The Reformed Pastor*, 100.

ministries. John Bunyan's (1628–1688) picturesque language captures the pastor's ongoing need to pray for God's blessing upon his work: "Prayer is as the pitcher that fetcheth water from the brook, therewith to water the herbs: break the pitcher and it will fetch no water, and for want of water the garden withers."[8] Thomas Foxcroft elaborated on the pastor's need for prayer by saying:

> Hence it behooves ministers to be very much in the exercise of prayer. They who would become fit for and faithful in the ministry of the Word must give themselves to prayer continually. The prayer of the upright is the most likely method to procure the tongue of the learned, the diligent hand, and an able head. The more fervent and frequent one is at the throne of grace, the better prospect he has of excelling in strength, of growing mighty in the Scriptures, and being skillful in the Word of righteousness.[9]

Shepard offered a sample of his prayer requests for strength and power for himself and the church in another journal entry:

> In prayer I was cast down with the sight of our worthiness in this church to be utterly wasted. But the Lord filled my heart with a spirit of prayer not only to desire small things but with a holy boldness to desire great things for God's people here and for myself, viz, that I might live to see all the breaches made up and the glory of the Lord upon us and that I might not die but live to show forth God's glory to this and the children of the next generation. And so I arose from prayer with some confidence of answer (1) because I saw Christ put it into my heart to ask; (2) because I saw the cry of the humble (Ps. 34:18).[10]

Another reason Puritan pastors made prayer and personal devotions a priority was so they might see the face of God and His glory. They shared David's desire "to behold the beauty of the LORD" (Ps. 27:4) and to see His power and glory, "so as I have seen thee in the sanctuary" (Ps. 63:2). Foxcroft described the effects of such communion with God on the minister of the Word: "To be often in the mount,

---

8. John Bunyan, *The Riches of Bunyan*, ed. Jeremiah Chaplin (New York: American Tract Society, 1851), 309.

9. Foxcroft, *The Gospel Ministry*, 62.

10. Shepard, *Works*, 3:87.

having his conversation much in heaven, will admirably warm him in his work, will make his affections glow with a holy heat, and his mind sparkle with rays of glorious light, even as the face of Moses did when he had been with God in Sinai."[11]

Thomas Watson, who died while in prayer, wrote about the blessing that prayer imparts to the man who prays: "A spiritual prayer is that which leaves a spiritual mood behind upon the heart. A Christian is better after prayer. He has gained more strength over sin, as a man by exercise gets strength. The heart after prayer keeps a tincture of holiness, as the vessel favours and relishes the wine that is put into it."[12]

Prayer for Puritan pastors was more than just a way to obtain gifts of grace for ministry; it was also a way to keep their hearts and minds focused upon the glory of the Lord. It was a way to put all things in proper perspective, viewing them in the light of eternity while enjoying the compelling beauty and excellence of Christ. The challenge for pastors today is to develop the kind of personal communion that the Puritans had with the Lord.

Enjoying Friendship with God

Pastors who are constantly bombarded with information and intrusions on their time and attention via cell phones, BlackBerries, the Internet, and iPods may think it's impossible to find more time to commune with the Lord. But what is your primary calling as a pastor? Unless you are marketing spiritual novelties or religious trinkets, your business as a pastor is first and foremost to spend time with the Lord. We can be grateful to the Puritans for their examples of how to enjoy friendship with God. Thomas Goodwin (1600–1679) offered four directives for establishing and maintaining such a friendship with God:

- Take occasion to come into His presence intending to have communion with Him. This is truly friendly, for friendship is maintained and kept up by visits; and the more free and less occasioned these are by urgent business, or solemnity, or custom, the more friendly they are.

---

11. Foxcroft, *The Gospel Ministry*, 62.
12. Watson, *The Godly Man's Picture*, 93.

- A second way of…expressing friendship to God is this: when thou comest into His presence, be telling Him still how well thou lovest Him; labour to abound in expressions of that kind, than which (when founded in a reality in the Spirit) there is nothing more taking with the heart of any friend.

- Delight much in Him. Friendship well placed affords the highest delight.

- A fourth particular wherein the communion of friendship lies, is [the] unfolding [of] secrets [Ps. 25:14].[13]

Goodwin's list contains the four basic building blocks of having an intimate time with the Lord: purpose, praise, pleasure, and privileged communications.

Samuel Rutherford said that prayer need not always be offered in the pastor's study or in a private prayer closet. He drew near to God on horseback. He wrote, "I have benefited by riding alone on a long journey, in giving that time to prayer…by abstinence, and giving days to God."[14] Cotton Mather (1663–1728) suggested that pastors set apart whole days for prayer and fasting:

That you may be good men, and be mightily inspired and assisted from heaven to do good, it is needful that you should be men of prayer…. In the pursuance of this intention, there appears more than a little need of it, that you should ever now and then keep whole days of prayer, in an holy retirement before the Lord; often set apart, whole days, for prayer with fasting, in secret, and perfume your studies with devotions extraordinary: and usually with a mixture of alms, to go up in the memorial before the Lord…. You may obtain, a certain afflatus [wind blowing] from Heaven upon your minds, and such an indwelling of the Holy Spirit, as will render you, grave, discreet, humble, generous, and men worthy to be greatly beloved. You may obtain those influences from above, that will dispel the

---

13. Thomas Goodwin, *The Works of Thomas Goodwin* (Grand Rapids: Reformation Heritage Books, 2006), 7:198–202.

14. Rutherford, *Letters*, 73.

enchantments, and conquer the temptations, which may else do a world of mischief in your neighborhood.[15]

Meditation on the Scriptures

Maintaining a consistent prayer time is an important prerequisite for intimate communion with the Lord. A right spirit and desire to be with the Lord and to delight in Him are also important if we would see the Lord of glory. The Puritans found that meditating on the words of Scripture was an effective way to keep the mind focused on God during prayer and to feed the soul for serving the Lord all day.

Today's pastors have a plethora of devotional booklets, study Bibles, and websites to help them develop personal devotional time with the Lord. Many Puritans read published sermons and lectures for their personal benefit. Even so, the Christian today has both a duty and a need to be in the Word every day. Sadly, many pastors today are hard-pressed to find time to read the Bible and to meditate upon it in a personal way to hear God's voice through its words. Puritan pastors, on the other hand, provided guides and other helps to assist their people in the profitable reading of the Bible. One guide was Lewis Bayly's *The Practice of Piety,* which offers directions on how to read the Bible through in a year. Another popular guide was John White's *A Way to the Tree of Life: Discoursed in Sundry Directions for the Profitable Reading of the Scriptures.*[16]

Meditating on Scripture is a particularly helpful practice. Thomas Manton (1620–1677) defined meditation as "that duty or exercise of religion whereby the mind is applied to the serious and solemn contemplation of spiritual things, for practical uses and purposes."[17]

---

15. Cotton Mather, *Bonifacius: An Essay upon the Good* (Cambridge: Harvard University Press, 1966), 70–71.

16. Charles E. Hambrick-Stowe, *The Practice of Piety: Puritan Devotional Disciplines in Seventeenth-Century New England* (Chapel Hill: University of North Carolina Press, 1982), 159.

17. Thomas Manton, *The Complete Works of Thomas Manton* (London: James Nisbet, 1874), 17:270.

Thomas Hooker (1586–1647) said, "Meditation is a serious intention of the mind whereby we come to search out the truth, and settle it effectually upon the heart."[18]

Without meditation on the Word, our prayers will become vague and dull and directed by the world rather than God's Spirit. Bunyan understood that to pray we must have a vision of the throne of grace "by the sight that God gives, not by any excellency that there is in my natural understanding," so that though we may begin in prayer with a heart that is "flat, dull, savorless, lifeless, and has no warmth in the duty," nevertheless by God's help "it mounts up with wings like an eagle when the throne is truly apprehended."[19]

The Puritans offered the following directives for meditating on Scripture:

1. Pray for the power to harness your mind. Focus by faith on the task of meditation. For example, use Psalm 119:18, 36–37 as a prayer: "Open thou mine eyes, that I may behold wondrous things out of thy law.... Incline my heart unto thy testimonies, and not to covetousness. Turn away mine eyes from beholding vanity; and quicken thou me in thy way."

2. Read a passage of Scripture, then select a verse or two or a particular doctrine upon which to meditate.[20]

3. Memorize these verses to facilitate meditation, to strengthen faith, to help you witness to and counsel others, and to serve as a means of divine guidance.

4. Think on what you know about these verses or subjects and how you have experienced their truths by probing the book of Scripture, the book of conscience, and the book of nature.[21] Develop particular

---

18. Thomas Hooker, *The Application of Redemption by the Effectual Work of the Word, and Spirit of Christ, for the bringing home of lost Sinners to God. The Ninth and Tenth Books* (London: Peter Cole, 1657), 210.

19. Bunyan, *Riches of Bunyan*, 305–6.

20. For a list of profitable subjects for meditation, see Stephen Charnock, *The Works of Stephen Charnock* (Edinburgh: James Nichol, 1865), 5:307.

21. George Swinnock, *The Works of George Swinnock* (Edinburgh: Banner of Truth, 1998), 2:417.

applications to your own life. As Thomas Watson said, "Take every word as spoken to yourselves."[22]

5. Stir up affections such as love, desire, hope, zeal, and joy to glorify God.[23] Preach the truth to your own soul (Ps. 42:5; 103:1).

6. Rouse your mind to some specific duty and a holy resolve to do it by God's grace.[24]

7. Conclude with prayer, thanksgiving, and psalm-singing.[25]

In meditation you may choose to focus on one verse of God's Word or a key word in a verse. In his memoir, Edwards described how he meditated upon Matthew 18:3: "Verily I say unto you, Except ye be converted, and become as little children, ye shall not enter into the kingdom of heaven." He used his imagination to visualize himself as a little child: "It has often appeared to me delightful, to be united to Christ; to have him for my head, and to be a member of his body; also to have Christ for my teacher and prophet. I very often think with sweetness, and longings, and pantings of soul, of being a little child, taking hold of Christ, to be led by him through the wilderness of this world."[26]

Bible study should be mingled with meditation and prayer. The Puritans prayed for the Spirit's illumination when they studied the Scriptures, whether for personal devotion or sermon preparation. When John Cotton was in his study, "he neither sat down unto, nor

---

22. Thomas Watson, "How We May Read the Scriptures with Most Spiritual Profit," in *Heaven Taken by Storm*, ed. Joel R. Beeke (Morgan, Pa.: Soli Deo Gloria, 1992), 113–29.

23. Richard Baxter, *The Saints' Everlasting Rest* (Ross-shire, U.K.: Christian Focus, 1998), 579–90, and Jonathan Edwards, *The Religious Affections* (London: Banner of Truth, 1959), 24.

24. William Bates, *The Works of the Rev. W. Bates D.D.* (Harrisonburg, Va.: Sprinkle, 1990), 3:145, and Thomas White, *A Method and Instructions for the Art of Divine Meditation* (London: for Tho. Parkhurst, 1672), 53.

25. See Nathanael Ranew, *Solitude Improved by Divine Meditation, or A Treatise Proving the Duty, and Demonstrating the Necessity, Excellency, Usefulness, Natures, Kinds, and Requisites of Divine Meditation* (Morgan, Pa.: Soli Deo Gloria, 1995). For a fuller treatment of Puritan meditation, see Simon Chan, "The Puritan Meditative Tradition, 1599–1691: A Study in Asceticality" (Ph.D. diss., Cambridge University, 1986); Joel R. Beeke, *Puritan Reformed Spirituality* (Darlington, England: Evangelical Press, 2006), 73–100.

26. Edwards, *Works*, 1:lxxxix.

arose from his meditations without prayer: whilst his eyes were upon his book, his expectation was from God. He had learned to study, because he had learned to pray."[27] Cotton Mather suggested that the time of sermon preparation can be a spiritual experience that rivals (but does not replace) a time or day of prayer, if it is mingled with prayer:

> And, what if while you are studying your sermons, you should at the close of every paragraph, make a pause, and endeavor with acknowledgements and [brief prayers] to Heaven, and with self-examinations, to feel some impressions of the truths in that paragraph on your own souls, before you go any further? By such a practice, the hours which you take, to make and write a sermon, will prove so many hours of devotion with you. The day in which you have made a sermon will even leave upon your mind, such a savor as a day of prayer uses to do.[28]

Manton wrote, "Faith is lean and ready to starve unless it be fed with continual meditation on the promises."[29] The Puritans did not want to approach subjects such as the Trinity, Christology, or Scripture from a purely scholastic or intellectual light. They wanted to see the God of the Trinity, not just with the thoughts of the mind but in union with the heart. In conclusion, Thomas Shepard said, "I have seen a God by reason and never been amazed at God. I have seen God himself and have been ravished to behold him."[30]

Journaling: Crystallizing the Present for the Future

The third tool the Puritans used to keep their minds focused upon the Lord, both in daily devotional times and times of discouragement, was journaling or keeping a personal diary. Puritans such as Thomas Shepard and Cotton Mather were prolific journal writers. Some diaries, memoirs, and autobiographies were written by Puritan pastors, often just before they died, as a legacy for future generations.

Journaling was encouraged by the Puritans for several reasons. The first reason was self-examination. The Puritans were concerned

---

27. Norton, *Abel Being Dead, Yet Speaketh*, 27.
28. Mather, *Bonifacius*, 72.
29. Manton, *Works*, 17:270.
30. Shepard, *Works*, 3:103.

about the condition of their own souls so they would record their personal failings and besetting sins. But they didn't catalog their sins merely to create shame and guilt; rather, they did so to memorialize the grace and mercy of God shown to them as sinners. It was the ongoing testimony of God's mercy in Christ that awakened in them a greater desire to walk in close fellowship with the Lord. Baxter exhorted his fellow pastors with these words:

> O, Brethren, watch therefore over your own hearts; keep out lusts and passions and worldly inclinations; keep up the life of faith and love and zeal; be much at home, and be much with God. If it be not your daily business to study your own hearts, and to subdue corruption, and to walk with God—if you make not this a work to which you constantly attend, all will go wrong, and you will starve your hearers; or, if you have an affected fervency, you cannot expect a blessing to attend it from on high.[31]

A second reason the Puritans encouraged journal writing was to record the ordinary and extraordinary instances of God's grace and mercy in day-to-day life. Increase Mather (1639–1723) kept a journal from the time he was a young man traveling in Europe until his death. One result of his constant journaling was the book he wrote titled *Remarkable Providences in Colonial New England*. Mather encouraged all pastors to record and publish "illustrious" examples of God's providences to strengthen the faith of ministers and to encourage their posterity.[32] The Puritans found it "angelic" to study

---

31. Baxter, *The Reformed Pastor*, 101.

32. "In order to the promoting of a design of this nature, so as shall be indeed for God's glory and the good of posterity, it is necessary that utmost care shall be taken that all and only remarkable providences be recorded and published. Such divine judgements, tempests, floods, earthquakes, thunders as are unusual, strange apparitions, or whatever else shall happen that is prodigious...remarkable judgments upon noted sinners, eminent deliverances, and answers of prayer, are to be reckoned among illustrious providences.... Inasmuch as we find in scripture, as well as in ecclesiastical history, that the ministers of God have been improved in the recording and declaring the works of the Lord, and since they are in divers respects under peculiar advantages thereunto, it is proposed, that each one in that capacity may diligently enquire into and record such illustrious providences as have happened.... Although it be true that this design cannot be brought unto perfection in one or

the works of God both in nature and in the life of the church. Flavel wrote, "Give me leave to say, it is an angelic employment to stand upon it, and behold the consent of God's attributes, the accomplishment of his ends, and our own happiness in the works of providence. For this is the very joy of the angels and saints in heaven, to see God's ends wrought out, and his attributes glorified in the mercy and peace of the church (Rev. 14:1–3, 8)."[33]

Third, Puritan pastors also wrote journals to provide direction for life. Recording daily events and answers to prayer were helpful for determining God's specific will for their lives. These pastors were also conscientious about time and the wise use of it, heeding Paul's admonition in Ephesians 5:16, to be ever "redeeming the time, because the days are evil." The Puritans lived each day in the light of Christ's return and the day of judgment. Recording daily events kept them accountable for their use of time and encouraged them to be faithful and diligent in their calling.

Finally, journaling also helped keep the memory of spiritual experiences with the Lord fresh and vivid. These records were constant reminders of how richly they had experienced the loving-kindness of the Lord. Some Puritans wrote poetry in their journals to recall their intimate experiences with the Lord. When these authors died, many of these diary entries and poems were destroyed because of their personal nature. Thankfully, the journals of Cotton Mather and Thomas Shepard survived. We will finish this chapter citing a diary entry from both men. The first is from Cotton Mather, who wrote about what he experienced at the end of a long day of public ministry of the Word:

> This day after my public labours, retiring into my study, at the evening, I there cast myself prostrate in the dust, on my floor before the Lord. And there, a wonderful thought with an heavenly force,

---

two years, yet it is much to be desired that something may be done therein out of hand, as a specimen of a more large volume, that so this work may be set on foot, and posterity may be encouraged to go on therewith." Increase Mather, *Remarkable Providences* (London: John Russell Smith, 1856), preface [n.p.].

33. John Flavel, "The Mystery of Providence," in *The Whole Works of the Rev. Mr. John Flavel* (London: W. Baynes and Son, 1820), 5:440.

came into my mind; that God loved my Lord Jesus Christ infinitely, and had given worlds unto him, and made him the Lord
of all; and that I had, thro' the efficacy of his grace upon me, my
heart exceedingly set upon the glorifying of my Lord Jesus Christ
and was entirely devoted unto him. Hereupon, an unutterable joy
fill'd my mind, from assurance, that God, for the sake of my Lord
Jesus Christ, had great things to do for me; that he would even
delight in me, and delight in using me, and use me in eminent
services for Him, who is dearer to me, than all things.[34]

The second diary entry is from Thomas Shepard:

Sept. 5. I was on Sabbath day night secretly swelling against God,
that he did not bless my ministry. But then remembering my
sins, how I deserved death eternally, I was soon quieted; and I
blessed God exceedingly for my life, and that the Lord was not
yet gone out hearing but that I might come to him privately, and
in extraordinary duties, and pray. So I prayed earnestly for favor
and love of Christ, and God in Christ and for a multitude of mercies. And I prayed so long, until my heart was made suitable unto
mercy; so as I prized nothing else but God's favor, so as my heart
did find rest there, and was quiet with it, and did rest on it, and
with it. For I considered, the heart of all ungodly men is ravished
and runs out to creatures, and finds rest there only. And so I fell to
blessing God, and praying for the fruits of God's reconciled love;
and among other things to bless my ministry. And in doing this
a desire came in, viz., that the Lord would not bless my words,
but his own word, because it is his own. Because I am sure he will
bless his own children, and make them blessings; so I was sure
the Lord would bless his own word, because it is his own.[35]

If you would experience the same kind of encouragement in your
own life and work, turn to God in prayer, meditate on God's Word,
and keep a journal, recording accounts of the Lord's faithful dealings.
By grace, you, too, will experience the sweetness of communion with
the living God (Ps. 73:23–28).

---

34. Cotton Mather, *Diary* (New York: F. Ungar, 1957), 1:255.
35. Shepard, *Works*, 424.

CHAPTER 3

Encouraged by God's Promises

It is difficult to make the glory of God the primary desire, goal, and motivation for our ministry. As one Puritan writer said, it is "as hard as to keep our eye fixed on a single object through an optic glass, held by a trembling hand."[1] In the last chapter, we said the Puritans kept their focus by enjoying daily communion with the Lord. At the heart of their piety was a thirst for communion with Christ. Communing with the Lord kept their eyes on their goal, giving them a right perspective on who they were in Christ and what they were called to do in their ministry.

However, Moses had to come down from his mountaintop experience with God to endure the shouts and perverse revelry of idol worship in the camp of Israel. Christ Jesus had glorious fellowship with Moses and Elijah on the Mount of Transfiguration, but He too had to come down to earth to face the weakness of His disciples and the unbelief of His generation. So too we must come down from the mountaintop of communing with God. We cannot live forever in our devotions but must go into the world to serve Christ.

When we do, all kinds of misery begin to seep into our lives, dampening our spirits. We and church members have such high expectations for our ministry. We are tempted to use worldly methods to produce visible results, as if God's work in the soul was nothing more than an assembly line in which the right parts matched with the

---

1. Gurnall, *The Christian's Labor and Reward*, 11.

right process will result in the right product in predictable numbers. Often the pressure of peoples' demands and needs is so immense that it makes our hands tremble. A single counseling session, pastoral call, or elders' meeting can leave us drained and discouraged.

What can strengthen our trembling hands? John Flavel offers the answer in a work titled *The Best Work in the Worst Times*. He wrote, "But what is this Christian fortitude, and wherein doth it consist. I answer briefly, It is an holy boldness in the performance of difficult duties, flowing from faith in the call of God, and his promise to us in the discharge of them."[2]

The promises of God offer us the help we need to fulfill our calling. They also help us in our calling as Christians. Second Peter 1:3–4 tells us, "According as his divine power hath given unto us all things that pertain unto life and godliness, through the knowledge of him that hath called us to glory and virtue: whereby are given unto us exceeding great and precious promises: that by these ye might be partakers of the divine nature, having escaped the corruption that is in the world through lust." The Scriptures were given to us as ministers of the Word so "that the man of God may be perfect, thoroughly furnished unto all good works" (2 Tim. 3:17).

God's promises encourage us by bringing Christ to us. Jesus Christ is the "sum, fountain, seal, treasury of all the promises," Edward Reynolds (1599–1676) wrote.[3] In Him, the promises of God are yea and Amen (2 Cor. 1:20). Samuel Rutherford said in his catechism: "The new covenant is a mass of promises laying the weight of our salvation upon a [Person] stronger than we are, to wit upon Christ, and faith grippeth promises and maketh us to go out of ourselves to Christ as being homelie [i.e., familiar] with Christ."[4]

The promises are the pathways on which Christ meets the soul. Thomas Goodwin said, "For if one promise do belong to thee, then all

---

2. John Flavel, "The Best in the Worst of Times," in *Works*, 4:48.

3. Edward Reynolds, *Three Treatises of the Vanity of the Creature. The Sinfulnesse of Sinne. The Life of Christ* (London: R. B. for Rob Boftocke and George Badger, 1642), part 1, 365.

4. *Catechisms of the Second Reformation*, ed. Alexander F. Mitchell (London: James Nisbet & Co., 1886), 176.

do; for every one conveys [the] whole Christ in whom all the promises are made and who is the matter of them."[5] William Spurstowe (c. 1605–1666) wrote, "The promises are instrumental in the coming of Christ and the soul together; they are the warrant by which faith is emboldened to come to him, and take hold of him; but the union which faith makes, is not between a believer and the promise, but between a believer and Christ."[6]

Reynolds said: "All the promises are made in Christ, being purchased by his merits, and they are all performed in Christ, being administered by his power and office…. Promises…are the rays and beams of Christ the Sun of Righteousness, in whom they are all founded and established…. Every promise by faith apprehended carries a man to Christ, and to the consideration of our unity with him, in the right whereof we have claim to the promises."[7]

Therefore, a pastor of God's Word must not take his cues from the world but cling to the promises of God. Rutherford said, "Forward then, dear brother, and lose not your grips. Hold fast the truth; for the world sells not one dram-weight of God's truth, especially now when most men measure truth by time, like young seamen setting their compass by a cloud: for now time is father and mother to truth, in the thoughts and practices of our evil time."[8]

God's Promises and Our Strength

To find encouragement in the promises of God, consider how the Puritans applied the following promises as they struggled with spiritual, political, and personal opposition.

1. A promise of strength when we are zealous for the name of the Lord. If we are zealous for our own name and success in this world, we will experience crushing disappointments. But if we are zealous

---

5. Goodwin, *Works*, 3:321.

6. William Spurstowe, *The Wells of Salvation Opened: or, A Treatise discerning the nature, preciousness, and usefulness of the Gospel Promises and Rules for the Right Application of Them* (London: T. R. & E. M. for Ralph Smith, 1655), 44–45.

7. Reynolds, *Three Treatises*, part 1, 356–57, 345. For more information on how the Puritans taught people to make use of God's promises, see Joel R. Beeke and James A. LaBelle, *Living by God's Promises* (Grand Rapids: Reformation Heritage Books, 2010).

8. Rutherford, *Letters*, 27.

for God's glory, the Lord will sustain us. Second Chronicles 16:9 says, "For the eyes of the LORD run to and fro throughout the whole earth, to shew himself strong in the behalf of them whose heart is perfect toward him." "Perfect" here does not mean sinless, but rather, "whole" or "sincere," meaning that we show singleness of heart in seeking to do God's will and to glorify God's name.[9] God blesses zeal for His name because that is in the heart of His Son. Thomas Watson wrote,

> Zeal is a mixed affection, a compound of love and anger. It carries forth our love to God and anger against sin in the most intense manner. Zeal is the flame of the affections; a godly man has a double baptism—of water and fire. He is baptized with a spirit of zeal; he is zealous for God's honor, truth, worship: "My zeal hath consumed me" (Ps. 119:139).... Our blessed savior in his zeal whips the buyers and sellers out of the temple: "The zeal of thine house hath eaten me up" (John 2:17).... Zeal casts out fear. It is quickened by opposition. Zeal does not say, "There is a lion in the way." Zeal will charge through an army of dangers, it will march in the face of death.[10]

Watson experienced many trials in his life and ministry. He lost four of his seven children when they were young. He protested the execution of Charles I and labored to restore the monarchy, though it cost him his pastorate in Walbrook and almost cost him his life. After the Act of Uniformity in 1662, Watson was once again forced out of his church by the monarchy he had helped to restore. He was forced to preach in homes, barns, and wherever his people could gather in private.[11]

2. A promise of support in the hour of need. When Paul prayed, asking the Lord to remove the thorn in his flesh, the Lord said, "My grace is sufficient for thee" (2 Cor. 12:9). Knowing that, Paul had the confidence to look death in the face and write, "For I know that this shall turn to my salvation through your prayer, and the supply of the

9. William Wilson, *Old Testament Word Studies* (McLean, Va.: MacDonald Publishing Co., n.d.), 307.

10. Watson, *The Godly Man's Picture*, 112–14.

11. Joel R. Beeke and Randall J. Pederson, *Meet the Puritans* (Grand Rapids: Reformation Heritage Books, 2006), 605–6.

Spirit of Jesus Christ, according to my earnest expectation and my hope, that in nothing I shall be ashamed, but that with all boldness, as always, so now also Christ shall be magnified in my body, whether it be by life, or by death" (Phil. 1:19–20).

William Bridge (1600–1671) wrote, "But though the Spirit does not always work alike, yet if God calls you to any work or service, you shall have so much assistance as is needful for you. Only you must know, that it shall be given in that hour;[12] it shall not lie cold and stale by you; but when you come to use it, then it shall be given unto you, more or less, but sufficient."[13]

Thomas Foxcroft, a young second-generation Puritan pastor, preached his ordination sermon at First Congregational Church of Boston on November 20, 1717. He spoke with great boldness and assurance, particularly for one just entering the ministry. He said,

> Hence, then, faithful ministers may expect from the Lord Jesus Christ all those supplies of both skill and strength that they need in order to fulfill their ministry.... He will teach their fingers to fight, and the arms of their hands shall be made strong by the mighty God of Jacob. He will anoint them with fresh oil, and renew their bow in their hand. He will give them a new heart and a new spirit, give power to them when they are faint, and when they have no might he will give an increase of strength. They who wait upon the Lord, who wait on their ministry, shall renew their strength as the eagles and mount up with wings [Isa. 40:31].... Ministers are his ambassadors, and as long as they act by His authority and keep to their credentials, He will bear them up and bear them out.[14]

3. A promise of success when we are faithful to the Lord. The Lord said in 1 Samuel 2:30, "Them that honour me I will honour, and they that despise me shall be lightly esteemed." The greater part of this honor will appear in eternal glory when we reign with Christ, for now is the time of our suffering, says 2 Timothy 2:8–12. So this is

---

12. Matthew 10:19, Vulgate.

13. William Bridge, *A Lifting up for the Downcast* (Edinburgh: Banner of Truth, 1990), 221.

14. Foxcroft, *The Gospel Ministry*, 65–66.

not a promise of worldly honor and success but rather a promise that people whom we influence for good today will be our eternal reward. As 1 Thessalonians 2:19–20 says, "For what is our hope, or joy, or crown of rejoicing? Are not even ye in the presence of our Lord Jesus Christ at his coming? For ye are our glory and joy."

Gifts and talents for ministry are not nearly as important as grace and obedience. Flavel thus said to pastors: "Weaker gifts, rooted in a gracious heart, will grow by using; but nothing grows without a root. I think the plainest men have done the greatest service in the church of Christ."[15] That means our perceived success or lack of it is not all-important, for the main thing that matters is faithfulness to God in the work He calls us to do. Bridge thus wrote,

> If a man be employed for God in any special service and work, the Lord will not only pardon his failings, but if he be faithful in his work, God will bless him and set a character of love and favour upon him. What a character of love did the Lord set on Caleb and Joshua! Of all men in Scripture, it is said of Caleb, that he followed the Lord fully; and this character God himself did set upon him…. But why did God own and dignify Caleb thus? Even because he was faithful in that work, service, and employment which God did call him to.[16]

Because of his faithfulness to biblical truth and steadfast opposition to error, Bridge was excommunicated from his church in Norwich, England, in 1636. A warrant for his arrest was also issued. So Bridge left England and went to the Netherlands, where he became co-pastor of a congregation of English exiles in Rotterdam. When Archbishop Laud gave his annual report to Charles I, he said, "Mr. Bridge of Norwich rather than he will conform, hath left his lecture and two cures, and is gone into Holland." Charles I wrote in the margin: "Let him go: we are well rid of him." But Bridge later returned to England (1641), and God blessed his ministry.[17] The Lord vindicated

---

15. John Flavel, "The Character of a True Evangelical Pastor," in *Works*, 6:581.
16. Bridge, *A Lifting up for the Downcast*, 216.
17. William Barker, *Puritan Profiles* (Ross-shire, U.K.: Christian Focus, 1996), 85–87.

His faithful servant during his lifetime and will vindicate him all the more at judgment day.

God's Promises and Our Trials

The Lord promises that our trials in life and ministry, when sanctified, serve the greater purpose of promoting the glory of the Lord and furthering His kingdom. They are also profitable to us in the following ways:

1. *Trials strengthen us in faith, patience, and self-denial.* James 1:2–3 says, "My brethren, count it all joy when ye fall into divers temptations; knowing this, that the trying of your faith worketh patience." Flavel wrote,

> God hath been training us up in faith, humility, patience, and self-denial in this school of affliction. When we could not preach the doctrine of faith, we were reduced, by a blessed necessity, to live the life of faith. The rules of patience, humility, and satisfaction in the will of God, we were wont to prescribe from our pulpits to the people, we were necessitated to practice and apply to ourselves in our sad solitudes, and various distresses, through which the Lord hath led us.[18]

2. *Trials compel us to pray boldly and more consistently.* Hosea 5:15 says, "In their affliction they will seek me early." Goodwin wrote,

> When God stirs up in the heart a particular faith in a business, as sometimes he doth, and upholds the heart to wait for it, [in spite of] all discouragements. So he did in David, Ps 27:3. David was then in great hazards by reason of Saul, or Absalom, and those such and so often, as that to sense and outward probabilities he was like never to live quietly again at, Jerusalem, and enjoy God's ordinances there in peace; but for this David had prayed, and had made it as the grand request of his whole life…and accordingly God gave him a special faith in this thing above all other, because it was his great request; 'In this will I be confident.'[19]

---

18. Flavel, "The Character of a True Evangelical Pastor," in *Works*, 6:584.
19. Goodwin, *Works*, 3:378.

Goodwin knew from experience about God's encouragement. When he was age fifteen, Goodwin was not allowed to take communion because his tutor thought he was too young (he was small in stature). This experience so discouraged Goodwin that he went into spiritual decline for a few years. He decided to become a preacher who won acclaim by rhetoric and style rather than substance. He was finally brought to a profound conviction of sin after listening to a funeral sermon. That sermon prompted him to search Scripture and to pray earnestly for spiritual deliverance.

3. *Trials foster a greater love for the Lord.* Hosea 2:14 says, "Therefore, behold, I will allure her, and bring her into the wilderness, and speak comfortably unto her." It is in the wilderness that God betroths His people to Himself in love and mercy so that they know Him (vv. 19–20).

Rutherford wrote, "My sky shall clear, for Christ layeth my head in his bosom and admitteth me to lean there. I never knew before what his love was in such measure. If he leave me, he leaveth me in pain, and sick in love. And yet my sickness is my life and health. I have a fire within me; I defy all the devils in hell, and all the prelates in Scotland to cast water on it."[20]

Rutherford was a person of extreme emotions. He loved his congregation in Anwoth, Scotland, where he labored as a faithful pastor and effective preacher of Christ. But in 1636, he was called before the High Court for his nonconformity. He was removed from his church and sentenced to stay in Aberdeen. That was a sore trial for a man who loved to preach. Many of his letters drip with sorrow over the loss of his congregation. Later he was briefly restored to his church, then was appointed as a professor at St. Andrews, where he spent the last fourteen years of his life teaching, preaching, and writing.

Throughout his life, Rutherford suffered much personal loss. In 1630, his first wife died after suffering extreme pain for thirteen months. He lost all but one child from that marriage. Ten years later he remarried and had six children, all of whom died before him. When the monarchy was restored, Rutherford was deprived of his

---

20. Rutherford, *Letters*, 65.

church and his university chair and placed under house arrest. He expected to be put to death for treason, as other prominent leaders had, but he was already on his deathbed and was unable to appear before the tribunal. His response to the court was, "Tell them I have got a summons already before a superior judge and judicatory, and I behoove to answer my first summons; and ere your day arrives, I will be where few kings and great folks come."[21] Few in church history loved Christ as deeply as Rutherford did. By the Spirit's blessing, great trials drove him into deeper intimacy with Christ.

4. *Trials wean us from the pride that often accompanies success.* Psalm 119:67, 71 says, "Before I was afflicted I went astray: but now have I kept thy word…. It is good for me that I have been afflicted; that I might learn thy statutes." Prosperity often inclines us to forget God, but affliction teaches us to cleave to Him and to walk humbly in the way of His commandments. Bridge wrote,

> Hereby also you are kept from that great temptation of resting on your labours as we are very apt to rest on our duties, sufferings and enjoyments. That we may not rest on our duties, God sometimes suspends our duty, or our heart in it. That we may not rest on our spiritual enjoyment, God sometimes suspends that also. So here. What is the reason that God puts the sentence of death upon our employments, or suspends their success, but that we may be kept from resting on our labours? Were our labours more successful, we should rest more upon them, but by lack of success we are weaned from them. This is comfort even in the absence of comfort.[22]

5. *Trials prepare us for the work God has planned for us to do.* Hebrews 5:8–9 says of Christ, "Though he were a Son, yet learned he obedience by the things which he suffered; and being made perfect, he became the author of eternal salvation unto all them that obey him." Christ was already sinless, but He was prepared for His mediatorial ministry by what He suffered in obedience to the will of His Father. Suffering also prepares us for Christian service. Perkins said,

---

21. Beeke and Pederson, *Meet the Puritans*, 727.
22. Bridge, *A Lifting up for the Downcast*, 233.

Does God bring some great affliction on you? It may be he has some mighty work of grace to do in you, or some great work of mercy to be wrought by you in his church, and is preparing you for it. Learn to say with the holy prophet, "I was mute, I did not open my mouth, because it was You who did it" (Ps. 39:9). What God may intend you cannot tell; therefore, in silence and patience, possess your soul.[23]

Perkins likely gave this counsel to students in his career as dean of students at Christ College, Cambridge. He tutored and catechized students, often when they were greatly distressed. A moving story of Perkins's pastoral love for people comes from Samuel Clark. He said that when Perkins saw a condemned prisoner climbing to the gallows, he called out to him, "What man! What is the matter with thee? Art thou afraid of death?" The prisoner said he was mostly afraid of what would *follow* death. Instantly, Perkins said to the prisoner, "Come down again, man, and thou shalt see what God's grace will do to strengthen thee." When Perkins prayed earnestly with the prisoner, he was first moved to tears over his sins and then moved to tears over God's redemption in Christ. After prayer, the prisoner rose from his knees, went up the ladder with joy to the gallows, and testified to the gathered crowd of being washed in the blood of Christ.[24]

6. *Trials and our response to them are a witness to the world.* It is significant that after Christ said, "Blessed are ye, when men shall revile you, and persecute you," He went on to say, "Ye are the light of the world." You may feel that your trials hinder your ministry, but if you respond well to them, those trials will actually increase your spiritual influence. Thus ministers must remember that they are "always bearing about in the body the dying of the Lord Jesus, that the life also of Jesus might be made manifest in our body" (2 Cor. 4:10). Robert Bolton (1572–1631) wrote,

And we shall hereby excellently honor and advance the glory of profession; when it shall appear to the world, and even the contrary-minded are compelled to confess, that there is a

---

23. Perkins, *The Art of Prophesying*, 158.
24. Beeke and Pederson, *Meet the Puritans*, 469–73.

secret heavenly vigour, undauntedness of spirit, and nobleness of courage, which mightily upholds the hearts of holy men in those times of confusion and fear, when theirs melt away within them like water. Worldlings wonder, and gnash the teeth hereat, when they see, as Chrysostom truly tells us, the Christian differ from them in this; that he bears all crosses courageously; and with the wings, as it were, of faith, outsoars the height of all human miseries.[25]

Bolton experienced the truth of his own words on his deathbed. He had been a proud man prior to his conversion, even calling Perkins a "barren empty fellow" after listening to him deliver a commencement address. But the Lord shook him "to pieces" and humbled him for the remainder of his life. He entered the ministry, and was thereafter known for his spiritual counsel and his deep devotional life. He would pray at least six times a day. In the days of preparation for the Lord's Supper, he demonstrated such humility that he prayed like a child talking with a parent. He died in 1631 after a painful illness. Prior to that, he received numerous visitors who were deeply moved as he expressed his ardent longing to be with the Lord. Two days before his death he said, "I feel nothing in my soul but Christ, with whom I heartily desire to be."[26]

If you learn to live by God's promises, you will be greatly encouraged rather than devastated by disappointments, trials, and losses. Your eyes will be on Jesus Christ, and you will live and die in victory.

---

25. Robert Bolton, *The Four Last Things* (Pittsburgh: Soli Deo Gloria, 1994), 20.
26. Beeke and Pederson, *Meet the Puritans*, 78–80.

PART TWO

Sovereignty

God is worthy of all praise and honor, not only when he doth enrich and strengthen us, when he fills and protects us; but also when he doth impoverish and weaken us, when he empties and smites us, when he gives us up to the will of our enemies, to the will of devils, and wicked men, even then God is to be blessed.

—JOSEPH CARYL

❦

CHAPTER 4

God Gives the Increase

Few activities are as fulfilling and frustrating as gardening. Our diligent efforts to weed and water seeds may result in a bountiful harvest. On the other hand, promising plants may suddenly wilt into fruitlessness. All is in God's hands, for He controls both the weather and the worm. As Jonah 4:7–8a says, "But God prepared a worm when the morning rose the next day, and it smote the gourd that it withered. And it came to pass, when the sun did arise, that God prepared a vehement east wind; and the sun beat upon the head of Jonah."

Pastoral ministry is much like gardening. Laziness almost certainly guarantees that one's ministry will be soon be overrun by weeds (Prov. 24:30–34), while diligent and faithful work will be rewarded by the Master when He returns (Matt. 25:14–30). Yet all our cares, efforts, and tears cannot secure conversion in a person or growth in a church. Paul humbles all ministers of the gospel when he writes in 1 Corinthians 3:5–7, "Who then is Paul, and who is Apollos, but ministers by whom ye believed, even as the Lord gave to every man? I have planted, Apollos watered; but God gave the increase. So then neither is he that planteth any thing, neither he that watereth; but God that giveth the increase."

We affirm God's sovereignty with our lips, but our roller-coaster ride on the ups and downs of church attendance may betray our hidden fears that our work is useless. Many pastors face pain and disappointments in ministry, which, at times may result in anger against God Himself. Kent Hughes says that after a season of watching his church shrink, he faced the horrible thought: "God has called me to do something he hasn't given me the gifts to accomplish. Therefore, God is not good."[1] We might at least be tempted to say, "God is not good *to me*." Have you ever thought that?

Reminding a discouraged pastor of the sovereignty of God may seem like rubbing salt in a wound. The pastor may already think that God is punishing him, or he may secretly accuse God of failing to reward him for his obedience. In reality, though, he is failing to fully embrace God's sovereignty with all its implications. Wholeheartedly embracing God's sovereignty will bring us to full dependence on Him and submission to His will.

In this chapter we will examine the Puritans' teaching on the sovereignty of Christ as Savior and Head of the church to help us become more dependent on Him. In the next chapter we will discuss how we may submit to God in our sufferings.

Dependence is central to God's plan to manifest His glory. Jonathan Edwards wrote, "God is glorified in the wisdom of redemption in this, that there appears in it so absolute and universal a dependence of the redeemed on him."[2] This is not just partial dependence, for God has built "absolute and universal" dependence into His plan so that all glory will go to Him (1 Cor. 1:29–31).

To benefit from the Puritans' teaching, we will consider, first, what they taught about predestination and preaching; and second, what they taught about conviction and conversion. We trust that this teaching will provide practical encouragements to the pastor as he labors in the Lord's field.

Predestination and Preaching

God saves through the preaching of the Word, but preachers do not control whom God saves. Preachers are significant instruments in God's hand, but they are not sovereign agents. These truths may

---

1. Kent and Barbara Hughes, *Liberating Ministry from the Success Syndrome* (Wheaton: Tyndale House, 1988), 22.

2. Jonathan Edwards, "God Glorified in Man's Dependence," in *The Works of Jonathan Edwards, Volume 17, Sermons and Discourses 1730–1733*, ed. Mark Valeri (New Haven: Yale University Press, 1999), 202. Henceforth *WJE* 17.

bring balance and joy to our pastoral ministry, for they enable us to renounce our own wisdom, knowledge, and ability and depend on the Lord to save whom He will.

Perkins established a paradigm of dependency for later Puritan preachers in his teachings on predestination. Far from a harsh and cold doctrine, his view of predestination laid the foundation for a warm experiential faith in Christ that promotes hope and humility.[3] Here, specifically, are some of the encouraging truths of predestination.

1. God decreed the salvation of some and damnation of others for His own glory. Perkins wrote, "Election is God's decree whereby on his own free will, he hath foreordained certain men to salvation, to the praise of the glory of his grace (Eph. 1:4–6)."[4] Similarly, he wrote, "The decree of reprobation is that part of predestination, whereby God, according to the most free and just purpose of his will, hath determined to reject certain men unto eternal destruction, and misery, and that to the praise of his justice (Rom. 9:21)."[5] Though God is not the author of sin, He is firmly in control of everything that happens in the world He created, including the salvation of some sinners and the damnation of others.

Flavel wrote, "God hath chosen some to salvation, and passed by others; as the Scriptures speak (Rom. 8:30; Jude 4). Did God choose some because he foresaw they would be better than others? No: God's choice was not on foreseen works, but merely of his grace, and [the] good pleasure of his will (Eph. 1:5–6)."[6] This truth reminds us that every spiritual blessing comes to us by God's grace and that nothing God does for us, in us, or through us is based on what we are or deserve.

---

3. Portions of this chapter are summarized from Joel R. Beeke, "William Perkins on Predestination, Preaching, and Conversion," in *The Practical Calvinist: An Introduction to the Presbyterian and Reformed Heritage in Honor of D. Clair Davis,* ed. Peter A. Lillback (Ross-shire, U.K.: Christian Focus Publications, 2002), 183–213.

4. William Perkins, "A Golden Chaine: or, The Description of the Theologie, Containing the order of the causes of Salvation and Damnation, according to Gods word," in *The Workes of that Famous and Worthy Minister of Christ in the Universitie of Cambridge, Mr. William Perkins* (London: John Legatt, 1612), 1:24.

5. Perkins, "A Golden Chaine," in *Workes,* 1:105.

6. John Flavel, "An Exposition of the Assembly's Catechism," in *Works,* 6:174–75.

Preaching the gospel to sinners is the heart of a pastor's calling. Knowing that God has chosen to save some people while rejecting others encourages a pastor to labor in utter dependence upon God's will. God has not only determined whom He will save, but also when He will save them and how His Holy Spirit will operate in them through the preached Word (Gal. 1:15–16; 1 Thess. 1:3–5). Perkins said, "The time of all events is determined in the counsel of God." That includes conversion.[7]

So the pastor cannot bring anyone to Christ. His task is to preach the gospel, trusting God to bring sinners to repentance and faith by His Word and Spirit. If God saves those who listen, He glorifies His grace; if He damns them, He glorifies His justice. Either way, though the preacher yearn for the conversion of all who listen, he may rest in the assurance that God will glorify Himself. That is a comfort to all who love God above all. It takes the weight of man's eternal destiny off the frail shoulders of preachers and puts it on God.

2. God made Christ the center of predestination. Perkins said the execution of God's decree rests upon the foundation of "Christ Jesus, called of his Father from all eternity, to perform the office of the Mediator."[8] Since Christ is the Son of God, He chooses with the Father and the Spirit whom God will save. Yet as Mediator, Christ is also the center of how God will save His elect.[9] They are chosen "in him," not apart from Christ (Eph. 1:4).[10] So when Perkins made a chart with lines showing how God implements election and reprobation in people's lives, Jesus Christ was the center column from which radiated all the lines of His saving influence to the elect.

Figure 1. William Perkins's "A Survey of Table declaring the order of the causes of salvation and damnation according to God's word."[11]

---

7. William Perkins, *A Commentary on Galatians,* ed. Gerald T. Sheppard (New York: Pilgrim Press, 1989), 42.

8. Perkins, "A Golden Chaine," in *Workes,* 1:24.

9. William Perkins, "A Treatise of Predestination," in *Workes,* 2:607–8; "An Exposition of the Creed," in *Workes,* 1:282.

10. Perkins, "A Golden Chaine," in *Workes,* 1:24.

11. Edward Hindson, ed., *Introduction to Puritan Theology: A Reader* (Grand Rapids: Baker, 1976), 139.

Figure 1

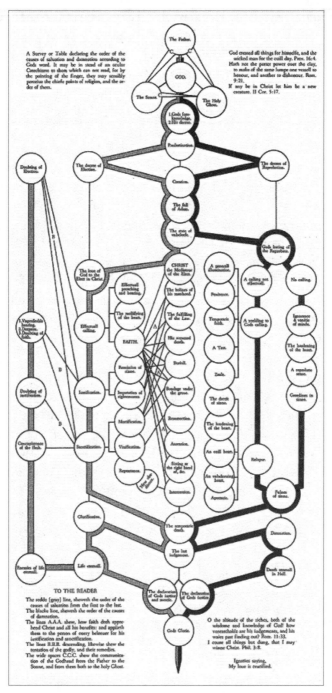

John Owen (1616–1683) wrote, "The person of Christ is the foundation of all the counsels of God, as unto his own eternal glory in the vocation [calling], sanctification, and salvation of the church."[12] The Father and the Son made this plan, commonly referred to as the covenant of redemption, with "ineffable delight," for God would make known in the Person of the Son His infinite wisdom, goodness, and love.[13]

Is your ministry centered on Christ? Perkins said the sum of all his instructions on preaching was to "Preach one Christ by Christ to the praise of Christ."[14] If that is so, be encouraged if you are in line with God's great purpose for all history (Eph. 1:9–10). Regardless of the results that you presently see, if you seek to honor Christ in your preaching, God will glorify Himself through you.

3. *God uses the preaching of Christ to save His chosen ones.* Perkins viewed the preaching of the gospel as God's mighty arm to gather in the elect and as Christ's chariot in which He rides victoriously into a sinner's heart. God executes His election through His covenant, specifically His covenant of works and covenant of grace.[15] So both the law and the gospel must be preached.

Rather than severing preaching from predestination, Perkins joined them, saying, "God doth not only ordain the end, but also the means whereby the end is compassed." And the means by which God saves His elect is "that we may be called by the ministry of the gospel." For those whom God predestinated, them He also called (Rom. 8:30).[16]

God's predestination comes to fruition through our preaching of Christ. Perkins reminds us that God promises to save all who truly believe in Christ (John 3:16). Indeed, he said that gospel ministers should "exhort all and every one to repent, considering that they are

---

12. John Owen, "Christologia: or, A Declaration of the Glorious Mystery of the Person of Christ," in *The Works of John Owen,* ed. William H. Goold (1850–1853; repr., Edinburgh: Banner of Truth, 2000), 1:54.

13. Owen, "Christologia," in *Works,* 1:56, 58.

14. William Perkins, "The Arte of Prophecying," in *The Workes of that Famous and Worthy Minister of Christ, in the Universitie of Cambridge, M. William Perkins* ([London]: John Legat, 1609), 2:762.

15. Perkins, "A Golden Chaine," in *Workes,* 1:31–32, 70.

16. William Perkins, "An Exposition of the Creed," in *Workes,* 1:283.

altogether ignorant, who, and how many be elected, and [are] to be converted."[17] When preachers tell people to turn from their idols and trust in Christ, they are not contradicting predestination but acting by faith in it, for Christ is the heart of predestination. Reformed Christians (sometimes called Calvinists) should never be afraid to preach Christ and to call and invite sinners to Him, for that is the very means God normally uses to realize His electing grace.

Pastors, the almighty will of God that predestined God's elect to glory now works through your preaching. People can oppose your ministry, but they cannot overcome God's predestination. That truth gave the apostle Paul much courage. He said, "Remember that Jesus Christ of the seed of David was raised from the dead according to my gospel: wherein I suffer trouble, as an evil doer, even unto bonds; but the word of God is not bound. Therefore I endure all things for the elect's sakes, that they may also obtain the salvation which is in Christ Jesus with eternal glory" (2 Tim. 2:8–10). So, as God's servant you may be bound, but God's Word cannot be bound.

4. God implements predestination through suffering servants. You might think that if God's sovereign power stands behind your ministry, you will crush all obstacles under foot and ride like a conquering hero to victory. In a sense, the opposite is true. God's servants triumph through suffering, weakness, apparent failure, and sometimes early death. This is hardly encouraging to those who approach the ministry with a desire for visible success. But this biblical truth may comfort you if you feel that you have failed God or that God has failed you.

Predestination unleashes God's power through human weakness and pain. We saw earlier that predestination centers on Christ. First Peter 1:19–20 says we were redeemed "with the precious blood of Christ...who verily was foreordained before the foundation of the world." One way to be encouraged to serve the Lord is to meditate on "Christ's predestination," for as William Ames (1576–1633) said, God's predestination of Christ was for Him to die as our redeeming lamb.[18]

---

17. Perkins, "A Treatise of Predestination, in *Workes*, 2:608.

18. William Ames, "A Commentary on the first Epistle of Peter," in *The Workes of the Reverence and Faithfull Minister of Christ William Ames* (London: for John Rothwell, 1643), 27.

Alexander Nisbet (c. 1623–1669) wrote, "Our Mediator was from all eternity designed [or designated] to the office of Mediatorship in that everlasting covenant of redemption wherein the Father gave the elect to His Son (Ps. 2:8), and appointed Him to assume human nature, therein to suffer for their redemption (Heb. 10:5)."[19] Therefore the heart of the gospel is the truth that God predestined His Son to redeem us through His mediatorial suffering. What could seem more futile than for the Messiah to be executed as a criminal while His disciples betrayed, denied, and forsook Him? Yet His sufferings and death have resulted in the redemption of an innumerable company of sinners.

Christians share in Christ's calling to be suffering servants (1 Peter 2:21–25). Philippians 1:29 says, "For unto you it is given in the behalf of Christ, not only to believe on him, but also to suffer for his sake." The God who predestined you to trust in Christ also predestined you to suffer for Him. Henry Airay (1560–1616) wrote, "Even both these, faith in Christ and persecution for Christ's sake, are the gift and grace of God towards you."[20]

God especially calls ministers to suffer for the good of others. When Christ took Paul captive to serve Him, He said, "He is a chosen vessel unto me, to bear my name before the Gentiles, and kings, and the children of Israel: for I will shew him how great things he must suffer for my name's sake" (Acts 9:15–16). Paul and Timothy profess that if "we be afflicted, it is for your consolation and salvation" (2 Cor. 1:6). A minister is never more effective for Christ than when he faithfully perseveres in the midst of great personal brokenness. For in this brokenness, as Sibbes said, you offer people a moving example, stir their minds to ask what keeps you faithful, provide public confirmation of the worthiness of Christ's cause, and demonstrate the power of the Holy Spirit in you. In short, you encourage all who have the same Spirit.[21]

---

19. Alexander Nisbet, *An Exposition of 1 & 2 Peter* (1658; repr., Edinburgh: Banner of Truth, 1982), 46.

20. Henry Airay, *Lectures upon the Whole Epistle of St Paul to the Philippians* (Edinburgh: James Nichol, 1864), 97.

21. Richard Sibbes, "Exposition of Second Corinthians Chapter 1," in *Works*, 3:94–95.

So do not let weakness and suffering bring you down. Your effectiveness has never depended on your own strength, so depend upon God to use you for His glory. The Lord loves His ministers. He decided from eternity past exactly how to work through us, even though we are often blind to how He is working in our circumstances. We can only be faithful to His Word.

Consider the experience of William Ames. Both of his parents died while he was young. Converted under the ministry of Perkins, Ames flourished as a teacher at Cambridge University. But after eight years of service, persecution against the Puritans forced Ames to leave Cambridge. Then the bishop of London forbad him to preach.

Ames went into exile in the Netherlands. For nine years he served as a military chaplain and preached to a small congregation. His wife died shortly after Ames married her in the Netherlands. He played a significant role in debates with the Arminians, particularly at the Synod of Dort. But his enemies in England managed to get him deposed from the chaplaincy. Then they blocked him from taking a promising position as a professor at Leiden University. Ames remarried and worked as a private lecturer and tutor to support his family.

God then opened a door for him to serve for eleven years as professor of theology at Franeker University. His work with students prospered, both in their theological training and spiritual growth. Once again, however, he found himself in the midst of controversy, this time with fellow professors. He also developed health problems. After accepting an invitation to help pastor a church in Rotterdam, Ames moved there, only to experience the flooding of his house. He caught pneumonia soon after that and died at the age of fifty-seven.

What a series of hardships and disappointments plagued Ames! Each time it looked like he might establish a foothold and make a difference in a church or school, he was forced to move. Yet he profoundly influenced the Reformed movement in the Netherlands, England, and especially in New England, where his books became the standard texts of theological students and pastors for more than a century.[22] Ames had no knowledge of how God would work through

---

22. In passing we should also take note of Ames's pervasive influence on the formulations of the Westminster Standards, adhered to by Presbyterian churches throughout the world today.

his efforts. Likewise, we are blind to God's plan for our lives. But we can trust that He who works all things according to His will has predestined us to the praise of His glory.

Conviction and Conversion

Ministers often needlessly suffer when they compare themselves to others and measure their ministries by today's standards of church growth. This worldly mindedness equates the advance of God's kingdom with numbers of people, expanding buildings, and rising budgets. But this mindset also arises from a mistaken view of conversion.

Many churchgoers today know the simple gospel that God loves us, sin separates us from God, Christ died for sinners, and therefore God forgives us and makes us His children when we trust in Christ. Each element of this gospel presentation is part of biblical truth. But important elements are missing. Just as some foods lack key vitamins and thus lead to malnutrition, so a simplistic gospel leads to a malnourished church because it omits key aspects of the biblical doctrine of salvation. An incomplete view of the gospel can greatly discourage a pastor or raise false hopes that will be dashed on judgment day. This is especially true when conversion is viewed merely as a human decision for Christ to gain forgiveness and entry to heaven.

The Puritans can help us recover the full biblical view of conversion. Consider how they understood God's great work of applying redemption to the individual sinner. They said that in conversion, we must remember that we are utterly dependent on God. Watson said, "Ministers knock at the door of men's hearts, the Spirit comes with a key and opens the door."[23] Jonathan Edwards said, "The ministers of the gospel are sent of God, and all their sufficiency is of him; 2 Cor. 4:7, 'We have this treasure in earthen vessels, that the excellency of the power may be of God, and not of us.' Their success depends entirely and absolutely on the immediate blessing and influence of God."[24]

Here are some of the ways God works in sinners to bring them to Christ.

---

23. Thomas Watson, "Body of Divinity," in *The Select Works of the Rev. Thomas Watson* (New York: Robert Carter, 1855), 148.

24. Jonathan Edwards, "God Glorified in Man's Dependence," in *WJE* 17:203.

1. God ordinarily prepares sinners for conversion by conviction of sin.[25] Before people come to Christ, normally they will be convinced that they need Christ. God pierces their proud hearts with a sense of their sin and His wrath so that they long to know how they can be saved (Acts 2:37). Perkins explained this in the questions and answers of his fundamental principles:

> Q. But how mayest thou be made partaker of Christ and his benefits?
>
> A. A man of a contrite and humble spirit, by faith alone apprehending and applying Christ with all his merits unto himself, is justified before God and sanctified....
>
> Q. How doth God bring men truly to believe in Christ?
>
> A. First, he prepareth their hearts, that they might be capable of faith, and then he worketh faith in them.
>
> Q. How doth God prepare men's hearts?
>
> A. By bruising them, as if one would break a hard stone to powder; and this is done by humbling them (Ezek. 11:19; Hos. 6:1–2).
>
> Q. How doth God humble a man?
>
> A. By working in him a sight of his sins, and a sorrow for them.[26]

Conviction of sin is a primary operation of the Holy Spirit (John 16:8). Goodwin wrote, "The Spirit will 'convince of sin,' that is, of that miserable and sinful estate which men live in by nature, and which, without belief in him, will prove matter of condemnation to them."[27]

Goodwin said the conviction of sin involves the Holy Spirit's use of God's law, just as John the Baptist prepared the way for Christ's coming by preaching against sin and calling for repentance.[28] The apostle Paul devotes considerable space in Romans to the themes of wrath, law, sin, and death (chaps. 1–3, 5, 7) to set the stage for the

---

25. See Joel R. Beeke and Paul M. Smalley, *Prepared by Grace, for Grace: The Puritans on God's Ordinary Way of Leading Sinners to Christ* (Grand Rapids: Reformation Heritage Books, forthcoming).

26. William Perkins, *The Work of William Perkins,* ed. Ian Breward (Appleford: Sutton Courtenay Press, 1970), 147, 156.

27. Thomas Goodwin, "The Work of the Holy Ghost in Our Salvation," in *Works,* 6:361.

28. Goodwin, "The Work of the Holy Ghost in Our Salvation," in *Works,* 6:362–63.

gospel.[29] The "law work" of humiliation takes away a man's ability to find comfort in anything but God and to trust no righteousness but what comes by faith in Christ.[30]

The message of God's love must be set in the context of the message of God's wrath against lawbreakers or it will produce shallow and half-hearted responses. We see this in some churches that outwardly thrive through popular programs while the behavior of attendees indicates a lack of wholehearted faith, devotion to Christ, hatred of sin, and renunciation of the world. They appear to have never been broken by their sins against God.

The Spirit's work begins with conviction of sin. Therefore we must pray to be bold like Micah, who said of preaching: "But truly I am full of power by the spirit of the LORD, and of judgment, and of might, to declare unto Jacob his transgression, and to Israel his sin" (Mic. 3:8). Never be ashamed of proclaiming God's law, God's wrath, or God's justice. Preach those in biblical balance with God's love, God's grace, and God's mercy in Christ, and trust that God's way of preparing sinners for conversion is by first awakening them to their true need instead of what they think they need.

2. God joins sinners to Christ by a hungry, militant faith. Perkins said that after God prepares the sinner with His law, He then stirs up his mind to consider the gospel. God kindles "sparks of faith" in the heart, thereby justifying the sinner even though at this point he is only aware of his desire to trust in Christ. God's grace then moves him to fight against doubt and mistrust. In due time the Lord grants him the assurance of faith that satisfies his conscience with the promise of eternal life in Christ.[31] Thus the first motions of faith are characterized, not necessarily by inward peace, but by "hungering and thirsting after that grace which is offered to him in Christ Jesus."[32]

The Puritans believed that faith was not merely "a bare acknowledgment that Christ is a Saviour," as Watson said, but also includes renouncing one's own righteousness and ability and resting upon

---

29. Goodwin, "The Work of the Holy Ghost in Our Salvation," in *Works*, 6:364–65.
30. Goodwin, "The Work of the Holy Ghost in Our Salvation," in *Works*, 6:382.
31. William Perkins, "The Whole Treatise of Cases of Conscience," in *Workes*, 2:13.
32. Perkins, "A Golden Chaine," in *Workes*, 1:79.

Christ and Him crucified "as bleeding and dying," that is, as the promises of the gospel present Him, and receiving Christ's merits as a hand receives gold. Watson said such faith can only be produced by the Holy Spirit: "The Spirit's working faith is called 'the exceeding greatness of God's power' [Eph. 1:19]. What power was put forth in raising Christ from the grave…the same power the Spirit of God puts forth in working faith [Eph. 2:4–6]. The Spirit irradiates the mind, subdues the will."[33]

A preacher can expound Scripture texts, explain sound doctrine, offer helpful analogies, make real-life applications, and express passion. But without the Spirit of God, those who listen to such preaching will remain as dead as the dry bones of Ezekiel's vision (Ezek. 37:1–14). Their responses will be as shallow and short-lived as the seed that fell by the wayside, into stony ground, or among the thorns (Matt. 13:3–9, 18–23).

Do not confuse intellectual assent with true, saving faith. Perkins said saving faith is "miraculous and supernatural" because it grasps hold of Jesus Christ by the operation of the Holy Spirit.[34] When you see such faith, give thanks to God (Eph. 1:15–16), for it is His creation. Never think that you can generate faith by your effectiveness as a communicator or as a winsome personality. You are not God. If pastors would truly accept that faith is a supernatural creation of God, they would spend less time agonizing over their inability to create it and more time in prayer and thanksgiving.

3. God turns sinners to Himself in repentance and new obedience. Though conviction of sin may move men to change their outward behavior, true repentance "is wholly begotten by the preaching of the gospel," Perkins said. It transforms a person into a gospel warrior who fights against Satan and sin.[35] Like true faith, true repentance is supernatural. Both the killing of sin and a life of obedience flow out of union with Christ in His death and resurrection (Rom. 6 and 8).[36]

Many pastors are heartbroken when people who profess faith in Christ rarely come to church or when others use external religious

---

33. Watson, "Body of Divinity," in *Select Works,* 145.
34. Perkins, "A Golden Chaine," in *Workes,* 1:79.
35. Perkins, "A Golden Chaine," in *Workes,* 1:85.
36. Perkins, "A Golden Chaine," in *Workes,* 1:83.

acts as a veneer to hide their wickedness. How many converts at evangelistic meetings have never shown the fruit of repentance? How many people have their names on church membership lists but do not live as members of Christ's body? The Puritans remind us that though our good works do not produce salvation, salvation produces good works (Eph. 2:8–10). Manton said, "Apples do not give life to the tree, but show it forth."[37] Christ taught us that we will know what men are by the fruit they bring forth (Matt. 7:15–20).

So pastors, get out of the trap of measuring yourself by the size of your ministry. Stop trying to produce fruit in other people's lives. Let go of trying to breathe life into corpses. Each branch must abide in the vine, but you cannot be that vine. You can only cling to Christ, let His Word abide in you, and bear the fruit of the Spirit to the glory and praise of God. Be faithful to proclaim both the law and the gospel. In so doing, you will show that you love Christ and truly care for His sheep. And you will discover the wondrous power of the Shepherd's voice to call His little flock to Himself "by the lively preaching of His Word."[38]

We should grieve over the lost, pray for their salvation, and preach the gospel to them. But let us not take responsibility for converting them or for building Christ's church. Take responsibility only for yourself. Remind yourself daily that you are not the Savior but only His servant.

Anthony Burgess (d. 1664) asked, "Is it God that giveth the increase?" He answered, "Then we ministers are not to be inordinately cast down, if people receive no divine stamp upon them. If we water not; if we plant not; then, woe be to us: but when both is done, yet if there be no increase, that is our misery, not our sin. God will give to every minister according to his work, not according to his success."[39]

---

37. Manton, *Works,* 4:243.

38. Heidelberg Catechism, Q. 98.

39. Anthony Burgess, *The Scripture Directory, for Church-Officers and People, or, A Practical Commentary upon the Whole third Chapter of the first Epistle of St Paul to the Corinthians* (London: Abraham Miller for T. U., 1659), 89.

CHAPTER 5

～❈～

Submission to God's Will

As servants of the sovereign Lord, pastors must be dependent on God's power and submit to His will. In the previous chapter, we talked about developing an attitude of dependence by recognizing the sovereignty of God. The Puritans help us see how the biblical doctrines of predestination and conversion promote a minister's absolute dependence on the Lord. This dependence humbles us and sets us free from the burden of trying to do what only God can do.

Submission to God walks hand in hand with dependence on Him. Indeed, submission strengthens dependence. However, even when we recognize that God alone saves sinners, we still face the pain of ministry. Sometimes this pain nags at us like a sore knee and slowly wears us down. Sometimes it tackles us like a three-hundred-pound defensive lineman.

We can become discouraged and despair. We may even become angry with God. But when we submit to His providence, we do so by humbly accepting the pain of ministry and persevere in doing God's will. We neither fight with the referee nor lie defeated on the ground. We get up and return to the line of scrimmage, knowing we have to pay for every yard gained.

Submission is crucial for our service to God and our own spiritual well-being. Owen said, "He that cannot live in an actual resignation of himself and all his concerns unto the sovereign pleasure of God, can neither glorify him in anything nor have one hour's solid peace in his own mind."[1] Still, we may go through the motions of ministry while our heart remains cold. Equally tragic, we may fail to model the kind of faith in God that we long to see in the lives of our people.

To learn about submission, we now turn to the example of Job. The Puritan Joseph Caryl (1602–1673) preached a lengthy series of sermons on Job. He said, "This book is written for this especially, to teach us the sovereignty of God, and the submission of the creature."[2] The submission of a godly man is shown in how Job responded to the news that his children had died and all his wealth had been lost in a single day, as recorded in Job 1:20–21: "Then Job arose, and rent his mantle, and shaved his head, and fell down upon the ground, and worshipped, and said, Naked came I out of my mother's womb, and naked shall I return thither: the LORD gave, and the LORD hath taken away; blessed be the name of the LORD."

In Job's response the Puritans recognized submissive grief, submissive humility, submissive faith, and submissive praise. Let us now examine those in detail.

Submissive Grief

First, Job expressed his overwhelming sorrow in a way that honored God. He rose from his seat, tore his clothes, shaved his head, fell to the ground, and bowed before God. Tearing his clothes and shaving his head were signs of intense grief and mourning. Falling down and worshiping God expressed Job's devotion to God.

We must never think that godliness will insulate us against pain. Love does not make us numb; it makes us feel losses all the more. We are wrong to think that submission means no tears, no breaking of the heart, no inward struggles, and no troubling questions. Job did not tear his clothes and shave his head merely out of custom. He tore his robe because his heart was torn to pieces. He cut his hair because

---

1. John Owen, *A Discourse on the Holy Spirit*, in *The Works of John Owen*, ed. William H. Goold (New York: Robert Carter & Brothers, 1852), 3:599.

2. Joseph Caryl, *An Exposition with Practical Observations upon… the Book of Job* (1644–1666; facsimile repr., Berkley, Mich.: Dust & Ashes Publications, and Grand Rapids: Reformation Heritage Books, 2001), 1:12.

all his hopes for his children were cut off. Can you imagine what it would be like to bury all your children in one day?

Further on in the book of Job, the good man wrestled with profound questions, responded to the accusation of friends by arguing his case, cried out to God, and eventually cursed the day he was born. There is not the slightest hint in Job of the rock-like indifference of the Stoic or the blind fatalism of the Muslim. Though Job was rebuked for calling God to account (chapters 38–41), for the most part he received God's commendation (Job 42:7). So Job's questions and wrestling were not wicked; they were signs of grief in a godly man.

Job exhibited both honest sorrow and holy submission, which are recommended in Hebrews 12:5, "My son, despise not thou the chastening of the Lord, nor faint when thou art rebuked of him." The Puritan Caryl said that we must avoid the extremes of grief, either by acting as though God's disciplines were a light thing, saying, "If my children die, let them die," or by falling into despair: "If when goods are taken away, the heart be taken away: and when children die, then the spirit of the parent dies too."[3] Neither extreme should be evident in our submission to God.

After hearing all the reports of his losses, Job bowed down and worshiped God. His outward body language expressed his inward heart of worship. Caryl said, "Internal worship is to love God, to fear God, and to trust upon him."[4] So let us learn in times of trouble not only to worship God with our bodies but also to pray to Him with our hearts. Caryl offered this expanded version of Job's prayer:

> Lord, though all this be come upon me, yet I will not depart from thee, or deal falsely in thy covenant. I know thou art still the same Jehovah, true, holy, gracious, faithful, all-sufficient; and therefore behold me prostrate before thee, and resolving still to love thee, still to fear thee, still to trust thee; thou art my God still and my portion forever. Though I had nothing left in the world that I could call mine, yet thou Lord alone art enough, yet thou alone art all.[5]

---

3. Caryl, *Exposition*, 1:186.
4. Caryl, *Exposition*, 1:190.
5. Caryl, *Exposition*, 1:190.

Job worshiped God with a broken heart, and so must we when God's hand lies heavy upon us.

Do not pretend that ministry doesn't hurt. Sometimes serving God hurts a lot. Perhaps you have seen your plans for ministry evaporate. You have poured your life into people only to suffer unfair criticism and rejection. Or perhaps you feel like a child who built sandcastles by the sea, only to watch your labors on behalf of the church be swallowed up by the inevitable tides of human sin, whether yours or someone else's.

It is best to respond to such trials with mourning and meekness. George Hutcheson (1615–1674), a minister in Edinburgh, said that to be "mournful under affliction…is very consistent with a patient and meek frame of spirit under trouble."[6] If we try not to feel the pain, we may harden our hearts. Hutcheson said the best way to manage grief is to "run to God with all that grieves us," with much humility and self-abasement.[7]

Whatever your grief is, acknowledge it and find appropriate ways to express it submissively before God. David cries out in Psalm 13:1–2, "How long wilt thou forget me, O LORD? for ever? how long wilt thou hide thy face from me? how long shall I take counsel in my soul, having sorrow in my heart daily? how long shall mine enemy be exalted over me?" If the Holy Spirit moved David to write such words, then surely there is nothing unspiritual about lying on the ground and crying out to God in your pain. Psalm 62:8 says, "Trust in him at all times; ye people, pour out your heart before him: God is a refuge for us." Other psalms model for us the spiritual discipline of writing our prayers in a journal or diary. Whether you compose freely flowing prayers or carefully crafted poetry, writing can help you to worship in your grief.

But beware of harboring anger against God, and beware of listening to people who tell you to forgive God for how He treated you. To forgive implies wrongdoing. If we are angry with God—and sadly we probably are more frequently than we are willing to admit—then we,

---

6. George Hutcheson, *An Exposition of the Book of Job* (London: for Ralph Smith, 1669), 14.

7. Hutcheson, *Job,* 14–15.

not God, need forgiveness. Cry out to Him in your pain and confess your anger for His cleansing by the blood of His Son. "Stand in awe, and sin not...offer the sacrifices of righteousness, and put your trust in the LORD" (Ps. 4:4, 5).

Submissive Humility

Second, we learn that Job humbled himself before God and man. He fell to the ground, saying, "Naked came I out of my mother's womb, and naked shall I return thither" (1:21a).[8] In this, Job revealed a profound degree of self-knowledge. He knew his utter nakedness and the utter destitution of his beginning and his end.

Job acknowledged his humility as a mere creature. How easy it is to forget that we came into the world with nothing! Paul reminds us, "Who maketh thee to differ from another? and what hast thou that thou didst not receive? now if thou didst receive it, why dost thou glory, as if thou hadst not received it?" (1 Cor. 4:7).

We thus have no right to hold onto the things we accumulate while we live, whether children, livestock, houses, lands, or money. Our humble birth reminds us that we came with nothing, so nothing is truly ours to claim or retain. Even the chair you sit on in your office is not ultimately yours. As sinners, we do not deserve any of the good things that we have. We have no reason to think that God will allow us to keep them forever, even while we live. Therefore we should humbly accept the loss of loved ones, earthly treasures, and riches.

The Bible reminds us that we must all die, and we cannot take our earthly riches with us. Ecclesiastes 5:15 says, "As [the rich man] came forth of his mother's womb, naked shall he return to go as he came, and shall take nothing of his labour, which he may carry away in his hand." Psalm 49:17 says, "When [the one made rich] dieth he shall carry nothing away: his glory shall not descend after him."

---

8. The latter part of Job's statement may strike us as a curious expression, for no one returns like a baby to his mother's womb (John 3:4). It may be that Job was speaking metaphorically, identifying his mother's womb with the earth from which man was first taken (Gen. 2:7; Ps. 139:13, 15). In this case Job is affirming that man comes from dust and returns to dust, in fulfillment of the penal curse imposed upon Adam after the fall (Gen. 3:19).

Paul says in 1 Timothy 6:7, "We brought nothing into this world, and it is certain we can carry nothing out." This is the futility of our fallen condition in Adam. Instead of expecting a life of increasing achievement and prosperity, we know that sin has doomed us to a brief, fleeting, insubstantial existence, "a vapour, that appeareth for a little time, and then vanisheth away" (James 4:14). "Man is like to vanity: his days are as a shadow that passeth away" (Ps. 144:4).

Ministers have various degrees of visible success. Some, like Nehemiah, make substantial, tangible contributions to the establishment and building up of God's church. Some, like Jeremiah, water their fields with tears but see no harvest. Yet others gather large crowds for a time, only to watch them walk away over a hard teaching, as did our Lord Jesus Christ. In the end, however, every minister will experience the truth that "the LORD hath taken away." Disability, old age, sickness, and death will inevitably remove us from ministry. And in that time, Hutcheson recommended, "Right reason will teach that we ought not to take it ill when we lose that at any time, of which we are certain within a short time to be stripped forever."[9] It makes no sense to fight with God over something that He has already told us would inevitably be taken away.

When you are sitting in a nursing home while younger men take your pulpit, how important will be the size of the church you served a decade ago? After you die, how many people will even remember your name? And if they do, what difference will it make to you? You will be with the Lord. If earthly honors and achievements mean so little in eternity, why put much stock in them now? Treasure only what will last.

Rutherford said, "Build your nest upon no tree here; for ye see God hath sold the forest to death."[10] He also wrote, "All that is here is condemned to die, to pass away like a snowball before a summer sun.... Let the movables go; why not? They are not yours. Fasten your grips upon the heritage."[11] Our heritage is Christ and His eternal kingdom, not what we hold in our hands.

---

9. Hutcheson, *Job,* 15.
10. Rutherford, *Letters,* 41.
11. Rutherford, *Letters,* 98–99.

We are servants temporarily assigned to do a task by our Master. When our appointed time is up, the Lord will quickly replace us as He sees fit. We run for a few decades in a relay race that started centuries ago and may continue after us for many generations. Be faithful in running your leg of the race, and be ready at any moment to pass on the baton. Realize that your ministry, while significant to those under your care, is miniscule in the grand scheme of God's plan. In that plan, there are no mega-pastors or mega-churches, only a magnificent Christ, the King whose greatness is beyond our thought.

Submissive Faith

The third lesson we learn from Job is that he trusted in the sovereign God. The second part of Job 1:21 says, "The LORD gave, and the LORD hath taken away." Job acknowledged Jehovah God as the eternal, unchanging, ever-faithful, covenant-keeping God, the "I AM THAT I AM" of Exodus 3:14. Job looked past himself, past all sorrows, past all secondary causes of grief, past rampaging enemies, lightning blasts, deadly wind storms, and Satan himself by acknowledging that everything comes from God (Rom. 11:36). He said, "*The LORD* gave, and *the LORD* hath taken away."

He saw first that everything he had was given to him by God. Job didn't speak of wages here, saying, "The Lord has paid me back; He has given me my earnings." Rather, he humbly recognized that what the Lord had given Job was given freely. He acknowledged the sovereignty of the Lord in giving.

Many preachers acknowledge that God gave them what they have, but they think and act as though God no longer had authority over these things. Their possessiveness swells to infernal proportions as they speak of "my church," "my preaching," and "my ministry." In truth, everything we have is a gift from God and remains His rightful property to dispose of as He sees fit. He is Lord of all. We are only His stewards, entrusted with His goods for a short time.

This Lord gives and gives and gives. We tend to complain when we lose something, but Job paused in his grief to remember the source of all his blessings. Why did he have children? Why did he have wealth? The Lord gave that to him. Before we moan our losses, we should remember why we had anything in the first place. The Lord gave us everything. Job said later, "Shall we receive good at the hand of God, and shall we not receive evil?" (Job 2:10). So respond to trials and tragedies by remembering God's generosity in everything He has given you.

Faith in God's sovereignty helps us to submit to God. According to Caryl, faith is a sword that can slay four monsters of the sinful heart: discontent, envy, pride, and contempt. So in times of loss or sorrow, ask yourself the following questions:

- Are you *discontent*, feeling you have too little? Submit to God, knowing that He gives you your portion with a Father's love. Is your Father not wise?

- Do you *envy* others for having more than you? "The Lord gave." Doesn't He have the right to do as He pleases with His possessions? Does God have to ask for your permission? Is it wrong for God to show grace to someone other than you?

- Are you *proud* because you are abundantly blessed? All good things are gifts from God, but if you obtained your riches by dishonest or violent means, they are the devil's gifts that will be cursed by God.

- Do you *look with contempt* on those who have less than you do? "The Lord gave," so He could as easily have given them more than you, for He gives freely.[12]

Much of the strife in our hearts and competition with other pastors could be avoided if we would look at every blessing and say, "The Lord gave." Nothing is more encouraging than submitting to God's will and thanking Him for offering good gifts to us.

Job acknowledged God's sovereignty in the gifts that He had given, but Job also owned God's sovereignty in the removal of those gifts. God is not only the great Giver; He is also the rightful Remover. Notice that Job did not say, "The Lord gave, and men have taken away." Nor did he say, "The Lord gave, and Satan has taken away." He did not regard secondary causes or agents. He went straight to the Source and said, "The LORD gave, and the LORD hath taken away."

---

12. Caryl, *Exposition*, 1:205–7.

Caryl wrote, "We should from hence learn, in all our afflictions to look beyond the creature. In all the evils we either feel or fear, let our hearts be carried up unto God."[13] He said, "It doth but set forth the supreme power and sovereignty of God in ordering all things.... Job knew that God had all men and devils, fire and wind, all creatures in his hand. He saith, 'The Lord hath taken,' because none could take but by the will of God."[14]

Preachers, tell yourself that God rules over everything in your life. Both good and bad things come to us by the sovereign decree of God (Isa. 45:7; Lam. 3:37–38). God hates sin, but He has planned so that His good purposes are accomplished, even through the sinful acts of men (Gen. 50:20). The Assyrian king arrogantly thought that he had conquered nations by his own might and wisdom, but he was merely a tool in the hand of the Lord to accomplish His purposes (Isa. 10:5–15). Thus Hutcheson wisely wrote: "Eye God more than instruments."[15]

If we receive all things from God's hand, we will more readily submit when God's hand takes them away. Manton advised a couple at their wedding to receive one another as from "God's hands."[16] He explained, "It is an help to make us more ready to part with one another when God willeth it."[17] The Lord gives; the Lord takes away. This must be our testimony regarding even the most precious gifts in our lives.

Submissive Praise

Job not only grieved submissively, owned his lowliness, and honored God's sovereignty; he also triumphed in adoration. The place in the dust where this broken man had fallen was turned into an altar for the sacrifice of praise. Job lifted up heart and voice to say, "Blessed be the name of the LORD." This is the language of the angels, for Psalm 103:20 says: "Bless the LORD, ye his angels, that excel in strength." It is the language of heaven.

---

13. Caryl, *Exposition,* 1:209.
14. Caryl, *Exposition,* 1:209.
15. Hutcheson, *Job,* 15.
16. Manton, *Works,* 2:163.
17. Manton, *Works,* 2:168.

In his submission, Job was not resigned to an impersonal fate or the arbitrary decree of a remote and uncaring God. When he said, "Blessed be the name of the LORD," Job was confessing that God is not just all-powerful but also righteous and good and worthy of all praise. How else could he bless God when God sent him sorrow? The *name* of the Lord is His nature or character as revealed to men. Job could bless God in his sorrows because he knew who God is. As Psalm 9:10 says, "They that know thy name will put their trust in thee."

When disappointment tempts you to be bitter, focus your mind on God's character and set your heart on praising Him. Caryl wrote, "God is blessed by his creatures, when his goodness, and greatness, and mercy, and bounty, and faithfulness and justice are published [or proclaimed] with thanksgiving and praise. God is also blessed likewise, when we have high and glorious thoughts of God: when we inwardly fear and reverence, and love, and honor God, then we bless God."[18]

Such praise is the opposite of complaining. Manton said, "Murmuring is an anti-providence, a renouncing of God's sovereignty.... As if we could correct [His ways], and do better and fitter for the government of the world."[19] How horrible it is when men whose mouths preach the gospel of God then complain with the same mouths about what God has done! Let us therefore seek to be filled with the Spirit so we may praise Him with our lips and make melody in our hearts to praise the Lord, even if we must do it while sitting in the dust under sore afflictions.

Remember, too, that we are engaged in spiritual warfare. Watson wrote, "Our murmuring is the devil's music."[20] Satan likes nothing better than to get men to curse God, even if they do it under their breath or in their heart of hearts. He tried to get Job to curse God. Dear brothers, is the devil also tempting you in your affliction to curse God? Submit to God, and resist the devil. In blessing God, Job unwittingly crushed the serpent under his feet. Let us likewise turn affliction into adoration and join Job in his triumph.

---

18. Caryl, *Exposition,* 1:213.

19. Manton, *Works,* 15:249–50.

20. Thomas Watson, *The Art of Divine Contentment,* ed. Don Kistler (Morgan, Pa.: Soli Deo Gloria, 2001), 65.

Praising God in pain requires us to submit our limited minds to God's incomprehensible ways. Why do we think we can judge God? John Owen was one of the greatest Christian thinkers of all time. His twenty-four volumes of writings continue to stretch the minds of theologians today. But Owen knew how little he knew of God. He wrote, "Notwithstanding all our confidence of high attainments, all our notions of God are but childish in respect of his infinite perfections. We lisp and babble, and say we know not what, for the most part, in our most accurate, as we think, conceptions and notions of God. We may love, honour, believe, and obey our Father; and therewith he accepts our childish thoughts, for they are but childish."[21] As children of God, we must not criticize our Father but trust Him.

We may grow weary of praying and waiting for God's mercies. We should then remind ourselves that God will keep His promises. Habakkuk 2:3 says, "For the vision is yet for an appointed time, but at the end it shall speak, and not lie: though it tarry, wait for it; because it will surely come, it will not tarry." Flavel said God's timing is always "precise, certain, and punctual," but, "the Lord doth not compute and reckon his seasons of working by our arithmetic."[22]

We can praise God through our tears when we let go of the desire to understand the ways and means of our infinite God. So many of our questions in ministry go unanswered. We ask why the Lord chose not to convert anyone through our evangelistic messages. We ask why an elder persistently opposes us. Why did that church member attack me so viciously? Why is my church so small while the one down the road flourishes? Why did our church go through such a horrific split?

We need to move beyond the *Why* questions to the *Who* questions. Like Job, we must consider the glory of God and ask, "Who art Thou, Lord?" We must see the insignificance and sinfulness of our humanity and ask, "O man, who art thou that speakest against God?" We must meditate on God's covenant of grace with us and ask, "Who am I, O Lord God?" When we remember who God is and who we are, we can lay aside our questions and praise God from the ash heap.

---

21. John Owen, *The Mortification of Sin*, in *Works*, 6:65.
22. Flavel, "The Mystery of Providence," in *Works*, 5:472.

Conclusion

The submission of a Christian glorifies God, so submission is the goal of our lives regardless of pain. "God is worthy of all praise and honor," wrote Caryl, "not only when he doth enrich and strengthen us, when he fills and protects us; but also when he doth impoverish and weaken us, when he empties and smites us, when he gives us up to the will of our enemies, to the will of devils, and wicked men, even then God is to be blessed."[23]

Submission to God's will is radical, Christ-like self-denial. For this reason it is both hard and healthy for us. Thomas Hooker got to the root of the matter when he said, "A man's self naturally is a God to his soul," so the wicked "will have no other God than their own selves."[24] Our submission to God's painful providences is a form of repentance for self-worship. Therefore, do not be discouraged when you are frustrated or disappointed in ministry. God is cleansing you of idolatry and growing you as a true worshiper. One day you will see how you needed that thorn in your flesh to make you into a better minister for the glory of the Lord.

---

23. Caryl, *Exposition*, 1:213.

24. Thomas Hooker, *The Christians Two Chiefe Lessons, viz. Selfe-Deniall, and Selfe-Tryall, as also the Priviledge of Adoption and Trial Thereof* (London: by T. B. for P. Stephens and C. Meredith, 1640), 38.

PART THREE

Clarity

The ministry [of the Word] is not only a seed to beget us, milk to feed us in childhood, but strong meat, by benefit of which we are to grow up further and further in the knowledge of the will of God.

— PAUL BAYNE

∞

CHAPTER 6

Taking Heed to Doctrine

We pastors are busy with countless worship services, classes, committees, small groups, one-on-one meetings, funerals, weddings, home visits, hospital visits, luncheons, lectures, and board meetings. In the midst of our busyness, are our books of theology gathering dust? Many men took their first steps toward ministry impelled by a passionate love for biblical truth and the desire to share it with others. They consumed theological books like well-cooked steaks. But after seminary, many of their theological works have become monuments to a bygone era of study.

You may object, saying, "I'm a pastor, not a theologian." But what do you think it means to be a theologian? If you think that means being a teacher of theology in a seminary or university, then, yes, most pastors are not theologians. But in another sense, a pastor must always be a theologian.

Herman Witsius (1636–1708) wrote, "By a theologian, I mean one who, imbued with a substantial knowledge of divine things derived from the teaching of God Himself, declares and extols, not in words only, but by the whole course of his life, the wonderful excellencies of God and thus lives entirely for His glory."[1] Shouldn't every pastor be a theologian in that sense? Shouldn't it be every pastor's goal that "their plain and chaste mode of teaching did not soothe itching ears but, impressing upon the mind an exact representation of sacred

---

1. Herman Witsius, *On the Character of a True Theologian*, ed. J. Ligon Duncan III (Greenville, S.C.: Reformed Academic Press, 1994), 27.

things, inflamed the soul with their love"?[2] Studying doctrine is no mere academic task but a deeply spiritual exercise, engaging the truth with faith and love by the power of the Holy Spirit (2 Tim. 1:13–14).

Continuing theological study is a primary duty of the pastor.[3] Paul says in 2 Timothy 2:15, "Study to shew thyself approved unto God, a workman that needeth not to be ashamed, rightly dividing the word of truth." Timothy received from Paul the equivalent of a seminary education (and more!); he traveled with the apostle for several years, listening to him expound his doctrine (2 Tim. 3:10). Paul now tells Timothy, however, that he must continue to "take heed unto the doctrine," reflecting on what he had already learned to increase his knowledge of biblical truth, and to profit from careful study and meditation as he preached the Word, "in season, out of season."

This chapter's goal is to encourage you in the delightful discipline that is close to the heart of the work of the pastorate: the reading of Holy Scripture and books of sound biblical theology.

Enrich People with Our Greatest Treasure

Why should pastors continue to read books of solid theology? The answer may be summed up in Paul's prayer that "the eyes of your understanding being enlightened…ye may know what is the hope of his calling, and what the riches of the glory of his inheritance in the saints, and what is the exceeding greatness of his power to us-ward who believe" (Eph. 1:18–19). God the Father has given us immense riches in His revelation of Christ.

The most important reason that Christian ministers should study doctrine all their days is that Christ is truth (John 14:6). If we love Christ, we must also love the truth (2 Thess. 2:10). As Christians, we are saved by believing the truth (2 Thess. 2:13). Faithful preaching is the "manifestation of the truth" (2 Cor. 4:2). To fully proclaim Christ, we must teach sound doctrine as "the unsearchable riches of Christ" (Eph. 3:8). Edward Leigh (1602–1671) said,

---

2. Witsius, *Character of a True Theologian*, 27.

3. For a helpful article on promoting continuing theological study, see Ryan M. McGraw, "Continuing Education for Ministers: A Guide for Ministers and Congregations," *Puritan Reformed Journal* 4, no. 1 (2012): 307–22.

Truth is precious and should be maintained: error is dangerous and should be opposed. "Buy the truth and sell it not," saith Solomon. Jerusalem is called a "city of truth" (Zech. 8:3). The church is called "the pillar and ground of truth" (1 Tim. 3:15). Christ came into the world, "that he might bear witness to the truth" (John 18:[37]). The prophet Jeremiah complains, "That none were valiant for the truth" (Jer. 9:3). "Contend earnestly for the faith, which was once delivered to the saints" (Jude 3). "We can do nothing against the truth but for the truth," saith Paul (2 Cor. 13:8).[4]

The glorified Christ gives pastors and teachers to the church to lead God's people from doctrinal immaturity to "the unity of the faith, and of the knowledge of the Son of God" (Eph. 4:11–14). In texts like these, "the faith" refers to an established system of teachings received by the church from the Lord, confessed before the world, and passed down from generation to generation.[5] Thus Paul wrote in Romans 6:17, "But God be thanked, that ye were the servants of sin, but ye have obeyed from the heart that form of doctrine which was delivered you."

Teaching these truths and urging believers to apply them builds up the body of Christ (Eph. 4:12). Thomas Watson said, "Knowledge of the grounds of religion much enricheth the mind. It is a lamp to our feet; it directs us in the whole course of Christianity, as the eye directs the body."[6]

If Christ's riches are "unsearchable," how can we ever be done searching them? Laziness, arrogance, and neglect of our calling tempt us to rest from studying and pressing on for a deeper knowledge of God. But the pastor who ceases to study deprives himself of one of the greatest joys he can know in this life and undercuts his usefulness as a servant of the Lord. Witsius said, "Nothing can be more delightful to a believing soul, nothing more useful to the Church, than that the

---

4. Edward Leigh, "The Epistle Dedicatorie," in *A Systeme or Body of Divinity* (London: by A. M. for William Lee, 1654), no pagination in the epistle. The original mistakenly reads John 18:27.

5. Acts 6:7; 13:8; 14:22; 16:5; 24:24; 2 Cor. 13:5; Gal. 1:23; Eph 4:13; Phil. 1:27; Col. 1:23; 2:7; 1 Tim. 3:9; 4:1; 5:8; 6:10, 21; 2 Tim. 3:8; Titus 1:13; Jude 3.

6. Watson, "Body of Divinity," in *Select Works,* 7.

theologian should, day by day, learn fresh lessons from the Scriptures, form more accurate ideas of spiritual things, discern with growing clearness the closeness of that connection by which saving truths are linked into one chain."[7]

Build God's Temple with Gold, Silver, and Precious Stones

While speaking about the ministry of the Word, Paul says in 1 Corinthians 3:10–13,

> According to the grace of God which is given unto me, as a wise masterbuilder, I have laid the foundation, and another buildeth thereon. But let every man take heed how he buildeth thereupon. For other foundation can no man lay than that is laid, which is Jesus Christ. Now if any man build upon this foundation gold, silver, precious stones, wood, hay, stubble; every man's work shall be made manifest: for the day shall declare it, because it shall be revealed by fire; and the fire shall try every man's work of what sort it is.

In verse 16, the building is the church, or the people of Christ. The builder is God's servant, the minister of the Word (vv. 4–9). The building materials are the contents of a pastor's preaching and teaching. Precious materials represent God's wisdom, revealed by God's Spirit in the Word of Christ, while cheap and perishable materials represent man's wisdom (1 Cor. 2).

Burgess wrote, "The ministers of God are greatly to take heed, that they preach no other thing, that what is already contained in the Scripture."[8] We must not assume that if we hold onto the true gospel our preaching will always be biblical. In using the metaphor of a building, Paul speaks not only of the foundational truths of Christ (v. 11) but also how we may build on the gospel with further teaching on the Word (v. 12). Paul's warning reminds us that it is not always easy to find and preach these precious truths. But Burgess said, "They ought to be esteemed and desired by us, as much as the covetous man desires his gold and silver."[9]

---

7. Witsius, *Character of a True Theologian*, 42.

8. Burgess, *The Scripture Directory*, 141.

9. Burgess, *The Scripture Directory*, 158.

So be encouraged to regularly read and study theology. Your time and effort are justified as an investment in the life and growth of your church. You are seeking silver and gold and jewels to give to the flock of God entrusted to your care. Indeed, you are making sure that you are building the church with materials that God approves, which will stand the final test of fire.

Defend the Church against False Teachings

Christ's half-brother (Matt. 13:55; Jude 1) wrote in Jude 3, "Beloved, when I gave all diligence to write unto you of the common salvation, it was needful for me to write unto you, and exhort you that ye should earnestly contend for the faith which was once delivered unto the saints." William Jenkyn (1613–1685) explained this, saying, "The faith which was once delivered unto the saints" is the "revelation of God's will, as they to whom it is delivered are bound to preserve and keep as their treasure."[10]

As revelation once delivered, this faith is an unchanging legacy that should be passed down to our spiritual heirs. Jenkyn said, "A ring, a jewel which belonged to our father or predecessors of old, how precious is it!… [Since it is] a precious *depositum* or treasure for children and successors, we should endeavor that the generation that is yet to come may also serve the same God, and enjoy the same Christ and gospel."[11]

To contend or fight for the faith is a primary duty of the elders of a church. Titus 1:9 says the elder must be a man "holding fast the faithful word as he hath been taught, that he may be able by sound doctrine both to exhort and to convince the gainsayers." Jenkyn said ministers must be tenacious with the truth, holding it "with both their hands, with all their strength; holding it in their understanding, in their affections, in their preaching and delivery, in their life and practice."[12]

The church needs pastors who tenaciously hold onto the truth. As the divines wrote in the preface to the Westminster Confession, "It

---

10. William Jenkyn, *An Exposition upon the Epistle of Jude* (Minneapolis: James & Klock, 1976), 63.

11. Jenkyn, *An Exposition upon the Epistle of Jude*, 67.

12. Jenkyn, *An Exposition upon the Epistle of Jude*, 64.

is one of the arch devices and principal methods of Satan to deceive men into sin; thus he prevailed against our first parents, not as a lion, but as a serpent, acting his enmity under a pretence of friendship, and tempting them to evil under an appearance of good.... A most sovereign antidote against all kinds of errors, is to be grounded and settled in the faith."[13] If a doctor must continually study medicine, how much more should a physician of souls study the eternal truths of God's Word, bearing in mind that Satan never ceases to spread his spiritual diseases?

Because of the danger of spiritual seducers, Christians must "continue in the faith grounded and settled" (Col. 1:23). Having received Christ, they must be "rooted and built up in him, and stablished in the faith, as ye have been taught" (Col. 2:7). *Grounded, settled, rooted,* and *established* suggest increasing stability in doctrine (Eph. 4:14). Watson thus said Christians should "not be meteors in the air, but fixed stars."[14] Pastors, your calling is to teach sound doctrine and refute error, for it is crucial for the salvation of the elect and the spiritual health of the flock.

Lay Foundations for Effective Evangelism

Too much evangelism today operates on the assumption of common beliefs. It offers a truncated gospel. It tries to graft biblical concepts such as "God loves you" onto a pagan and worldly mindset, resulting in syncretism and hypocrisy. Easy believism also encourages counterfeit faith. While the Spirit is free to work as He pleases (John 3:8), it is best to lay a solid foundation of truth in the mind of unbelievers so that they can rightly respond by the Spirit's grace to our appeals to come to Christ. It is not whipped-up emotions but well-instructed minds that best prepare people to receive the Spirit's illumination. The Westminster divines said, "The two great pillars upon which the kingdom of Satan is erected, and by which it is upheld, are ignorance and error; the first step of our manumission from this spiritual

---

13. "To the Christian Reader, Especially Heads of Families," in *Westminster Confession of Faith* (Glasgow: Free Presbyterian Publications, 2003), 6.

14. Watson, "Body of Divinity," in *Select Works*, 5.

thralldom [slavery] consists in having our 'eyes opened, and being turned from darkness to light' (Acts 26:18)."[15]

An excellent tool for laying the foundations of saving knowledge is a catechism. This once-common method of teaching fundamental biblical truths is now sadly neglected by many Protestants. Leigh said, "Catechizing is a plain and easy instructing of the ignorant in the grounds of religion, or concerning the fundamental principles, familiarly by questions and answers, and a spiritual applying the same for practice."[16]

Baxter said, "We must use all the means we can to instruct the ignorant in the matters of their salvation; by our own most plain familiar words; by giving, or lending, or otherwise helping them to books that are fit for them: by persuading them to learn catechisms."[17] He explained the benefits of catechizing people for the purpose of evangelism:

> It will be the most hopeful advantage for the conversion of many souls that we can expect; for it hath a concurrence of those great things which must further such a work. (1) For the matter of it, it is about most needful things; the principles or essentials of the Christian faith. (2) For the manner of exercise; it will be by private conference, where we may have opportunity to set all home to the heart."[18]

Catechizing enables you to evangelize people, from children to adults, who already attend your church. In a small group or one-on-one meetings, teaching a catechism with discussions of personal application is a powerful way to reach outsiders with the gospel.

By visiting homes with a catechism in hand, you can also train parents how to catechize their children. The benefit of teaching ordinary people to catechize their families is inestimable. One Puritan wrote, "Doubtless many an excellent magistrate hath been sent into the commonwealth, and many an excellent pastor into the church,

---

15. "To the Christian Reader," in *Westminster Confession of Faith,* 5.

16. Leigh, "Prolegomena," in *A Systeme or Body of Divinity,* no pagination in section.

17. Richard Baxter, "The Reformed Pastor," in *The Practical Works of the Rev. Richard Baxter* (London: James Duncan, 1830), 14:96.

18. Baxter, "The Reformed Pastor," in *Works,* 14:247.

and many a precious saint to heaven, through the happy preparations of a holy education, perhaps by a woman that thought herself useless and unserviceable to the church."[19]

If you want the Spirit to light a fire in someone, stack up dry kindling and seasoned wood in his mind, then pray for the divine spark. Tracts may introduce the gospel, but a catechism puts truth into a context in which words like *God, sin*, and *salvation* make sense. Nothing will equip you to teach a catechism to others more than reading a good exposition of the catechism yourself, which is exactly what many Puritan "bodies of divinity" are.

Equip Yourself for Edifying Preaching

The Puritan method of preaching was not to inject a few Scripture references into a motivational speech or essay. The Westminster Directory for the Publick Worship of God instructed a pastor to preach from a specific text of Scripture, then draw from that text doctrines or teachings that are "the truth of God...contained in or grounded on that text, that the hearers may discern how God teacheth it from hence." After selecting the doctrines that are the main points of that text, a preacher should serve them in a way that would best edify listeners. Each doctrine (or point in an outline) should be taught in plain and simple terms. The preacher should then draw upon parallel Scriptures that clearly confirm each doctrine, offering arguments and reasons for it that are "solid and convincing."[20]

The preacher should use illustrations which, by the Spirit's help, "convey the truth into the hearer's heart with spiritual delight." They should remove doubts and prejudices by answering questions and objections. Then they should proceed to specific applications, including "instruction" in truths implied by this doctrine, "confutation of false doctrines" that endanger believers, "exhorting to duties" based on this doctrine, "admonition" against sins contrary to this doctrine, "applying comfort" related to the doctrine, and then suggesting ways

---

19. Quoted by Thomas Manton, "Epistle to the Reader," in *Westminster Confession of Faith*, 10.

20. "The Directory for the Publick Worship of God," in *Westminster Confession of Faith*, 379.

for people "to examine themselves" regarding their faith and obedience in this area. A preacher need not say everything that might be said but must select what is "most needful" for his flock and "may most draw their souls to Christ, the fountain of light, holiness, and comfort."[21]

Preaching this way requires the study of theology. It requires preachers to work on specific theological questions in sermon preparation, and to sharpen their grasp of general theology by wider reading and meditation. Theological study is hard work, but it gives preachers depth and clarity in their preaching and makes them more useful to the church.

Paul Bayne (c. 1573–1617) said, "The ministry [of the Word] is not only a seed to beget us, milk to feed us in childhood, but strong meat, by benefit of which we are to grow up further and further in the knowledge of the will of God."[22]

Enable People to See the Big Picture

We all come to Scripture with presuppositions that color how we interpret it. The goal of the minister is to form presuppositions based on the doctrines of the Bible. The Bible then provides positive feedback by drawing listeners deeper into the truth. Theology reflected in the confessional unity of the church helps us to see the big picture so that we know how to fit individual parts of Scripture together, just as the picture on a box helps us to know how to put together the individual pieces of a jigsaw puzzle.

In his book on the preparation and delivery of sermons, Perkins said pastors must be diligent in private study prior to preparing sermons. Theology is central to this task. His advice "concerning the study of divinity" is that a minister should first "diligently imprint both in thy mind and memory the substance of divinity described, with definitions, divisions, and explications of the properties." In other words, a preacher must study theology systematically as well as exegetically.

---

21. "The Directory for the Publick Worship of God," in *Westminster Confession of Faith*, 380–81.

22. Paul Bayne, *An Entire Commentary upon the Whole Epistle of St Paul to the Ephesians* (Edinburgh: James Nichol, 1866), 263.

Next, the preacher should study specific books of the Bible (beginning with Romans and John). Then he should read orthodox writings of other theologians, particularly of "the more ancient church." As the minister reads, he should take notes in his "common-place books," meaning personal theological journals arranged by specific topics and questions. This exercise provides a context in which he may study an individual text in its literal sense.[23]

Perkins emphasized systematic theology in sermon preparation because he was concerned with interpreting each text in context so that no Scripture was interpreted contrary to the mind of the Holy Spirit revealed in all of Scripture. Thus he urged that interpreting Scripture be done according to "the analogy of faith," meaning the "sum of the Scriptures" found in the Apostles' Creed and the Ten Commandments.[24] He wrote an extensive treatise on the Apostles' Creed, no doubt in part to help believers read Scripture according to the analogy or rule of faith.

No pastor should slight or neglect the Bible by reading the works of mere men, however, and then impose those views on the Bible. Witsius said our faith must rest in "God alone," whose Word fills the mind with truth that is heavenly, pure, solid, certain, without the "least mixture of error," unspeakably sweet, satisfying, penetrating, powerful, and breathing forth the fragrance of holiness into the soul.[25] We must also not presume to teach ourselves, when, as Witsius wrote, "illustrious men in the Church... have discerned in the Holy Scriptures, have drawn from them, have committed to writing and placed in the clearest light, many things of which we, in the thick darkness of this life, would otherwise, perhaps, have remained forever ignorant, unable by our own unassisted powers to discover them in the mines where they lay hid."[26] It is unnecessary and often dangerous to reinvent the wheel in writing our own theology. We ignore to our peril the great teachers whom the Spirit has given to the church through the ages. Let us also remember "that no faith is to be put in

---

23. William Perkins, "The Arte of Prophecying," in *Workes* (1609), 2:736–37.
24. Perkins, "The Arte of Prophecying," in *Workes* (1609), 2:737.
25. Witsius, *Character of a True Theologian*, 32.
26. Witsius, *Character of a True Theologian*, 33.

the assertions of any man respecting the meaning of the Scriptures unless he shall demonstrate from the Scriptures themselves that the meaning in question is indeed the true one."[27]

Studying theology also helps us to see the connections between different doctrines. Thomas Ridgley (1667–1734) wrote, "It will be of singular use to us not only to know the doctrines that are contained in Scripture; but to observe their connection and dependence on one another, and to digest them into such a method, that subsequent truths may give light to them that went before."[28] Sadly, our beliefs often float like fragments of timber in a sea of ignorance, error, and confusion shared with the world around us. We need to integrate each biblical truth into a coherent worldview, whether we express this as "a system of divine truths," or "the chief articles of our religion," or "a confession of faith," or "a catechism," or "a body of divinity."[29] In this way we will develop a biblically sound and rational, albeit limited, view of reality. We will also guard ourselves from so emphasizing some element of biblical truth that we lose sight of other biblical teachings. Many a heresy has risen from a lack of balance in the approach to truth.

Studying and teaching a systematic approach to doctrine also bears subjective fruits. The big picture fits our lives and questions into the meta-narrative or epic story of God's eternal plan and redemptive activity in history, thereby giving us an encouraging sense of meaning and direction. It helps us to answer questions such as, "Who am I?" "Where did I come from?" "Why is my existence so painful?" "What is the solution to my problems?" "Where is all this headed?" and "What is the purpose of life?" This last question leads to our final reason to study theology.

Glorify God and Enjoy Him Forever

The ultimate aim of everything you do should be to glorify God (1 Cor. 6:20; 10:31). How can you glorify God without great thoughts of God?

---

27. Witsius, *Character of a True Theologian*, 34.

28. Thomas Ridgley, *A Body of Divinity... Lectures on The Assembly's Larger Catechism* (London: for Daniel Midwinter, Aaron Ward, John Oswald, and Richard Hett, 1731), 1.

29. Ridgley, *A Body of Divinity*, 2.

Indeed without such a vision, faith will decline and perish. Theology is the discipline of thinking glorious thoughts of God. Watson said glorifying God consists of appreciation, adoration, affection, and subjection. Regarding appreciation he wrote, "To glorify God, is to set God highest in our thoughts, to have a venerable esteem of him.... There is in God all that may draw forth both wonder and delight; there is in him a constellation of all beauties." He further said, "This is to glorify God, when we are God-admirers; we admire God in his attributes, which are the glistering beams by which the divine nature shines forth; we admire him in his promises, which are the charter of free grace, and the spiritual cabinet where the pearl of price is hid; we admire God in the noble effects of his power and wisdom."[30]

The Westminster divines said in their preface to the confession, "The knowledge we especially commend, is not a brain-knowledge, a mere speculation...but an inward, a savoury, an heart knowledge."[31] The word *savoury* means tasty, appetizing, and delicious. While deep theology may mentally tax your mental resources, it may also engage your heart in doxology because it delights your mind with the glory of God.

When pastors study theology with both mind and heart, they learn how to live a God-centered life. Ames said, "Theology is the doctrine or teaching of living to God," explaining, "men live to God when they live in accord with the will of God, to the glory of God, and with God working in them" (1 Peter 4:2, 6; Gal. 2:19–20; 2 Cor. 4:10; Phil. 1:20).[32] What can be more encouraging than that?

Conclusion

If you want to study sound doctrine and promote what John Murray called "intelligent piety," you may be confused about what to read, since bookstores carry everything from Augustine to the theological equivalent of *Alice in Wonderland*. We recommend that you start precisely where this book starts, with the Reformed experiential writings of the Puritans. These writers combined solid biblical

---

30. Watson, "Body of Divinity," in *Select Works*, 9.
31. "To the Christian Reader," in *Westminster Confession of Faith*, 6.
32. William Ames, *The Marrow of Theology*, trans. John Dykstra Eusden (Grand Rapids: Baker Academic, 1997), 1.1.1, 6.

doctrine with warm spirituality. Hundreds of their books are now reprinted and available.

Learning from the great writers of the past will show that we are wise to listen to God's best messengers. Charles Spurgeon said, "He who will not use the thoughts of other men's brains, proves that he has no brains of his own." He then wrote, "Study as much as possible sound theological works, especially the Puritanic writers, and expositions of the Bible."[33]

If you have never read Puritan theology, whet your appetite by reading a few titles in the new Puritan Treasure for Today series, which updates short Puritan works into contemporary language, such as John Flavel's *Triumphing Over Sinful Fear* or William Greenhill's *Stop Loving the World*.[34] Then move on to the Puritan Paperback series, such as Thomas Watson, *All Things for Good,* or John Bunyan's *Come and Welcome to Jesus Christ*.[35] For an overview of Puritan theology, pick up a copy of Watson's *A Body of Divinity*.[36] It is one of the best expositions of the Shorter Catechism ever written. If you want to go deeper into Reformed experiential theology, pick up Wilhelmus à Brakel's *The Christian's Reasonable Service*.[37] This Dutch "puritan" knew how to wrap up theology and doxology into one, and to apply biblical doctrine and ethics to the soul with remarkable pastoral insight and warmth. If you had to choose only one title besides the Bible, Brakel would be an outstanding choice. Once you've mastered Brakel, consider reading the giants of Puritan theology: Thomas Goodwin and John Owen, especially on the doctrines of sin, Christ,

---

33. C. H. Spurgeon, *Metropolitan Tabernacle Pulpit* (repr., Pasadena, Tex.: Pilgrim Publications, 1979), 9:668.

34. John Flavel, *Triumphing Over Sinful Fear* (Grand Rapids: Reformation Heritage Books, 2011); William Greenhill, *Stop Loving the World* (Grand Rapids: Reformation Heritage Books, 2011).

35. Thomas Watson, *All Things for God* (Edinburgh: Banner of Truth, 1986); John Bunyan, *Come and Welcome to Jesus Christ* (Edinburgh: Banner of Truth, 2004).

36. Thomas Watson, *A Body of Divinity* (Edinburgh: Banner of Truth, 1965). This volume contains Watson's messages on the first part of the catechism. The rest of the catechism is covered by companion volumes *The Ten Commandments* (Edinburgh: Banner of Truth, 1965) and *The Lord's Prayer* (Edinburgh: Banner of Truth, 1965).

37. Wilhelmus à Brakel, *The Christian's Reasonable Service,* trans. Bartel Elshout, ed. Joel R. Beeke, 4 vols. (Grand Rapids: Reformation Heritage Books, 2011).

and the Holy Spirit.[38] For a biographical summary of 140 Puritans reprinted in the last fifty years, together with brief reviews of their nearly seven hundred reprinted titles, read *Meet the Puritans: With a Guide to Modern Reprints*.[39] For the theology of the Puritans read *A Puritan Theology: Doctrine for Life*.[40]

On the battlefield of life and ministry, nothing is more worthwhile than clarity. Clarity of mind enables us to remember what we must do at every point of the battle. Clarity of vision allows us to see what is actually happening, good and bad. And clarity of hope gives us the courage to keep fighting. Read sound doctrine and discover the encouragement of greater clarity for the spiritual battle.

---

38. *The Works of Thomas Goodwin* (Grand Rapids: Reformation Heritage Books, 2006), volumes 4, 5, 6, and 10; *The Works of John Owen* (Edinburgh: Banner of Truth, 1965), volumes 1, 3, 6, and 10. Some of these treatises have been published separately in paperback form, such as Thomas Goodwin, *Christ Set Forth and The Heart of Christ in Heaven towards Sinners on Earth* (Ross-shire, U.K.: Christian Focus Publications, 2011) and John Owen, *The Glory of Christ: His Office and Grace* (Ross-shire, U.K.: Christian Focus Publications, 2005); *The Holy Spirit: His Gifts and Power* (Ross-shire, U.K.: Christian Focus Publications, 2005); *The Death of Death in the Death of Christ* (Edinburgh: Banner of Truth, 1984); *Indwelling Sin in Believers* (Edinburgh: Banner of Truth, 2010); *The Mortification of Sin* (Edinburgh: Banner of Truth, 2004).

39. Joel R. Beeke and Randall J. Pederson, *Meet the Puritans* (Grand Rapids: Reformation Heritage Books, 2006). Try reading one life-story each day to supplement your devotional reading. For a good source for purchasing Puritan books, see Reformation Heritage Books (www.heritagebooks.org).

40. Joel R. Beeke and Mark Jones, *A Puritan Theology: Doctrine for Life* (Grand Rapids: Reformation Heritage Books, 2012).

CHAPTER 7

❦

Practicing What Is Preached

It's Thursday afternoon, and you're staring at your unfinished sermon notes on the computer. You're stuck. Part of the problem is the nagging memory of that comment at the last elders' meeting, "Your preaching needs to be more practical, more relevant to people's lives." *I thought I was being practical,* you think.

When the phone rings, it's a welcome interruption. But then Mrs. Smith fills your ear with concerns about her husband. He is depressed. Even going to church is hard; he just wants to sit at home. "Can you come over?" she asks.

"What time?" you respond. Hanging up the phone, you pray for the wisdom to know what to say. Mr. Smith has struggled with depression for years. *Lord, how can I make a difference?* you pray.

Before getting back on your sermon, you notice someone standing in the doorway. It's Bill, a young man you are mentoring. He closes the door behind him and slumps into a chair. Once again he is battling evil thoughts that seem to come out of nowhere. After he pours out his heart, you offer a few words of encouragement. You then pray. Bill stands up with renewed vigor, saying, "Pastor, you don't know how much it means to talk with you."

For the first time that afternoon, you smile. *Thanks, Lord, for the privilege of being a pastor.*

"A word fitly spoken is like apples of gold in pictures of silver," says Proverbs 25:11. As pastors we are often called to speak words of wisdom to people who are struggling. It can be an overwhelming task. "Who is sufficient for these things?" (2 Cor. 2:16). Thankfully, we have the Word of God and the Spirit of God to direct us.

The Puritans applied their mental powers and spiritual fervor to find divine wisdom to shepherd the flock of God. In this chapter, we will offer some ways the Puritans can encourage you to apply the truths of Scripture to people, leading believers to full assurance of faith, helping them face affliction and depression, and arming them for spiritual warfare.

Applying Truth to Life

One major difficulty in preaching is finding the link between doctrine and application. Some preachers rush into application in a sermon with no apparent connection to the text of Scripture. Others spend so much time expounding the meaning of the text that application becomes little more than a blurb at the end of the message. Or the application is so general that it has no heat or power. We want to do better. Pastors who love the Word of God must preach what the Bible says as well as how it applies to the hearts and lives of listeners.

The Puritans can help us link doctrine to application. Most of their published works consist of edited series of sermons. Puritan sermons usually followed a pattern containing the announcement of the text, introduction to the context, exposition of the text, systematic development and defense of some doctrines taught by the text, and, finally, the improvement, or uses, to be made of those doctrines. Puritan preachers drew a line from the Bible to doctrine to application. We don't necessarily need to adopt this exact form of preaching, but we can learn from the Puritans how to derive practical applications from the teachings of Scripture.

The "uses" section of most Puritan sermons is extensive, detailed, and profound. Consider Flavel's sermon on Christ's words on the cross, "It is finished" (John 19:30). The doctrine he derived from this text was "Jesus Christ hath perfected and completely finished the great work of redemption, committed to him by God the Father."[1] Half of the sermon then offers these practical inferences drawn from

---

1. John Flavel, "The Fountain of Life," in *Works*, 1:431.

the doctrine: (1) *comfort*: believers need not fear condemnation for all the imperfections of our works for God; (2) *warning*: trusting anything besides Christ for our justification is dangerous to us and dishonoring to Christ; (3) *hope*: if Christ finished His work for us, then He will finish His work in us; (4) *exultation*: rejoice in this finished work and the way of justification by faith in Christ alone; (5) *imitation*: if Christ worked, then all Christians must labor to glorify God by hard work; and (6) *exhortation*: strive to finish the work God gives you before death closes your life.[2]

The Puritans encourage us by example to devote much time to practical application. We might think of the Puritans primarily as theologians, yet they poured the most energy into application. The Directory for the Publick Worship of God produced by the Westminster Assembly said of the preacher,

> He is not to rest in general doctrine, although never so much cleared and confirmed, but to bring it home to special use, by application to his hearers: which albeit it prove a work of great difficulty to himself, requiring much prudence, zeal, and meditation, and to the natural and corrupt man will be very unpleasant; yet he is to endeavor to perform it in such a manner, that his auditors may feel the word of God to be quick and powerful, and a discerner of the thoughts and intents of the heart; and that, if any unbeliever or ignorant person be present, he may have the secrets of his heart made manifest, and give glory to God.[3]

The Puritans viewed the Bible as the revelation of God but also as the revelation of human nature, especially the fallen human heart. They studied the Bible as a mirror that reflected their own hearts and then preached from their hearts to the hearts of listeners. Though at first you might find their analyses quaint or contrary to today's opinion, prayerful reflection will show you that the Puritans had astonishing insight into the thoughts and motives of men. This was not because of a direct, mystical insight into the heart or theory built on human reasoning but was due to a careful, Spirit-led study of

---

2. Flavel, "The Fountain of Life," in *Works,* 1:436–42.

3. "Directory for the Publick Worship of God," in *Westminster Confession of Faith,* 380.

biblical psychology that expounds what the Word reveals about the souls of men.

The study of biblical psychology led the Puritans to reflect on the various spiritual conditions of listeners so they could give to each what was needed. Perkins advised preachers to use the following categories to characterize their hearers:

1. Unbelievers who are both ignorant and unteachable. They need reproof to expose sin.

2. Unbelievers who are teachable but ignorant. They need catechizing in basic truths.

3. Unbelievers who have knowledge but are not humbled. They need to hear the law and its curse against sinners.

4. Unbelievers who are humbled. If they are partially humbled, continue to show them the terrors of God's law but tempered with the promises of the gospel. If they are fully humbled, offer them the gospel doctrines of faith, repentance, and comfort.

5. Believers. Offer them the gospel of justification, sanctification, and perseverance as well as the law for new obedience, that is, the law which still commands obedience and condemns sin but no longer condemns believers.

6. Fallen believers. If they have fallen into false teachings, they must hear true doctrine and a call to repent. If they are despairing of their salvation, help them to discern whether they hate sin and desire reconciliation with God. Once more offer them the promise of the gospel. If they have fallen into disobedience they need both law and gospel to renew their faith and repentance.

7. Mingled: "A mixed people are the assemblies of our churches." This may refer to the mixture of both believers and unbelievers in a church, or it may refer to individuals who contain within themselves a combination of the first six kinds of listeners. If the latter is what Perkins intended, much wisdom is needed to know how much law and how much gospel to bring to them.[4]

---

4. Perkins, "The Arte of Prophecying," in *Workes* (1609), 2:752–56.

Perkins did not offer a rigid set of rules to follow in preaching but an exercise to help preachers address the real needs of people. Reflection upon the state of your church will help you craft a balanced mix of sermons that target people with different spiritual conditions.

Puritan sermons will encourage and equip you both as a preacher and pastor. Their theology will help you, as the previous chapter showed, and their method of deriving practical uses will help you to move from doctrine to application in a variety of ways suited to the needs of your hearers. Along the way, they may help you personally as they apply the Word to your own spiritual state and its needs.

Numerous collections of Puritan sermons have been reprinted, such as the six-volume set of morning sermons preached at Cripplegate, now titled *Puritan Sermons 1659–1689*,[5] and the Puritan Pulpit series of sermons by various Puritan preachers.[6] There are also scores of reprinted sermon volumes by English Puritans, as well as by puritan-minded ministers from other countries, particularly Scotland. One of my favorite volumes of sermons was written by the Scottish minister, Andrew Gray (1633–1656), titled *Loving Christ and Fleeing Temptation*.[7] Gray died at age twenty-two but was considered a spark from heaven while he lived. His sermons include puritan-type application from beginning to end.

Finding Assurance of Faith

The Puritans were very concerned about personal salvation and the assurance of faith. Perkins wrote *A treatise tending unto a declaration, whether a man be in a state of damnation, or in the estate of grace* (1589) and *A Case of Conscience...how a man may know whether he be the child of God, or no* (1592).[8] In his *Christian Directory* (1673),

---

5. *Puritan Sermons 1659–1689: Being the Morning Exercises at Cripplegate, St. Giles in the Fields, and in Southwark by Seventy-Five Ministers of the Gospel in or near London*, 6 vols. (London, 1674; repr., Wheaton, Ill.: Richard Owen Roberts, 1981).

6. Published by Soli Deo Gloria, this series includes volumes of sermons by Jonathan Edwards, Ebenezer Pemberton, Solomon Stoddard, James Ussher, and Thomas Watson.

7. Andrew Gray, *Loving Christ and Fleeing Temptation*, ed. Joel R. Beeke and Kelly Van Wyck (Grand Rapids: Reformation Heritage Books, 2007).

8. J. I. Packer, *A Quest for Godliness: The Puritan Vision of the Christian Life* (Wheaton: Crossway, 1990), 58.

Baxter gave "unconverted, graceless sinners" seventeen reasons to listen to his spiritual advice, twenty directions for seeking salvation in Christ, thirty temptations Satan uses to hinder the conversion of sinners with directions on how to resist them, and ten temptations by which Satan convinces the unconverted that they are safe in Christ.[9]

The Puritans were first concerned with how a person may know he is saved. Gross ignorance and willful blindness allow many people to assume they are Christians, when that is not likely so. Second, the Puritans addressed the issue of godly persons who lacked assurance of salvation. The Reformation doctrine of justification by faith alone had raised the important question, "How do I know if I have justifying faith?" Finding a satisfying answer to that question often proved difficult.

Today's pastor can profit much by reading the writings of the Puritans on assurance.[10] In today's theological climate, many people assume they are Christians, presuming upon the love of God as if it were a cosmic broom sweeping everyone into heaven. It is rare indeed to find preaching that properly binds assurance of salvation to a living faith in Christ which produces good works, thus distinguishing hypocrites from humble believers.

The Puritans help us see that assurance belongs only to those who are broken over sin. As Matthew 5:3 says, "Blessed are the poor in spirit: for theirs is the kingdom of heaven." Jeremiah Burroughs (c. 1600–1646) pointed out that the Greek word for "poor" in this text does not refer to a lower-class laborer who lacks the luxuries of life, but to a beggar who lacks the basic necessities to live.[11] That is our spiritual condition apart from Christ. A man who is truly poor in spirit "is emptied of himself; whatsoever he hath in himself, or whatsoever he doth, he dares not rest upon it, not for his spiritual and eternal good, but is delivered as it were from himself, looking upon himself as undone, utterly undone in respect of what he is, of

---

9. Richard Baxter, "Christian Directory," in *Works*, 2:6–88.

10. For an in-depth study of this subject in its theological emphases and historical connections, see Joel R. Beeke, *The Quest for Full Assurance: The Legacy of Calvin and His Successors* (Edinburgh: Banner of Truth, 2000).

11. Jeremiah Burroughs, *The Saints' Happiness* (Beaver Falls, Pa.: Soli Deo Gloria, [1988]), 11.

what he hath, or of what he can do," and so rests his hope "merely upon the grace of God revealed in Christ in the gospel."[12] Sadly, many people who are confident of their salvation are merely trusting in themselves that they are righteous (Luke 18:9), not in Christ and His righteousness alone.

The Puritans did not cut people off from hope, however, but applied the paradoxical promise of Scripture that the poor in spirit are the richest people on earth. To them belong the "present comforts" of the kingdom of heaven, the reign of Christ that "is begun in the work of grace in the hearts of the saints, and so carried on till it comes to eternal glory."[13] Through Christ and the Spirit, true believers engage in free trade with heaven and already enjoy its commodities of "grace, comfort, happiness, and glory."[14] They have "heaven on earth," as Thomas Brooks said.[15]

Thus the Puritans taught the doctrine of assurance to cultivate both humility and hope. In doing this, they had to exercise a delicate balance, which is also true of the preacher today. He should aim to penetrate all the deceptions and evasions of the hypocrite to expose his lost condition. Yet he must also offer comfort to saints who are fearful and nearly despair over their sins and unworthiness. As Thomas Cole (c. 1627–1697) asked, "How may we steer an even course between presumption and despair?"[16]

Puritan writings on assurance will help you rightly speak to men and women about their salvation.[17] A classic book on the assurance of salvation is *The Christian's Great Interest* by William Guthrie

---

12. Burroughs, *The Saints' Happiness*, 19.
13. Burroughs, *The Saints' Happiness*, 23–24.
14. Burroughs, *The Saints' Happiness*, 35.
15. Thomas Brooks, "Heaven on Earth," in *Works*, 2:303ff.
16. Thomas Cole, "How may we steer an even course between presumption and despair?" in *Puritan Sermons 1659–1689* (Wheaton, Ill.: Richard Owen Roberts, 1981), 2:507.
17. As in all things, we must weigh the teachings of men in the balance of the Bible. Some Puritans, especially the New England divines such as Thomas Hooker and Thomas Shepard, went too far in requiring submission to God as a preparation for saving faith. Indeed, though sound in overall doctrine, Hooker so belabored the point of conviction of sin that his imbalanced presentation probably left some people wallowing in fear instead of rushing to Christ. Yet even in the matter of preparation

(1620–1665).[18] John Owen read this book and said its author was one of the greatest theological writers who ever lived. People who struggle with doubts about their salvation may also find help in Richard Sibbes's *The Bruised Reed* or Obadiah Sedgwick's (1600–1658) *The Doubting Believer.*[19]

Facing Affliction and Dealing with Depression

As a pastor you have the privilege of sharing in some of the greatest joys of your people and also in their deepest sorrows. As a shepherd, you must feed your flock, strengthen the weak, heal the sick, bind up the broken, restore those driven away, and seek the lost (Ezek. 34:3–4). You will encounter people struggling with all kinds of troubles. How will you help them?

Tenderhearted shepherds will find much wisdom in Puritan writings to help them serve people in sorrow. The Puritans themselves went through many trials. They lacked the advantages of modern medicine and sanitation. Parents commonly buried half of their children before they reached adulthood. They suffered government persecution under King Charles I, Archbishop Laud, and King Charles II; starvation in New England; civil war in England and Scotland; repeated epidemics of the plague; and the Great Fire of London. Of course, they also had many joys to celebrate, but overall life was hard in the seventeenth century.

In their sorrows the Puritans discovered how the Lord uses affliction to give His people experiential knowledge of Him, which goes far beyond theoretical or intellectual knowledge. A classic Puritan treatise on affliction is Thomas Brooks's *The Mute Christian under the Smarting Rod.* Brooks said, "Afflictions are the golden key by which the Lord opens the rich treasure of his word to his people's souls."[20]

---

by conviction, we can learn from the Puritans because today the church has gone to the opposite extreme of neglecting conviction of sin or regarding it as unhealthy.

18. William Guthrie, *The Christian's Great Interest* (Edinburgh: Banner of Truth, 1969).

19. Richard Sibbes, *The Bruised Reed* (Edinburgh: Banner of Truth, 1998); Obadiah Sedgwick, *The Doubting Believer* (Pittsburgh: Soli Deo Gloria, 1993).

20. Thomas Brooks, "The Mute Christian under the Smarting Rod," in *Works,* 1:287.

The doctrine driving his book is "that it is the great duty and concernment of gracious souls to be mute and silent under the greatest afflictions, the saddest providences, and the sharpest trials that they meet with in this world."[21] This teaching may seem severe, but Brooks offers it with sensitivity and sympathy in seeking to promote submission to the Lord's will.

Brooks said silence under affliction is not stoic, unfeeling silence nor sullen, forced silence. It is holy, gracious silence that springs from a "sight of God" in His "majesty, sovereignty, dignity, authority, and presence."[22] It is worshiping inwardly while suffering pain. Psalm 39:9 says, "I was dumb, I opened not my mouth; because thou didst it." Brooks called the sufferer to submit quietly to God as Lord over one's sufferings, charging Him with no injustice but trusting that afflictions work for the good of God's children in the development of holiness and humility (Lam. 3:27). God does not delight in His children's pain but afflicts them with the loving hand of a father. Brooks wrote, "God's heart was not in their afflictions, though his hand was."[23] We are to obey His command to wait upon Him (Pss. 27:14; 37:7), surrendering ourselves to God in patient expectation of deliverance in due time (Pss. 40:1–3; 62:5; Lam. 3:26).[24]

The Puritans pursued this theme in great detail for people who struggle with deep and specific questions. Brooks explains eight ways of feeling and expressing grief that are consistent with a quiet spirit, eight reasons why a Christian should receive sadness quietly, five kinds of people rebuked by this doctrine, six reasons not to sin by avoiding suffering, twelve exhortations to honor God with silent submission in troubles, twelve evils of murmuring, ten answers to objections, and twelve helps for quieting your soul under affliction. Yet Brooks is never tedious, but tender and wise in dealing with suffering Christians. Reading his works can also help make pastors tender and wise.[25]

---

21. Brooks, "The Mute Christian under the Smarting Rod," in *Works,* 1:295.
22. Brooks, "The Mute Christian under the Smarting Rod," in *Works,* 1:298–99.
23. Brooks, "The Mute Christian under the Smarting Rod," in *Works,* 1:304.
24. Brooks, "The Mute Christian under the Smarting Rod," in *Works,* 1:304–6.
25. Another helpful book on submission to difficult providences is Thomas Boston, *The Crook in the Lot* (Morgan, Pa.: Soli Deo Gloria, 2001); also found in

The worst affliction, perhaps, is depression, which oppresses the soul with darkness and dims the color of all we see. Depression is also one of the most difficult cases for pastoral counseling. The Puritans understood the complexity of depression, which they called "melancholy." They traced its potential roots to a variety of causes: physical illness, poor diet, particular sins, inordinate love of the world, and demonic attack.[26] William Bridge, in *A Lifting Up for the Downcast,* offered Christ-centered comfort for people discouraged over great sins, a weak spiritual life, failure to do their duty, lack of assurance, temptations, spiritual desertions, outward afflictions, a sense of uselessness in the service of God, and overall discouragement.[27]

Perhaps you have also suffered depression. It is not uncommon among ministers. Timothy Rogers (1658–1728), a gifted preacher, was crippled for two years by an incapacitating depression. He felt he was abandoned by God in a land of darkness, where the sun never shone. The cause of his suffering is hard to trace, but it did happen soon after the death of a young friend who was studying for the ministry. Depression was also evident in Rogers's family. Though Rogers recovered enough to fruitfully minister for two decades, depression continued to dog him. In 1707, he retired, feeling like a broken vessel. But he continued to glorify God during his remaining two decades on earth.

Rogers wrote *Trouble of Mind and the Disease of Melancholy* out of his reflections on Scripture and his experience with depression. He said, "Melancholy is the worst of all distempers, and those sinking and guilty fears which it brings with it are inexpressibly dreadful."[28] He also confessed that this experience "may be sadly felt, but cannot be fully expressed."[29]

---

volume 3 of *The Complete Works of the late Rev. Thomas Boston* (Wheaton: Richard Owen Roberts, 1980).

26. See Richard Baxter, "What are the best preservatives against melancholy and overmuch sorrow?" in *Puritan Sermons 1659–1689,* 3:253–92.

27. William Bridge, "A Lifting Up for the Downcast," in *The Works of the Rev. William Bridge* (Beaver Falls, Pa.: Soli Deo Gloria, 1989), 2:3ff; also published separately as *A Lifting Up for the Downcast* (Edinburgh: Banner of Truth, 1988).

28. Timothy Rogers, *Trouble of Mind and the Disease of Melancholy* (Morgan, Pa.: Soli Deo Gloria, 2002), xxi.

29. Rogers, *Trouble of Mind,* xxii.

Rogers advised the friends of depressed people to treat them as people who suffered from a terrible, painful disease. He said we should look upon them with great pity and compassion, as upon a torn and wounded man. We should not speak harshly to them but with gentleness and tenderness. We should accept what they say about their painful experiences, not attributing it to mere imagination. Rogers cautioned against a heavy-handed approach to counseling people with depression. Do not urge them to do what they cannot, such as engaging in intense reasoning, he said. Do not attribute all their troubles and actions to the devil. Do not be amazed by their strong words or strange actions, for they are in great pain. Do not tell them sad or frightening stories. Do not speak as if their troubles will last a long time. Tell them about others who have suffered such anguish but were delivered. Pray for them with fervency, since they may have difficulty praying for themselves. Get other Christians to pray for them. Speak to them often of the sovereign grace and love of God in Jesus Christ.[30]

Rogers, like other Puritans, directs us to respond to depression with biblical truth and Christ-like compassion. His work is a great resource for a pastor who seeks to serve the broken people of his congregation.

Arming Believers for Spiritual Conflict

The Puritans embraced the Bible's realistic view of human sin and struggle. They viewed the Christian life not as an experience of unwearied success and easy triumph but as a conflict, wrestling, and war that lasts all of life. Though Christ has won the victory, Satan will claw at us until the bitter end.

The Puritans searched the Scriptures to arm people for spiritual conflict.[31] William Spurstowe (c. 1605–1666) wrote *The Wiles of Satan;* William Gurnall, *The Christian in Complete Armour;* Thomas

---

30. Rogers, *Trouble of Mind*, xxiv–xlvii.

31. Portions of this section are adapted from "The Puritans on Demons," in Joel R. Beeke and Mark Jones, *A Puritan Theology* (Grand Rapids: Reformation Heritage Books, 2012). See that chapter for much more detail.

Brooks, *Precious Remedies against Satan's Devices;* and John Downame (d. 1652), *The Christian Warfare.*[32]

Spurstowe warned, "Satan is full of devices, and studies arts of circumvention by which he unweariedly seeks the irrecoverable ruin of the souls of men."[33] But Brooks also spoke of the way to help: "Christ, the Scripture, your own hearts, and Satan's devices, are the four prime things that should be first and most studied and searched."[34]

Spiritual warfare calls us to be watchful because Satan's chief means of destroying people is through lies and deception (Gen. 3:1–5, 13; John 8:44; 2 Cor. 11:3; 1 Tim. 2:14; Rev. 12:9). Spurstowe wrote, "We ought rather to be all the more watchful since we have such a serpent to deal with that can hide his deadly poison with a beautiful and shining skin."[35] In particular, Satan targets the elect, to harm them in any way possible. Spurstowe wrote, "If not to extinguish their light, yet [Satan tempts them] to eclipse their luster; if not to cause a shipwreck, yet to raise a storm; if not to hinder their happy end, yet to molest them in their way."[36]

Satan usually crafts his temptations to fit each person. Spurstowe said Satan tempts a young man with sexual lust, a middle-aged man with "an itch for honor and to be great," and an old man with "covetousness and peevishness."[37] Gurnall said no actor has so many outfits "to come in upon the stage with as the devil hath forms of temptation."[38] In various writings, the Puritans described many forms of temptation and the equipment needed to fight them.

Most importantly, the Puritans directed the believer to Christ, who is the victorious Captain against all the forces of evil. Downame wrote,

---

32. Thomas Brooks, "Precious Remedies for Satan's Devices," in *Works*, 1:1–166; John Downame, *The Christian Warfare against the Devil, World, and Flesh* (1604; facsimile repr., Vestavia Hills, Ala.: Solid Ground Christian Books, 2009); William Gurnall, *The Christian in Complete Armour: A Treatise of the Saints' War against the Devil* (1662–1665; repr., Edinburgh: Banner of Truth, 2002); William Spurstowe, *The Wiles of Satan* (1666; Morgan, Pa.: Soli Deo Gloria, 2004).

33. Spurstowe, *The Wiles of Satan*, 6.

34. Brooks, "Precious Remedies," in *Works*, 1:3.

35. Spurstowe, *The Wiles of Satan*, 14.

36. Spurstowe, *The Wiles of Satan*, 21.

37. Spurstowe, *The Wiles of Satan*, 61.

38. Gurnall, *The Christian in Complete Armour*, 1:382.

If we did indeed regard our enemies' strength and our own weakness only, we might well be discouraged from undertaking this combat, but if we look upon our grand Captain Christ, whose love towards us is no less than his power, and both infinite, there is no cause of doubting.... He hath already overcome our enemies.... Our Saviour hath spoiled principalities and powers, and hath made a show of them openly, and hath triumphed over them upon the cross (Col. 2:15).[39]

In writings such as these, pastors will find specific answers to questions about spiritual warfare. These insights come from the revelation of Holy Scripture, not human speculation, vain imagination, or superstition. Puritan writings will encourage and equip you to fight against Satan and to serve the flock of God.

Conclusion
Puritan writings offer a wealth of biblical wisdom for pastors and laypeople. Rather than developing a theology abstracted from human life, the Puritans traced God's golden chain from eternity past to our personal history. In doing so, they applied the gospel to real life. While we may not agree with all their conclusions, we may learn much from their biblical, doctrinal, experiential, and practical approach to life.

In this chapter, we have suggested helpful books on various subjects. See the previous chapter for series and volumes to get you started if reading Puritan literature intimidates you. Consider also the small but solid Pocket Puritan books such as Jonathan Edwards's *Heaven, A World of Love,* or *When Christians Suffer* by Thomas Case.[40]

Some additional books present Puritan teachings in contemporary language, such as Kris Lundgaard's *The Enemy Within: Straight Talk about the Power and Defeat of Sin,* a presentation of John Owen's teachings on the mortification of sin. The Deepen Your Christian Life series includes titles such as *Living by God's Promises* and *Living Zealously.*[41]

---

39. Downname, *The Christian Warfare*, 14.

40. This series is published by the Banner of Truth (www.banneroftruth.org).

41. Kris Lundgaard, *The Enemy Within: Straight Talk about the Power and Defeat of Sin* (Phillipsburg, N.J.: P&R, 1998); Joel R. Beeke and James A. La Belle, *Living*

Why not commit yourself to reading one of the Puritan practical writings for fifteen minutes a day? If you do that consistently over the years, you will find yourself progressing through books that will encourage your soul and empower your ministry.

---

by God's Promises (Grand Rapids: Reformation Heritage Books, 2010); Joel R. Beeke and James A. La Belle, *Living Zealously* (Grand Rapids: Reformation Heritage Books, 2012).

CHAPTER 8

The Calling of the Shepherd

The ideal pastor loves the old people of the church and visits them daily yet spends all his time with the youth. He is always on his knees in prayer but is constantly available at the church office. He preaches convicting sermons against sin yet is ever positive and upbeat. He upholds the doctrine of God's sovereignty over all things while unfailingly leading sinners to trust in Christ each week. He manages all the church's programs for optimal results but gives volunteers freedom to serve as they see best. He attends every committee and ministry function and is always refreshing and deep in his knowledge of the Bible. He is content to live on a meager income but tithes thousands of dollars to the church. He is thirty-nine years old and has preached for twenty years.

You get the point?

One reason pastors become discouraged is the lack of clarity regarding their calling. In previous times, the vocation of a Protestant pastor was well-defined, but today the rise and growth of parachurch organizations has brought the business mindset into Christian ministry, clouding our vision of the pastoral office. The work of a Christian businessman is noble, as is the calling of a Christian soldier, magistrate, mother, student, or laborer. Yet we must not fail to recognize the distinct vocation of pastoral ministry, specifically as ministers of the Word in Christ, the anointed Servant of the Lord.

Every Christian has a gift to use in service to others for their mutual edification (Eph. 4:7, 16), but the ascended Lord specifically charges ministers of the Word to build up the whole body in the knowledge of Christ and in likeness to Him (Eph. 4:11–14). Pastoral ministry is a special office and a special calling that requires special qualifications of character, ability, and experience (1 Tim. 3:1–7).

The world pressures us to woo people to church by entertaining them and their children. This entertainment can turn worship into a show and the sermon into an emotional pep-rally. Or, more subtly, it teaches people to use God to get more satisfaction out of earthly relationships and acquire more of this world's goods, rather than commanding them to be reconciled to God. This distortion of the calling of a pastor makes him an administrator of a religious form of worldliness.

The Puritans remind us that the minister is a steward of divinely revealed truth and an ambassador from heaven. This chapter does not attempt to present a comprehensive Puritan theology of the duties of the pastoral office. Rather, it offers practical helps to clarify the pastor's calling to relieve the pastor from some of the burdens imposed upon him by people, not God.

What God Has Not Called Ministers to Do

Saying yes to what is best may mean saying no to many things which, under God, are not your responsibility. Ministers are servants of God, but they are not God. Ministers serve people, but no mere person or group of people is their lord. The Puritans can help you to clarify your calling by dispelling some of the following misconceptions that produce false guilt in pastors.

1. *God has not called you to produce converts.* As Edwards said, lost sinners are "forsaken of God." They are separated from all life, happiness, and hope because God has departed from them. Ministers cannot save sinners because they cannot reconcile or reunite sinners to God. Edwards said, "They have no power to help the poor, lost soul except they have power of the Almighty and have him at command." The perishing are "spiritually dead," and ministers cannot raise the spiritually dead any more than doctors can raise the physically dead (Eph. 2:1; Col. 2:13). Sinners are "in a state of captivity to Satan" (cf. 2 Tim. 2:26),

thus they are beyond our power to save, "unless ministers are stronger than the powers of darkness."[1]

Ministers are mere creatures, not divine saviors. Indeed, they suffer from the same weaknesses as those to whom they minister. Edwards wrote,

> If ministers knew perfectly the circumstances of every soul, knew all his thoughts and the workings of his heart, and so knew how to suit the word exactly to his case; if he could set forth the Gospel in the most powerful, moving, and convincing manner that the nature of words will allow of, yet if the matter be left there and God does nothing, nothing will be done. The soul will remain as dead as before.[2]

This does not excuse laziness and lack of zeal in the ministry. Fenner said that as a hen stays upon her eggs until the chicks hatch, so the true minister of the Word labors for the conversion and salvation of his hearers. He counts it "a misery to be unprofitable." We are given gifts to be used for the salvation of sinners. When sinners are saved, we rejoice and are encouraged to press on. We must thus labor to "sharpen our ministry that it may pierce into men's consciences," and "study how to do good," even while we acknowledge that "the best ministers may have little takings."[3] We must gladly suffer all things for the salvation of whomever God has chosen, though He alone knows who they are (2 Tim. 2:10, 19). Fenner said, "Maybe some of God's elect are among you, and if there be, the Word will find them out."[4]

Remembering our inability to save men will make us more prayerful and dependent on Christ. Fenner talked about a man who heard about the many victories a mighty warrior won by his sword. When the man saw the sword, he told the soldier he was surprised by how ordinary it was. The warrior replied that his weapon was just a

---

1. Jonathan Edwards, *The Salvation of Souls: Nine Previously Unpublished Sermons on the Call of Ministry and the Gospel,* ed. Richard A. Bailey and Gregory A. Wills (Wheaton, Ill.: Crossway, 2002), 46–47.

2. Edwards, *The Salvation of Souls,* 47–48.

3. William Fenner, *Christs Alarm to Drowsie Saints* (London: for John Rothwell, 1650), 13–15.

4. Fenner, *Christs Alarm to Drowsie Saints,* 17.

sword, but he had the arm that wielded it to do all it did. "So, beloved," Fenner wrote, "we have Christ's sword, but we have not Christ's arm, and therefore let us pray."[5]

Cry out to God for conversions. Robert Traill (1642–1716) said, "This may be the reason why some ministers of [lesser gifts] are more successful, than some that are far above them in abilities; not because they preach better, so much as because they pray more. Many good sermons are lost for lack of much prayer in study."[6] Only God can save sinners.[7]

2. God has not called you to comfort unrepentant sinners. Edwards observed from Scripture that men have always preferred to silence prophets who proclaim God's wrath against sin, choosing rather to promote preaching that soothes unrepentant sinners (Mic. 2:11; Isa. 30:9–10). He said, "If the business of ministers was to further the gratification of men's lusts, they would be much better received by many than they are now."[8] Popular preaching offers salvation from the punishment of sin without true repentance for sin. It presents Christ as Priest without Christ as King. It proclaims God as a means of gratifying greed and making men rich and great on earth instead of bowing before God and His glory as the great goal of our lives.[9]

The Spirit fills true preachers of the Word with power to confront men with their sin (Mic. 3:8). Their preaching calls people to faith and repentance and a life of gratitude in works that always accompany justifying faith (Acts 20:21; 26:18–20). Fenner wrote,

> Every minister should show his people what cursed creatures they are, until they be converted and renewed; every minister should press the evil of sin, and open the wiles of Satan, the guilt of the conscience, the spiritualness of the law, the necessity of

---

5. Fenner, *Christs Alarm to Drowsie Saints,* 33.

6. Robert Traill, "By What Means May Ministers Best Win Souls?" in *The Works of the Late Reverend Robert Traill* (1810; repr., Edinburgh: Banner of Truth, 1975), 1:246. The words in brackets were originally "meaner gifts and parts."

7. For a deeper development of this idea, see chapter 4. The idea that we are responsible for the presence or absence of converts in our ministry is so subtle and pervasive that we thought it worthwhile to repeat its refutation here.

8. Edwards, *The Salvation of Souls,* 60.

9. Edwards, *The Salvation of Souls,* 62–63.

humiliation, and repentance, and amendment of life, that there is no mercy but in Christ, no salvation but by Christ, except people take him to live in their hearts by faith.[10]

Referring to Acts 20:21, Perkins said the duty of a minister in his public speaking is "first, to preach repentance, which a man must perform to God, whom by his sins he hath grievously offended; secondly, to preach faith in Christ, and free forgiveness, and perfect salvation through that faith in Christ, to all that truly believe in him."[11]

3. *God has not called you to be like other ministers but like Christ.* Do not compare your ministry and church with others. Your ministry should reflect your particular place and people. Fenner said some audiences need a son of thunder ("Boanerges"), while others need a comforter ("Barnabas"). Some people need milk, while others are ready for meat.[12] Some churches are dead regardless of the spiritual vibrancy of their pastor. Fenner wrote, "The minister may be lively, and yet the people dead. The Lord tells us that Ezekiel had a stiff-hearted people (Ezek. 2:4), and yet he was not to be blamed, the people were all the fault."[13]

Your ministry should also reflect your particular strengths and weaknesses. All pastors are not equal in gifts. Fenner said, "Stars are of different magnitudes, some stars are greater, some lesser." Ministers who have few gifts might be greater used by God, so long as they are truly godly and are called to the ministry. God's power is not tied to particular men, means, or gifts. Fenner said, "Paul calls Epaphroditus who was much inferior to him, his brother, and companion in labor, and fellow soldier (Phil. 2:25)...so that there may be unity for all this, and a gracious sympathy and agreement between ministers, though of never so different parts [abilities]."[14]

Beware, however, that your ministry does not suffer from your lack of holiness. It is one thing to accept with humility your limited

---

10. Fenner, *Christs Alarm to Drowsie Saints,* 25.

11. William Perkins, "Of the Calling of the Ministerie, Two Treatises: Describing the Duties and Dignities of that calling," in *Workes* (1613), 3:434.

12. Fenner, *Christs Alarm to Drowsie Saints,* 21.

13. Fenner, *Christs Alarm to Drowsie Saints,* 45.

14. Fenner, *Christs Alarm to Drowsie Saints,* 22.

gifts, ability, and opportunities. It is another to complacently accept your sins, immaturity, or lack of zeal for the kingdom. Perkins warned that "leaden lives" hurt ministry more than "golden words." He wrote,

> All ministers therefore, as they would see any fruit of their ministry, let them first sanctify themselves, and cleanse their hearts by repentance, before they presume to stand up, to rebuke sin in others.... As no man is more honorable than a learned and holy minister, so none more contemptible in this world, none more miserable for that to come, than he that by his loose and lewd life doth scandalize his doctrine.[15]

Be especially careful that your Christianity does not cool into religious professionalism. Traill said to ministers, "Take heed unto thyself, that thou be a lively thriving Christian. See that all thy religion run not in the channel of thy employment." He warned, "When we read the word, we read it as ministers, to know what we should teach, rather than what we should learn as Christians. Unless there be great heed taken, it will be found, that our ministry, and labour therein, may eat out the life of our Christianity."[16] This need not be so. Make your ministry a context for your own growth in grace and the pursuit of closer communion with Christ.

Brothers, may the Lord release you from the false expectations of men and propel you to pursue God, preaching His Word and doing His will with all your might. Let nothing distract or hinder you from that.

What God Has Called Ministers to Do

The Lord Jesus has entrusted you with some of His goods or talents (Matt. 25:14–29), and He expects you to use those faithfully and diligently to build up His kingdom. So let us strengthen your hands with a picture from the Puritans about what God *does* call you to do.

1. God calls you to serve Christ for His pleasure and glory. Paul said in 2 Corinthians 5:9–11a, "Wherefore we labour, that, whether present or absent, we may be accepted of him. For we must all appear before the judgment seat of Christ; that every one may receive the things

---

15. Perkins, "Of the Calling of the Ministerie," in *Workes* (1613), 3:450.
16. Traill, "By What Means May Ministers Best Win Souls?" in *Works*, 1:241–42.

done in his body, according to that he hath done, whether it be good or bad. Knowing therefore the terror of the Lord, we persuade men."

Edwards wrote, "The ministers of the Gospel are sent forth by Jesus Christ. It is Christ that has appointed the order or office of the gospel ministry. The ministerial commission is from [him] who is the Great Shepherd of the sheep. The word which they preach is his Word, and the ordinances which they administer are his ordinances. And they have no authority to minister in holy things but as they derive it from him."[17] He added, "There is a time coming when ministers of the Gospel must return to him that sent them, to give him an account of their ministry. As they have been sent forth from him, so they must return again to him."[18]

A pastor serves best when he serves in the fear of the Lord (Mal. 2:5). Perkins said ministers who are called by God to represent Him must be struck with fear, "yea, into an amazement and astonishment, in the admiration of God's glory and greatness," and "the more they are afraid and shrink, so it be under the contemplation of God's majesty, and their own weakness, the more likely it is that they are truly called of God."[19]

People need ministers who are God-fearers, not people-pleasers. That does not mean a pastor should not be concerned about his reputation in the church and community (Prov. 22:1; 1 Tim. 3:7). Thomas Fuller (1608–1661) wrote, "He endeavors to get the general love and good-will of his parish…. Otherwise he may preach his own heart out before he preacheth anything into theirs." But this is no justification for doctrinal or moral compromise. You will win the respect of men by living consistently in the fear of God. Fuller said, "He shall sooner get their goodwill by walking uprightly than by crouching and creeping."[20]

Likewise, a love for God's glory and for our neighbor's eternal welfare will motivate effective ministry. The weapons of our warfare are not "pride, vain glory, and self-conceit," said Perkins, so "let us be content that God give any occasion or means to pull us down."

---

17. Edwards, *The Salvation of Souls*, 76.

18. Edwards, *The Salvation of Souls*, 77.

19. Perkins, "Of the Calling of the Ministerie," in *Workes* (1613), 3:442.

20. Thomas Fuller, *The Holy and Profane States* (Boston: Little, Brown, and Co., 1865), 80.

We must "ever look to be made instruments of God's glory in the saving of souls."[21]

As servants of Christ, we should love the people to whom we are sent. Nothing is more pleasing to Christ than when we lay down our lives for others, for this is how He demonstrated His great love for us (John 13:34; 1 John 3:16). His loving self-sacrifice is the pattern for all Christians in serving one another (Eph. 5:2), but especially for ministers and elders. Paul says in Acts 20:28, "Take heed therefore unto yourselves, and to all the flock, over the which the Holy Ghost hath made you overseers, to feed the church of God, which he hath purchased with his own blood." Edwards drew this conclusion: "Now Christ so loved the souls of men, and had so great a regard to the salvation, that he thought it worthy for him so to lay out himself. Shall not his ministers and servants be willing [to do the same]?"[22]

As ministers we represent Christ. The Puritans viewed the pastoral office as an extension of the office of Christ (2 Cor. 5:18–6:1). Burroughs said, "God the Father appoints Him...and the Holy Spirit anoints Jesus Christ to be a preacher of the gospel. He being the prime and chief Prophet of the Church, He appoints others to exercise, as it were, some work of His prophetic office, that is, to preach the great doctrine of reconciliation."[23]

Edwards said that through preaching Christ applies what He accomplished: "the salvation of souls." Ministers are the agents of Christ, coworkers with Christ, and ambassadors for Christ. They should strive to be earthly images of the heavenly Bishop of souls, Prophet, Teacher, Light of the World, Head of the church, Intercessor, King, and Example of the saints.[24] All they say and do should be done in the name of Jesus Christ.

2. God calls you to care for the spiritual needs of men. Edwards viewed the list of spiritual gifts in Romans 12:4–8 as a twofold division of labor among church officers, focusing on either the soul or the

---

21. Perkins, "Of the Calling of the Ministerie," in *Workes* (1613), 3:442.

22. Edwards, *The Salvation of Souls,* 170.

23. Jeremiah Burroughs, *Gospel Reconciliation* (Morgan, Pa.: Soli Deo Gloria, 1997), 225.

24. Edwards, *The Salvation of Souls,* 176–77.

body. He wrote, "Bishops or elders were to wait on [attend to] their teaching, exhorting and ruling, and the deacons on their ministering, giving, and showing mercy."[25] Just as "earthly princes" hire two kinds of servants to care for their children's souls (chaplains and tutors) and for their bodies (nurses and cooks), so "Christ, the King of kings" cares for His family with two kinds of servants, elders and deacons.

Therefore pastors should not devote much time to the physical needs of the flock. Certainly the church must care for the poor and the widowed. Buildings must be raised and maintained. Funds must be gathered, distributed, and accounted for. Together with the elders, ministers are responsible for the general oversight of all church ministries, but they should delegate physical and temporal concerns to the deacons of the church, saying with the apostles, "It is not reason that we should leave the word of God, and serve tables.... But we will give ourselves continually to prayer, and to the ministry of the word" (Acts 6:2, 4).

Do not delegate tasks with contempt as if such things were beneath you. You are not worthy to take off Christ's sandals or be a doorkeeper in Christ's house, much less to preach His Word. So in all humility devote yourselves to the particular calling that Christ extends to you, realizing that you need others to do their jobs as part of the body of Christ, the church, while you do yours (1 Cor. 12:21).

Caring for eternal needs requires keeping watch over the spiritual condition of individual sheep in the flock. God commands you to watch over their souls, and will call you to account for your shepherding of them (Heb. 13:17). The words of Proverbs 27:23 apply to more than physical sheep: "Be thou diligent to know the state of thy flocks, and look well to thy herds." Fenner said ministers should always be watching and listening to learn "what courses are in their town, what sins break out, what corruptions appear, what proficiency the good ones make, who grow, who decline, who stand at a stay, who go aside, and wax [grow] worse and worse."[26] You must view men with spiritual eyes, assessing their spiritual needs and speaking spiritual words, for you are accountable for their spiritual welfare.

---

25. Edwards, *The Salvation of Souls,* 98. Edwards considered prophecy to be an extraordinary gift which has ceased (*The Salvation of Souls,* 98–99).

26. Fenner, *Christs Alarm to Drowsie Saints,* 34.

3. God calls you to preach His Word and nothing but His Word.
Edwards said, "Ministers are not to preach those things which their
own wisdom or reason suggests, but the things already dictated to
them by the superior wisdom and knowledge of God."[27] They must
not reject any doctrine revealed in Scripture which "contains difficulties and seeming inconsistencies that their reason cannot solve."[28]
We must not "make our mere reason our highest rule in our search
after truth, and God's revelation but a subordinate rule."[29] Nor may
we avoid teaching the doctrines of the Bible just because they are puz-
zling and difficult. Edwards wrote, "To say this is greatly to reproach
the wisdom of God and to make ourselves wiser than he. God in his
wisdom thought it best that those mysterious doctrines should be
taught, otherwise to what purpose did he teach them?"[30]

Edwards urged a newly ordained minister to hold fast to the Word
no matter how much people accuse him of evil motives. He said,

> Sir, I would now humbly and earnestly recommend to you that
> Holy Book which God is about to commit into your hands, and
> containing that message which you are to deliver to this people
> in his name. God gives you this Word—which is his Word—to
> preach that, and not the dictates of your own reason. You are to
> preach the dictates of God's infinitely superior understanding,
> humbly submitting your reason as a learner and disciple to that,
> renouncing all confidence in your own wisdom and entirely
> relying on God's instructions.
>
> God is now about to deliver to you a summary of doctrines
> already discovered and dictated to your hand, which you are to
> teach and zealously to maintain. And if the time should come that
> you should be reproached for so doing…and you should be called
> a bigoted zealot, one whose zeal runs before your knowledge, one
> that durst not indulge a freedom of thought, one that dare not
> presume to think otherwise than your forefathers thought, one
> of those that judge of God by themselves, that think that God is
> a morose, ill-natured sort of being because they are so, one that

27. Edwards, *The Salvation of Souls,* 116.
28. Edwards, *The Salvation of Souls,* 119.
29. Edwards, *The Salvation of Souls,* 124.
30. Edwards, *The Salvation of Souls,* 126.

is a person of little sense or reason—if such proud contemptuous reproaches are cast upon you, merely because you rely more on God's testimony than the dictates of your own reason, the time will soon come when they will be wiped away. Your Lord and Master, that commanded you to preach these doctrines, will defend you.[31]

To rightly preach the Word, we must preach it from the heart. Fuller said, "Having brought his sermon into his head, he [the minister] labors to bring it into his heart before he preaches it to his people. Surely, that preaching which comes from the soul most works on the soul."[32] Perkins said, "He must not only read the book, but eat it, that is, not only have the knowledge of divine things flowing in his brain, but engraved in his heart: and printed in his soul, by the spiritual finger of God, and therefore for this end, after all his own study, meditation, conference [talking with other godly people], commentaries, and after all human helps, he must pray with David, 'Open thou mine eyes, that I may see the wonders of thy law.'"[33]

Applying the Word to our own hearts before we preach it will give us greater spiritual insight and power. You will more clearly perceive what the needs of the heart are and be equipped to more closely address them. You will treat them in a more suitable manner. Fenner warned against preachers who use the Scriptures like a rattle for children to shake or like a tennis ball to toss back and forth. We should not draw attention to our cleverness.[34] Ministers must rather preach "the naked Word," speaking "from God to the consciences of men; as when a constable comes in the name of a king, [saying,] I charge you in the king's name."[35]

Conclusion: Persevering in Hope

Fuller said God ordains some pastors to be as clouds that rain on rocky deserts and rewards them "not by their success but endeavors,"

---

31. Edwards, *The Salvation of Souls*, 128–29.

32. Fuller, *The Holy and Profane States*, 83.

33. Perkins, "Of the Calling of the Ministerie," in *Workes* (1613), 3:431.

34. Fenner, *Christs Alarm to Drowsie Saints*, 26.

35. Fenner, *Christs Alarm to Drowsie Saints*, 27. A "constable" was a law enforcement officer.

that is, not according to what they achieve, but according to their faithfulness in persevering. Ministers must persevere and be patient, for ministry may be like "the planting of woods" that take twenty years to grow up. Or the work may be like that of David, who did not build the temple but laid up materials for Solomon, his successor.[36]

Jonathan Edwards said, "Let it be considered that if we are faithful, though we have but little success, we shall [not] fail of a glorious reward.... Ministers' faithfulness has in itself no sufficiency or efficacy to obtain success.... When therefore the want of success has not been for want of sincere endeavors and earnest diligence, their want of success will not be an occasion of their failing of reward."[37]

Regardless of the immediate visible results of our ministries, God honors the faithful minister even today in his high calling. The work of pastors, Edwards said, "is to be the instruments of Christ's success in the work of redemption, which God looks on and speaks of as the most glorious of all his works."[38]

There is nothing nobler than a servant of the living God who defies the world but has the ear and heart of a disciple regarding the Scriptures. As a pastor, be a faithful guide to God's pilgrims. Men will try to mold you into their image of a minister. Resist them and submit to God, serving Him with gladness. He has His eye upon you. He extends His hand of blessing toward you and has laid up for you a crown of glory to reward you on the last day.

---

36. Fuller, *The Holy and Profane States*, 86.
37. Edwards, *The Salvation of Souls*, 89.
38. Edwards, *The Salvation of Souls*, 86.

PART FOUR

Creativity and Community

The ministers and the saints that have been in former ages, being tied unto us by bands and ligaments, have propagated the truth unto us.... It is the church in one age that helpeth forward the church in another.... And the body (take the whole compass of it in all ages) is fitly joined together, that it may cause every age and every saint to increase according to his proportion.

— THOMAS GOODWIN

~~✦~~

CHAPTER 9

History and Science

You may not be especially talented or creative. But if you are serious about finding biblical encouragement for daily ministry, there are many ways to plant the many promises and truths of Scripture in your mind and heart.

Puritan pastors were very conscious of God's hand of providence in their lives and in the lives of others. Whenever possible, they would record examples of how "all things work together for good to them that love God, who are the called according to his purpose" (Rom. 8:28). Many Puritans were also encouraged to study God's handiwork in nature to discover biblical truths.

In this chapter, we will highlight some Puritan pastors who were creative in finding ways of encouragement and encouraging others through God's visible activity in history, nature, and personal experience. Perhaps these pastors will give you some ways to transform your personal interests and observations into spiritual insights that will give you strength in the Lord.

History: Observing God's Hand in God's Story

As Christians we know that the past, present, and future are in the hands of the Lord. History is the record of God's purposes being fulfilled for His glory and the advancement of His kingdom. It truly is "His story." A study of God's providence in ancient and more recent history can yield a gold mine of encouragement for pastors and congregations. The Puritan pastors were well aware of the wealth of spiritual help in such observations.

Solomon Stoddard once preached a sermon titled "The Acceptable Year of the Lord," addressing the need for revival. He was encouraged to keep praying for revival by the promises of Scripture, the biblical account of God's dealings with Israel, and the history of his own congregation. He wrote, "There is encouragement to beg for this. There are encouragements in the word of God.... There is encouragement also in the providence of God. He has many times revived His work in Israel formerly, and we should take notice of God's mercy to ourselves once and again, and now a third time."[1]

In chapter 11, we'll look at how pastors may be encouraged by reading Christian biographies of leaders, a practice that can serve as part of the communion of saints. But in this chapter, we will focus on how and why you should take time to make creative observations of the hand of God in your life and in the world. Puritan pastors such as Increase Mather believed it was important for pastors to record such observations[2] to preserve a record for years to come.

John Flavel suggested three reasons we should keep a record of the providences of God: (1) Our memories often fail us. A written account becomes a permanent memorial for us and future generations.

---

1. Solomon Stoddard, "The Acceptable Year of the Lord," in *The Puritan Pulpit: Solomon Stoddard*, 310.

2. Increase Mather records the following resolution of the colonial ministers in 1681 that a record of extraordinary providences be produced: "In order to the promoting of a design of this nature, so as shall be indeed for God's glory and the good of posterity, it is necessary that utmost care shall be taken that all and only remarkable providences be recorded and published. Such divine judgements, tempests, floods, earthquakes, thunders as are unusual, strange apparitions, or whatever else shall happen that is prodigious...diabolical possessions, remarkable judgments upon noted sinners, eminent deliverances, and answers of prayer, are to be reckoned among illustrious providences.... Inasmuch as we find in scripture, as well as in ecclesiastical history, that the ministers of God have been improved in the recording and declaring the works of the Lord, and since they are in divers respects under peculiar advantages thereunto, it is proposed, that each one in that capacity may diligently enquire into and record such illustrious providences as have happened.... Although it be true that this design cannot be brought unto perfection in one or two years, yet it is much to be desired that something may be done therein out of hand, as a specimen of a more large volume, that so this work may be set on foot, and posterity may be encouraged to go on therewith" (Increase Mather, *Remarkable Providences Illustrative of the Earlier Days of American Colonisation*, ed. George Offor [London: John Russell Smith, 1856], unpaginated preface).

(2) Recording God's providential acts and deliverances in a book will help us recall God's past mercies. (3) An accurate record of our experiences will help us keep present trials in perspective, reminding us that we, by the mercy of God, have endured similar or even greater trials in the past.[3]

Pastors would be wise to become skilled in articulating God's truths and recording them. It doesn't take a poet or author to write down such experiences. The only prerequisite is a good pen, an eye for detail, and a heart that seeks to bring glory to God.

Cotton Mather, following in the footsteps of his father, Increase Mather, wrote an extensive account of the early history of New England. While Increase Mather was particularly interested in the miraculous providences of God, his son demonstrated the broader scope of God's providential activity in establishing New England. In his work *Magnalia Christi Americana* ("The Great Works of Christ in America"), Mather offered a historical collection of works, including many of his sermons, books, and other biographical materials. His ultimate goal for the work was stated in his general introduction:

> I write the wonders of the Christian Religion, flying from the Depravations of Europe, to the American Strand; and, assisted by the Holy Author of that Religion, I do, with all Conscience of Truth, required therein by Him, who is the Truth itself, Report the wonderful displays of His infinite Power, Wisdom, Goodness, and Faithfulness, wherewith His Divine Providence hath Irradiated an Indian Wilderness.[4]

Historical accounts of God's providences in New England had already been written by John Winthrop (*Winthrop's Journal*), Edward Johnson (*Wonder-Working Providence*), and William Bradford (*Of Plymouth Plantation*). But other Puritans were also gifted in writing about God's providential acts in history. Stephen Charnock, military chaplain under Henry Cromwell and pastor at Crosby Hall in London, wrote *Divine Providence* about his experiences of the providence of

---

3. Flavel, "The Mystery of Providence: A Treatise upon Psalm 57:2," in *Works*, 4:496–97.

4. Cotton Mather, *Magnalia Christi Americana* (New York: Russell & Russell, 1967), 1.

God in his life and ministry. After the Restoration in 1660, Charnock was without a church for fifteen years in London. He made ends meet by practicing medicine. During that time he lost his entire library in the Great Fire of London. As he grew older, his eyes weakened and his memory faded, making ministry difficult for him and his congregation.[5] Like many people going through trials, he likely asked, "What is the Lord doing? Why is this happening to me?"

How can a twenty-first-century pastor journal his experiences of the divine providences of God? What should he record of the wonderful acts and mercies of God to encourage his own faith and that of his congregation? Some pastors put much effort into journaling. Others benefit from researching the genealogy and history of their family. Still others travel to explore historical places and to participate in archeological digs. No matter what your historical interest is, Flavel gives us helpful directions on how to meditate and record the providential acts of God in your history and that of the world.[6] Here is a paraphrase of some of those tools.

1. Work faithfully and regularly to produce a detailed record of experiences, bearing in mind the following:

    a. Be extensive in your study of God's providential acts. Go back to your earliest memories of life, asking questions such as *How was God's providence evident in the circumstances of my birth and upbringing? When did God first work in my heart in an evident way? What has God meant to me and done for me across the years?*

    b. Be intensive in your study of God's providential acts. Focus on the timeliness of God's mercies, and the loving kindness He showed in them. Ask questions such as *How do such mercies fulfill the promises of God made to me in my baptism? How do they confirm the truth of His Word? What do they reveal about the character and heart of God?*

---

5. Beeke and Pederson, *Meet the Puritans*, 142–43.
6. Flavel, "The Mystery of Providence," in *Works*, 4:416–35.

c. Record the beginning of a chain of events, then how one event led to another, then how everything led to a gracious end.

d. Consider the human instruments God used to accomplish His purpose. Ask questions such as *Whom did God use to bring me comfort in my time of need? How has God worked in my life through family, friends, neighbors, strangers, or even enemies?*

e. Meditate on the design and scope of God's actions. Ask yourself *How can God use this trial for His purposes? How has God glorified His name through other such events? How has God caused all things, even the bitterest ones, to work for my salvation?*

f. Observe how the providential acts of God are connected to prayers offered to Him. Flavel said: "Prayer honours providence and providence honours prayer." Reflect upon these questions, asking *How did God answer your prayers in the past? How did He answer the prayers of others on your behalf? What does that teach you about what role prayer should play in your life?*

2. Observe God's providential acts with Scripture in hand so that you might do the following:

a. Confirm your faith in the truth of God's Word.

b. Understand your duty under all providences, what they signify, what you should do, and how you should conduct yourself as a believer. Flavel said, "The Word interprets the works of God. Providences in themselves are not a perfect guide. They often puzzle and entangle our thoughts; but bring them to the Word, and your duty will be quickly manifested."

c. Strengthen your trust in God's care. Learn to lean upon the Lord instead of your own strength or the strength of other people.

d. Show you if sin is the cause of your afflictions and how God is leading you to repentance.

e. Teach you how sure God's promises are and that God will avert all evil or turn it to your profit.

   f. Assure you of the reward of grace promised to those who persevere in faith. Flavel said, "Providence hath doubled all they have laid out for God in ways unexpected to them."[7]

  g. Remind you that God will never leave or forsake you.

  h. Encourage you to direct your ways to please the Lord and to trust in Him at all times. "For he is our peace" (Eph. 2:14).

Science: Observing God's Glory in His Handiwork

Perhaps you're not an artist, poet, painter, or historian. You may be like many Puritans who simply enjoyed God's creation, keeping it "before our eyes as a most elegant book, wherein all creatures great and small, are as so many characters leading us to contemplate the invisible things of God, namely, His eternal power and divinity."[8] Many Puritan pastors were greatly encouraged by studying nature. Some became leading experts in the sciences. Cotton Mather was the first American-born fellow of the Royal Society for Improving Natural Knowledge, a scientific and mathematical organization led by Isaac Newton as president. Mather wrote *The Christian Philosopher,* an early encyclopedia of scientific knowledge. It includes many observations and writings of noted experts of the day in astronomy, geology, horticulture, and anthropology.

One need not be a scientist to make observations about the natural world. Bunyan wrote a book for children titled *A Book for Boys and Girls, Divine Emblems, or Temporal Things Spiritualized.* In this collection of poetry, Bunyan described many objects and creatures of nature, often with a bit of humor. For example, he wrote three meditations about eggs, the second of which prompted a theological lesson from a rotten egg:

> But chicks from rotten eggs do not proceed,
> Nor is a hypocrite a saint indeed.
> The rotten egg, though underneath the hen,
> If crack'd, stinks, and is loathsome unto men.

---

7. Flavel, "Mystery of Providence," in *Works,* 4:424.

8. Belgic Confession, art. 2, in *Doctrinal Standards, Liturgy, and Church Order,* ed. Joel R. Beeke (Grand Rapids: Reformation Heritage Books, 2003), 6.

> Nor doth her warmth make what is rotten sound;
> What's rotten, rotten will at last be found.
> The hypocrite, sin has him in possession
> He is a rotten egg under profession.[9]

Bunyan wrote about larks, vines, flying fowl, light, flint, fish, swallows, bees, clouds, candles, the sun, spiders, moles, cuckoo birds, butterflies, flies, trees, rose bushes, frogs, cackling hens, snails, sluggards, and fire.

Flavel wrote poems to end each chapter in his book of husbandry and in his book on navigation. In those two books, he offered suggestions on growing, caring for, and harvesting crops. He also made observations about grafting fruit trees, caring for cattle, and the proper care of title deeds. The following quote illustrates his typical approach to a topic:

> Husbandmen find, by experience, that their arable lands may be dressed too much, as well as too little; if the soil be over-rank, the seed shoots up so much into the stalk, that it seldom ears well; and if too thin and poor, it wants its due nutriment, and comes not to perfection. Therefore their care is, to keep it in heart, but not to overdress, or under-dress it. The end of all their cost and pains about it is fruit; and therefore reason tells them, that such a state and temperament of it, as best fits it for fruit, is best both for it and them.[10]

In this observation Flavel taught readers not to seek too much prosperity from the hand of providence but to rest in the daily supply of their needs.

In his book on navigation, Flavel wrote on subjects such as launching into troubled seas, a ship's helm, winds and tide, fishing, and trade winds. Flavel had some experience with the sea through his ministry to people in the seaport of Dartmouth. As noted in the first chapter, Flavel was zealous to preach even when he was forced into hiding. Sometimes his pulpit was on a small rock or island in

---

9. John Bunyan, "Divine Emblems, or Temporal Things Spiritualized," in *Works*, 3:749.

10. John Flavel, "Husbandry Spiritualized," in *Works*, 5:41.

the water, to which people rowed their boats to hear him expound God's Word.

We might ask why Puritan pastors spent so much time writing about nature. To understand why they did so, let us concentrate on three writers: Cotton Mather, John Bunyan, and John Flavel.

Cotton Mather wrote in his introduction to *Christian Philosopher*:

> The essays now before us will demonstrate, that Philosophy is no enemy, but a mighty and wondrous Incentive to Religion; and they will exhibit that Philosophical Religion, which will carry with it a most Sensible Character, and victorious Evidence of a reasonable Service. Glory to God in the Highest, and Good-Will Towards Men.[11]

Mather wanted to reconcile religion with science. He used nature as an apologetic to prove the existence of a powerful and benevolent Creator. But he also wrote his book to bring glory to God. Editor Kenneth Murdock, in introducing some of the works of Mather in the American Authors Series, said about Mather's book:

> *The Christian Philosopher* shows constantly not only that Cotton Mather saw the wonders of nature with the observant eye of the scientist, but also that his feeling for them was akin to the poet's.... The passage in which he writes of the moon is prosaic enough, perhaps, and certainly far removed from Henry Thoreau's passionate outburst of pagan adoration of the same luminary, but the next line, referring to what has gone before, reads, "These are some of the Songs, which God, the Maker of us, has given me in the night."[12]

Mather's observations on the natural world resulted in spiritual insights that encouraged him. Likewise Jonathan Edwards often rode into the woods to be alone with the Lord, while absorbing the sights and sounds and lessons of nature, so as to glorify God.

---

11. Cotton Mather, *The Christian Philosopher* (Urbana: University of Illinois Press), 286–87.

12. Kenneth Murdock, *Selections from Cotton Mather,* The American Authors Series (New York: Harcourt, Brace and Company, 1926), lii–liii.

John Bunyan explained in the introduction to his children's book how his observations of life and nature could profit readers. He wrote:

> Wise Solomon did fools to piss-ants[13] send,
> To learn true wisdom, and their lives to mend.
> Yea, God by swallows, cuckoos, and the ass,
> Shows they are fools who let that season pass,
> Which he put in their hand, that to obtain
> Which is both present and eternal gain.
> I think the wiser sort my rhymes may slight
> But what care I, the foolish will delight
> To read them, and the foolish God has chose
> And doth by foolish things their minds compose,
> And settle upon that which is divine;
> Great things, by little ones, are made to shine.[14]

Bunyan loved children and was not ashamed to get on their level to teach them. He wrote, "Nor do I blush, although I think some may call me a baby, [because] I with them play."

A biographer of Bunyan wrote of the author, "His outdoor habits and employments, and his sanctified contemplations on the beauties of nature, were calculated to strengthen the vigour of his imagination, and the decision of his character."[15] Bunyan appears to have combined his two loves of children and nature in writing this work. In the process, he also found strength in the Lord.

As noted above, Flavel also wrote about God's creation. He said he did so, first, because we are humbled that "man, who at first was led by the knowledge of God to the knowledge of the creature, must now by the creatures learn to know God." The second reason Flavel wrote about nature was to win people to Christ. He wrote,

> The motives inducing me to this undertaking, were the Lord's owning with some success, my labours of a like nature, together with the desire and inclination (stirred up in me, I hope by the

---

13. The "piss-ant" refers to a small ant often found in homes. The biblical reference is Prov. 6:6–8.

14. Bunyan, "Divine Emblems," in *Works*, 3:748.

15. George Offor, editorial introduction to Bunyan, "The Pilgrim's Progress," in *Works*, 3:11.

Spirit, of the Lord) to devote my vacant hours to his service in this kind. I considered that if the Pharisees, in a blind zeal to a faction, could compass sea and land, to proselyte men to their party, though thereby they made them sevenfold more the children of the devil than before; how much more was I obliged, by true love to God, and zeal to the everlasting happiness of souls, to use my utmost endeavours both with seamen and husbandmen, to win them to Christ, and thereby make them more than seventy-seven fold happier than before?[16]

Pastors today have even more opportunities than the Puritans did to experience and study God's beautiful creation. Consider the wealth of knowledge that has been mined in the past three or four centuries! That should stir our hearts to greater heights of praise and poetry than even the Puritans produced.

Some pastors today might profit by auditing an astronomy or biology course at a local college. Studying science through the lens of a maturing faith can be spiritually uplifting. Likewise, a pastor with a green thumb may enrich his faith in the Lord by reading what others have discovered about the plants in a garden and the insects that infest them. We can all make a hike into the woods a spiritual experience for ourselves and our children by studying God's wisdom that is displayed in the intricacies and interdependencies of ecosystems.

Some pastors love to watch birds. Others enjoy fishing, camping, deep-sea diving, hunting, or other outdoor activities. The Puritan pastors would counsel all of us, no matter what our particular interest, not to trivialize these experiences by simply treating them as diversions from ministry or, sadly, taking a break from the Bible. Allow God to use your hobbies and interests to help you find strength in Him and to teach others to glorify Him.

We will end this chapter and section with a quote from Flavel about his writings on finding the wings and ladders in nature that we need to mount up to heaven:

---

16. Flavel, "Husbandry Spiritualized," in *Works*, 5:5.

What pleasure you will find reading it I know not; but to me it hath been a pleasant path from first to last; who yet have been at far greater expense of time and pains in compiling it, than you can be in reading it.... May you but learn that lesson which is the general scope and design of this book, viz. How to walk with God from day to day, and make the several objects you behold...*wings and ladders to mount your souls nearer to him,* who is the centre of all blessed spirits.... O Sirs! What an excellent thing would it be for you, to make such holy improvements of all these earthly objects which daily occur to your senses, and cause them to proclaim and preach to you divine and heavenly mysteries.[17]

17. Flavel, "Husbandry Spiritualized," in *Works,* 5:6, emphasis added.

CHAPTER 10

❧

The Communion of Saints

H. B. London and Neil Wiseman wrote *Pastors at Risk* in 1993, dedicating it to the nearly 400,000 pastors in the United States and Canada. The book describes the various problems and hazards that are common in ministry, such as overwork and low self-esteem. Of the pastors surveyed for the book, 90 percent consistently worked more than forty-six hours a week, and 70 percent said their self-esteem had dropped since they began working in ministry.[1]

The book mentions other issues of ministry as well, such as dwindling public confidence, infidelity, and money concerns. It specifies twelve serious hazards for pastors and their families, then concludes with a twelve-step plan to help overcome these hazards of ministry. These steps include revising your ministry, daring to lead, treasuring the gifts of God, and knowing your environment. We would add to this list meeting with other pastors for prayer, mutual accountability, and support. These brothers can sympathize with you, pray for you, and give wise counsel. They can be a great blessing in ministry.

Seventeenth-century England was a blood-stained mosaic of churches, some desperately trying to enforce worship traditions, while others felt compelled for conscience's sake to embrace nonconformity. Some churches stressed evangelical purity, while others wanted a comprehensive national church. Still others were fired up in debating the teachings of Jacob Arminius versus historic Calvinism.

---

1. H. B. London and Neil B. Wiseman, *Pastors at Risk: Help for Pastors, Hope for Churches* (Wheaton, Ill.: Victory, 1993), 22.

The Puritans had their own internal debates over doctrine, the sacraments, worship practices, and church polity, particularly Congregationalism versus Presbyterianism. In New England debates raged over the "half-way covenant" and the role of the clergy in church and society. But by and large, the Puritans who considered themselves "nonconformist" in regard to the Book of Common Prayer and the requirement for Episcopal ordination stood together in opposing the established church in England. Together, they faced the threat of ejection, persecution, and imprisonment for preaching the gospel. As we will see in later chapters, the Puritans saw themselves as soldiers fighting a spiritual war against enemies beyond those of flesh and blood.

The counsel these seventeenth-century pastors offer us to find strength in the Lord is rich, indeed. Yet some of it may challenge our twenty-first-century love of autonomy, for the Puritans encourage us to deal with ministry risks and hazards within the context of the communion of saints, both present and past, beginning with our fellow pastors.

Mutual Edification among Ministers

Richard Baxter's classic work, *The Reformed Pastor*, began as a sermon to be preached at a county-wide gathering of pastors in Worcester. The meeting was to begin with fasting and prayer, then conclude with a sermon from Baxter. But Baxter was too weak to attend the meeting and preach about the importance of house visitation. Later, he took this unpreached sermon and fortified it with teachings on pastoral formation and practice, resulting in a book. When the book was finally published, Baxter offered this encouragement in the introduction:

> My last request is, that all the faithful ministers of Christ would, without any more delay, unite and associate for the furtherance of each other in the work of the Lord, and the maintaining of unity and concord in His churches; and that they would not neglect their brotherly meetings to those ends, nor yet spend them unprofitably, but improve them to their edification, and the effectual carrying on the work.[2]

---

2. Baxter, *The Reformed Pastor*, 85.

Baxter succinctly described the two purposes of regularly scheduled times of fellowship between pastors. The first purpose is edification. Mutual edification was desperately needed by all pastors in the seventeenth century, but, as Owen wrote, some pastors needed it more than others. When the church underwent persecution, it often began with strikes against church leadership. Bringing the shepherd down was one way to scatter the sheep. In England, during the heaviest years of persecution, many sheep could not or would not stand by their shepherds when they were in harm's way. Owen explained,

> In England, usually, no sooner had persecution laid hold of a minister, but the people willingly received another, perhaps a wolf, instead of a shepherd. Should a wife forsake her husband because he is come into trouble for her sake? When a known duty in such a relation is incumbent upon a man, is the crime of backslider in spiritual things less? Whilst a pastor lives, if he suffer for the truth, the church cannot desert him.[3]

You may have experienced similar kinds of betrayal in your ministry. If people in the church fail to encourage and provide support to a pastor undergoing trials, where does a servant of the Lord go to find it? Many Puritan writers who were sensitive to the plight of their fellow pastors encouraged other pastors to extend the right hand of fellowship to those who were suffering. William Perkins suggested that when pastors became "thinly sown on the ground" it was incumbent upon godly ministers to extend the right hand of fellowship to each other and unite together in love.[4]

The Puritan pastors who were Presbyterian already had the apparatus for mutual encouragement. Their form of church government called for meetings of pastors and elders on a regular basis. George Gillespie (1613–1648), speaking in favor of Presbyterianism, wrote:

> Finally, that the governors of particular churches may impart help mutually one to another against the cunning and subtle enemies of the truth, and may join their strength together (such as it is) by an holy combination, and that the church may be as

---

3. John Owen, "Eshcol, A Cluster of the Fruit of Canaan," in *Works,* 13:61.
4. Perkins, *The Art of Prophesying,* 98–99.

a camp of an army well ordered, lest while every one striveth singly all of them be subdued and overcome, or lest by reason of the scarcity of prudent and godly counselors (in the multitude of whom is safety) the affairs of the church be undone.[5]

The Independent, or Congregationalist, pastors were at a disadvantage, however, because any attempt to hold meetings of pastors and elders were judged by some to savor of Presbyterianism. However, in New England, the early generations of Congregationalist Puritan pastors were forced to form an association. They were inundated with civil and ecclesiastical questions and were struggling to define the roles of church and state and the relationship between them. They were fearful of "ecclesiastical tyranny" in any form, yet realized that some standards or guidelines were necessary in the Massachusetts Bay Colony. John Cotton, Nathaniel Ward (1578–1652), and other Puritan pastors produced a document, "The Body of Liberties," in 1641, which was then adopted by the General Court (or provincial legislature). Though this document was more a civil code than an ecclesiastical ordinance, it tried to delineate the roles of church and state, as well as relations between churches and church leaders. The document asserted that ministers, elders, and laypeople had "free libertie to meete monthly, quarterly, or otherwise, in convenient numbers, and places…by way of brotherly conference and consultations."[6]

These conference meetings, sometimes called the Private Meetings, were held in the homes of the laity. Puritan pastors and laypeople would gather either weekly or biweekly in homes to integrate new people into the church by encouraging mutual edification and accountability. Thomas Hooker listed six ways these small groups edified fellow Christians: (1) Christians could more easily express love to each other in a small group; (2) Christians could more easily exercise earnest prayer for the church; (3) Christians could admonish one another, applying the gospel in more direct ways;

---

5. George Gillespie, *The Works of George Gillespie* (Edinburgh: Robert Ogle and Oliver and Bound, 1846), 10.

6. *The Colonial Laws of Massachusetts. Reprinted from the Edition of 1660, with the Supplements to 1672. Containing also, The Body of Liberties of 1641* (Boston: William Whitmore, 1889), 57.

(4) Christians could instruct one another when necessary; (5) Christians could comfort each other in a time of need; and (6) Christians who were meek or less likely to use their gifts in public ways could exercise their gifts in a more private setting.[7]

When pastors met in New England without laypeople, they often gathered in a pastor's home. Often the host would choose a spiritual topic for the pastors to consider as well as provide an agenda or outline for their discussions. Baxter emphasized the importance of preparing a definite agenda to ensure that the gathering was profitable. He, like many other pastors after him, had found that without an agenda to keep the focus on spiritual things, groups would often end up wasting time with gossip or other trivial matters. They might even result in division. Peter Thacher, pastor of the church in Milton, wrote about a profitable gathering of Boston ministers in his home in 1681:

> The ministers meeting was at my house. Mr. Torry, Mr. Fisk, Mr. Hobard, Mr. Whiteman, Mr. Adams, Mr. Danfort. Question was what are those special spirituall acts of worship whereby, the soul doth set toward and upon God. 1. In his word, 2. in prayer, 3. in the sacraments. God did much warme and inlarge my heart in prayer and in speaking and made it a good day, blessed be his holy name; they all stayed this night.[8]

Prayer and fasting were often the most important parts of these gatherings.

The value of such close fellowship with other pastors is also apparent in some of the funeral sermons that Puritan pastors preached for their colleagues. At the funeral for his friend and colleague Richard Adams, John Howe described the relationship the two men had enjoyed over the years: "About fifty years I remember his course, and our conversation was not casual or at a distance, as that of mere colleagues, chosen by others, but as friends inward, and chosen by ourselves; many a day we prayed together; conferred and took sweet counsel together."[9]

---

7. Thomas Hooker, *Soules Vocation* (Ann Arbor: UMI, 1999), 522.

8. Peter Thacher, "Diary," as quoted in Hambrick-Stowe, *The Practice of Piety*, 142.

9. Howe, *Works*, 3:424.

Today a pastor might ask himself: "What relationships do you have with other pastors? How many of your colleagues know you well? How many of your peers know you well enough to speak at your funeral and accurately describe your spiritual life?"

The Effectual Carrying on of the Work

Promoting the spiritual welfare of pastors undoubtedly helps them to be more effective in their work. Sadly, many pastors and church members fail to see that connection until it's too late. Consider the time and energy that elders sometimes must invest in cleaning up the messy effects of their pastor's quick temper upon several disgruntled families in the church. What about the pastor who has an addiction problem? His oversized ego won't let him admit there is a problem, so without proper accountability and intervention, his picture ends up on the front page of the local newspaper after he crashes his car under the influence of alcohol. Or what do you say to the youth group about the pastor whose computer is full of pornography?

The Bible addresses the effect of sin on a person's life. King David evidently had no peers who dared to hold him accountable until God sent the prophet Nathan to confront the king with a conscience-piercing parable. But note how David's sin with Bathsheba exacted a heavy toll of suffering for himself and his family. Psalm 32 describes David's inner turmoil while living with a guilty conscience. He suffered long without the peace and joy of living with a conscience free of guilt and shame. Notice too what effects David's sin had upon his family. His son Absalom used his personality and good looks to attempt to usurp the throne from his father. The Israelites had to pay a high price after that attempt ended in disaster. Leaders who think they are above accountability can cause great damage to themselves and those they lead.

Encouraging pastors to take part in doctrinally sound ministers' conferences, accountability groups, or prayer meetings with each other is a proactive way of assuring pastoral accountability and effectiveness. These groups are usually the most effective when they are outside of a pastor's own church and church staff. When office bearers provide their minister with prayer and financial assistance for attending ministers' conferences, that money is well spent.

The Puritan pastors found such meetings beneficial in several ways. First, some of the pastors desperately needed support during the battles they were facing. Samuel Rutherford was barred from ministering to his congregation in Anwoth. He said to Robert Cunningham:

> My dear brother, let us help one another with our prayers. Our King shall mow down his enemies and shall come from Bozrah with his garments all dyed in blood. And for consolation shall he appear, and call his wife Hephzibah and his land Beulah (Isaiah 62:4) for he will rejoice over us and marry us, and Scotland shall say, "What have I to do any more with idols?"[10]

In a letter to members of his church in Kilmalcolm, Rutherford reminded them of the need to gather together for prayer in small groups. After quoting many Scripture passages proving his point, he explained why it was so important to pray in groups: "Many coals make a good fire, and that is a part of the communion of saints."[11]

The Puritans also cherished these collegial groups because of the time fellow pastors spent building each other up in love and encouraging the development of ministerial gifts. They also shared ideas and offered advice on how to build up the church of Christ. Flavel wrote,

> As to our brethren and fellow-workers in the Lord, prudence will dictate and enjoin it upon us, that by the firmest union with them, we make their gifts and graces useful as possible, for the furtherance and advancement of our great and difficult work.... Christ hath shed down a variety of glorious ascension-gifts upon them, which are not capable of a full improvement, but in union and in conjunction with each other. Gifts are improved in us by prayer and study, but the benefits of those gifts are shared among us by love and unity. Love and union bring every man's gifts and graces into the common bank, and instead of monopolies, they drive a free and open trade, to the great enriching of the church.[12]

---

10. Rutherford, *Letters,* 41.
11. Rutherford, *Letters,* 162.
12. John Flavel, "The Character of a True Evangelical Pastor," in *Works,* 6:574.

In his diary, Peter Thacher said the pastors of Boston invited him to join their ministerial fellowship even before he had a church. This young minister was greatly impressed by the wisdom of Samuel Torrey[13] who invited him to participate.

A third blessing derived from these meetings is the wisdom other pastors offer in helping a colleague determine God's will in a call to another church. John Cotton responded to Jeremiah Burroughs's inquiry about leaving his church for another, saying:

> The settling or removing of a minister is like the lying or removing of the stone of the well of Syria which must lye and not be removed till the shepherds were met together [Gen. 29:1–10], so neither ought you to pitch upon a place, or remove without the joint approbation [approval] of your brethren, met together to consider advisedly of your case.[14]

Thomas Shepard likewise recalled how his colleagues urged him to accept a call to serve the church in Earle's Colne: "He is the God that sent me by all these ministers to obey the voice of God in the call of the people of Earle's Colne, a most profane place, where the Lord blessed my poor labors."[15]

A final blessing of these spiritual retreats is the unity they foster among pastors, which then serves as a model for their churches. This unity built up concern for the well-being of other pastors and their congregations. Watson wrote, "What induces a godly man to love the saints is the fact that he is closely related to them. There ought to be love among relations."[16]

Twenty-First-Century Communion

We began this chapter lamenting that some pastors today are reluctant to meet with colleagues in small groups. They often encourage their own church members to get involved in small groups, yet they

---

13. Torrey was about twenty years older than Thacher.

14. John Cotton, *The Correspondence of John Cotton,* ed. Sargent Bush Jr. (Chapel Hill: University of North Carolina Press, 2001), 155–56.

15. Michael McGiffert, ed., *God's Plot: Puritan Spirituality in Thomas Shepard's Cambridge,* rev. ed. (Amherst: University of Massachusetts Press, 1994), 76.

16. Watson, *The Godly Man's Picture,* 142.

personally shy away from small groups for the same reasons their parishioners cite: lack of time, fear of intimacy, pride, competition, or just plain apathy.

Twenty-first-century pastors should avail themselves of the blessings of interacting with fellow pastors who have fought some of the same battles, experienced many of the same heartaches, faced similar challenges, and are familiar with the conditions that lead to burnout. It only makes sense to join with others for prayer and spiritual conference as often as possible, for this spiritual discipline will enrich your ministry and enable you to find strength in the Lord. In *Pilgrim's Progress,* Christian wasn't alone on his journey to the Celestial City. He almost always shared the pilgrimage with a fellow believer, and the two pilgrims helped each other along the way.

Where should you start? If there is no ministerial fellowship or prayer group in your area, take the initiative and start one. Follow the advice of George Herbert, who counseled pastors to correspond or meet regularly with neighboring pastors. Welcome colleagues into your homes, no matter how discouraged they are or how small their church may be, with a "joyful countenance as if…to entertain some great lord."[17]

Today pastors have many more ways to fellowship with each other than the Puritans did, but we make too little use of them. Let us not take our brethren for granted but establish friendships with them so that we may encourage each other to keep our hand on the plow and persevere in the great work that God has entrusted to us of serving the church.

---

17. George Herbert, *The Priest to the Temple, or The Country Parson* (New York: Thomas Whittaker, 1908), 79 [ch. 19].

CHAPTER 11

❧

A Cloud of Witnesses

Charles Haddon Spurgeon, the nineteenth-century "Prince of Preachers," was one of the first mega-church pastors. In his preaching and writings, he attracted huge audiences. But few people knew Spurgeon was a student of the Puritans.

At the age of six, Spurgeon stumbled upon some books that had belonged to his grandfather, a Congregationalist minister. Many of those were Puritan writings. From that time on, Spurgeon absorbed all the Puritan writings he could get his hands on. Puritan writers became his spiritual guides, theological instructors, and pastoral mentors.

Richard Ellsworth Day writes, "Spurgeon received his baptism of fire from hours without end of communing with the Bible at his right hand and the books of Puritan divinity at his left."[1] Spurgeon's ministerial fire was lit from the torches of his seventeenth- and eighteenth-century spiritual heroes. In turn, many believers have set ablaze their passion for the Lord and gospel ministry from Spurgeon's torch.

The Puritan pastors valued the writings and testimonies of earlier saints, just as Spurgeon did. But in the seventeenth century there was also an upsurge of interest in spiritual biography and church history. In his introduction to Joseph Alleine's biography, Richard Baxter writes,

---

1. Richard Ellsworth Day, *The Shadow of the Broad Brim* (Grand Rapids: Baker, 1976), 120.

As history is both useful and delightful to mankind, so Church-History above all hath the pre-eminence in both. For it treateth of the greatest and most necessary of subjects.... The report of one soul's conversion to God, and of the reformation of one family, city, or church, and of the noble operations of the blessed Spirit, by which he brings up souls to God, and conquereth the world, the flesh, and the devil; the heavenly communications of God, unto sinners, for their vivification, illumination, holy love to God and to his image, are so far better than the stories of these grand murderers and tyrants, and their great robberies and murders, called conquests.[2]

Baxter goes on to recommend that believers read literature that builds up and encourages their walk of faith. He asks, "Is it more pleasant to read of the building of cities, than of their ruins; or of the cures of a physician, than of the hurts done by robberies?"[3]

Puritan Biographies

William Haller believes that Puritan biography, or at least the mass publication of biographies, began with the publication of funeral messages. When a saint of renown died, a well-known preacher was engaged to give the funeral message. In the funeral sermon, the preacher spoke on a suitable text, then ended his sermon with a brief biographical appendix. This was often called a "lean-to" because it resembled a room or kitchen cobbled onto the back of a house. Haller says countless funeral sermons were published with lean-tos.[4]

Later on, spiritual biographies, especially the work of Samuel Clark (1599–1682), became bestsellers. Clark was groomed from childhood to become a powerful preacher like his father, Hugh Clark.

---

2. Richard Baxter, *The Life and Letters of Joseph Alleine* (Grand Rapids: Reformation Heritage Books, 2003), 21–22.

3. Baxter, *The Life and Letters of Joseph Alleine,* 22.

4. William Haller, *The Rise of Puritanism* (New York: Harper and Row 1957), 101. He suggests that this was often done by preachers in order to make money and grow in notoriety. While this may have sometimes been the case, we would not be so cynical. The Puritans saw the life of a godly preacher as a burning light which should continue to illuminate the church after his death. They also saw the death of such a preacher as a providential warning the church should heed.

Samuel Clark wasn't a gifted speaker, however, and he lost one pulpit after another because of it. However, he went on to make his mark as an author and publisher of Christian biographies. He put together biographies of famous kings, martyrs, reformers, and numerous eminent Puritans to edify seventeenth-century readers. Funeral sermons, unpublished manuscripts, and information supplied to him by relatives helped Clark flesh out the life and testimony of his subjects.

The biographies that Clark and other Puritans assembled for publication had a standard outline:

- An account of a person's sinful life or indifference to the gospel,

- The struggle for conversion through the influence of a godly preacher's preaching or by reading books by godly writers,

- A chronicle of the person's deliverance in Christ, and subsequent life-long battle against temptations of the heart, especially unbelief,

- God's encouragements in the form of temporal or spiritual success, and

- An account of how the subject died. This often included a deathbed battle with Satan, which ended in the saint's triumph and his blessed entrance to glory.[5]

Samuel Clark was not an especially gifted writer, as Haller points out, but served more like a reporter who related the facts and relied upon the Holy Spirit to encourage the reader. Clark's first biography was titled *The Marrow of Ecclesiastical Historie, Conteined in the Lives of the Fathers, and other Learned Men, and Famous Divines, which have Flourished in the Church since Christ's Time, to this Present Age* (London, 1650). The third edition of this work, published in 1675, was considerably enlarged to include scores of biographies.[6]

---

5. Haller, *The Rise of Puritanism*, 108.

6. Samuel Clark, *The Marrow of Ecclesiastical History, Divided into Two Parts: The First, containing the Life of our Blessed Lord & Saviour Jesus Christ; with The Lives of the Ancient Fathers, School-Men, First Reformers, and Modern Divines. The Second, Containing The Lives of Christian Emperors, Kings, and Sovereign Princes. Whereunto are Added The Lives of Inferiour Christians, who have lived in these latter*

Clark's next biography had an even longer title and was devoted to martyrs. It included a section devoted to "Sundry Modern Divines" who had died within the past twelve years. Many of those divines were Puritans whom Clark knew personally. He produced a second "martyr log" in 1652 that detailed the lives of Christian leaders who had died in England since the gospel had reached its shores. He wrote another book in 1662 titled *A Collection of the Lives of Ten Eminent Divines,* which featured well-known Puritans who lived in the first part of the seventeenth century.

Other Puritans wrote spiritual biographies. Often, family members wrote biographies that included the letters of their loved ones. For example, Joseph Alleine's widow, with the help of Richard Baxter, published *The Life and Death of that Excellent Minister of Christ Mr. Joseph Alleine.* A more somber biography was written by James Janeway titled *A Token for Children.* It was a collection of testimonies and conversion stories about children who had died prematurely. That book became one of the most popular works for children besides John Bunyan's *Pilgrim's Progress.*[7]

Janeway wrote another book, *The Saints' Encouragement,* which included the deathbed experience of a woman known only as "Mrs. B." Janeway wrote in detail about her last moments to encourage other believers in the faith. He wrote about Mrs. B's final struggles before death, "All this while she lay smiling and triumphing like one that was more than a conqueror through Christ that did strengthen her: and after a while she turned to me and said, 'O sir, I am one of those that you shall not be ashamed of in the day of judgment; the Lord hath made you a happy instrument to my poor soul.'"[8]

The Purpose of Biography

Puritan pastors encouraged people to read spiritual biographies. Richard Baxter gives one of the chief reasons why they should do so

---

Centuries. And Lastly, are subjoined the Lives of many of those, who by their Vertue and Valor obtained the Sir-name of Great... (London: Printed for W. B., 1675).

7. Beeke and Pederson, *Meet the Puritans,* 378.

8. James Janeway, *The Saints' Encouragement* (Pittsburgh: Soli Deo Gloria, 1994), 113.

in his introduction to Joseph Alleine's *Life and Letters*. He says, "In the lives of holy men we see God's image, and the beauties of holiness, not only in precept, but in reality and practice."[9] Spiritual biographies can also greatly encourage Christians when they see how the living God worked in the lives of others to transform them into the likeness of Christ. Testimonies of people, such as the apostle Paul, David Brainerd (1718–1747), or John Newton (1725–1807), offer strong evidence of the almighty and enduring grace of God.

Another reason for reading spiritual biographies is to spur Christians onward through real-life examples. Cotton Mather wrote about the righteous and courageous lives of the settlers who came from England to establish the colonies. He said his purpose in writing about these magistrates and ministers was to "leave unto posterity, examples worthy of everlasting remembrances."[10] Mather's father must have impressed upon his son the need to write about Christian history and the lives of eminent Christians. Increase Mather preached a sermon titled "David Serving His Generation" at the funeral of Rev. John Baily of Boston. In his message he said:

> We should consider how the holy prophets served their generations, and endeavor to do like them.... So we should take the prophets for an example of serviceableness in their generations. We should consider how the holy Apostles of the Lord Jesus Christ served their generation, according to the will of God, and take pattern by them.... And besides scripture examples, we should consider those whom we ourselves have known, that have faithfully served their generation: and in a special manner such faithful ministers of Christ as we have had knowledge of, and most of all, if we have lived under their ministry.[11]

A third purpose for reading Christian biography, and likely one of the most important to Puritan pastors, is evangelistic; that is, these books call for repentance. James Janeway wrote *Tokens for Children* to rescue his young readers from their "miserable condition by nature"

9. Baxter, *The Life and Letters of Joseph Alleine,* 22.
10. Mather, *Magnalia Christi Americana,* 2.
11. Increase Mather, "David Serving His Generation," in *Jeremiads* (New York: AMS Press, 1985), 24.

and "from falling into everlasting fire."[12] But lest we see Janeway as a dour Puritan fixated upon death and dying, his book on encouragement also highlights the joys of living and dying in the comfort of salvation through Christ.

A fourth purpose for reading biography is to trace the saving work of God in the experience of the human soul. While we should never make someone else's experience a law to dictate God's way with all people, we can learn much from the experiences of others. It is encouraging to hear of God's work in another Christian's soul and to realize that we have experienced the same thing or something very similar. Biographies of Christians generate in those who read them a sense of belonging to a spiritual family that transcends the centuries.

For example, John Owen used Augustine's autobiographical *Confessions* as a pattern for "the manner of conversion."[13] Owen wrote,

> I must say, that, in my judgment, there is none among the ancient or modern divines unto this day, who, either in the declarations of their own experiences, or their directions unto others, have equaled, much less outgone him, in an accurate search and observation of all the secret actings of the Spirit of God on the minds and souls of men, both towards and in their recovery or conversion.[14]

Fifth, reading Christian biography strengthens the reader's soul with accounts of people who have exercised godliness in the midst of great sufferings and trials. By nature we tend to indulge in self-pity and laziness. Reading about the labors and sufferings of other Christians should wake us out of our drowsy selfishness. John Bunyan wrote an account of his imprisonment for preaching without a government license, and the brave testimony of his wife on his behalf.[15] This account has strengthened the hearts of many believers since then.

---

12. Beeke and Pederson, *Meet the Puritans*, 378.

13. John Owen, "Pneumatologia, or, A Discourse Concerning the Holy Spirit," in *The Works of John Owen* (Edinburgh: Banner of Truth, 1965), 3:337–66.

14. Owen, "Pneumatologia," in *Works*, 3:349.

15. John Bunyan, "A Relation of the Imprisonment of Mr. John Bunyan," in *Works*, 1:50–62.

Bunyan recorded these events, he said, because long before he was imprisoned, he had heard rumors of his arrest. A friend urged him to cancel a meeting he was to speak at and flee for safety. Bunyan replied, "Come, be of good cheer, let us not be daunted; our cause is good, we need not be ashamed of it; to preach God's Word is so good a work, that we shall be well rewarded, if we suffer for that."[16] Bunyan understood that the news of his sufferings, if God willed that he must suffer, would honor God and strengthen the churches. So he wrote about his experiences to stir us up to labor and be willing to suffer for our Lord. That is the power of the examples of godly men and women who have gone before us.

Sixth, we read Christian biography so that we might be inspired to proclaim "the praises of the LORD, and his strength, and his wonderful works that he hath done" (Ps. 78:4). As we read about the lives of other saints, we are taught "reliance on Providence," which Daniel Shea observes, is "a thematic staple of Puritan autobiographies."[17] Often only in hindsight can we discern the wisdom of God in the circumstances that surround us. Biography offers us a kind of hindsight that expands beyond the narrow bounds of our own experience to see God working in history.

In his biography of John Cotton, John Norton said it was vitally important for people to write biographies of other Christians because the Bible is full of testimony about what the faithful have done in time past and how they suffered for the kingdom. These accounts were recorded for the benefit of succeeding generations, not only as a memorial, "but as so many practical demonstrations of the faithfulness of God."[18] Trials and difficulties were not the result of fate, but were given to us by the hands of an all-loving and all-wise God. In essence, the study of history gives Christians the unique advantage of seeing the "end of the story," or at least the greater good that God produces in the lives of the godly from trials, opposition, and persecution at the hands of wicked men.

---

16. Bunyan, "A Relation of the Imprisonment of Mr. John Bunyan," in *Works*, 1:51.

17. Daniel B. Shea Jr., *Spiritual Autobiography in Early America* (Princeton: Princeton University Press, 1968), 157.

18. Norton, *Abel Being Dead, Yet Speaketh*, 4.

Reading about others who have endured difficulties also helps us trust more deeply in the Father, through Christ. Increase Mather wrote in his autobiography, "I have thought that the relation of what the Lord has done for your father, and the wonderful experience which he has had of God's faithfulness towards him, might be a means to cause you to give yourselves entirely to the Lord Jesus and to endeavor to walk with God."[19]

Seventh, Christian biographies help pastors to serve as witnesses, tutors, and coaches by showing them how God worked through His servants in ages past. History thus becomes a textbook that warns us of dangers, while calling us to faithful service. One of Norton's reasons for writing about John Cotton was to encourage young pastors to stay in New England and serve the Lord as faithful shepherds in "the wilderness."

Finally, one more reason to read the biographies of eminent divines is that many of their passages on life experiences shed light upon the doctrinal treatises these men wrote or the sermons they preached. The biographies provide evidence that the Puritans lived the life of faith that they preached about and urged upon their listeners. Many of the challenges facing twenty-first-century pastors are the same, albeit in different dress, as the Puritans faced in former times. We can learn much from those who preceded us.

Conclusion

Hebrews 11 with its heroes of faith encourages us to listen to these faithful witnesses who today are in the grandstands of heaven, figuratively speaking, cheering us on by the lives they lived, the things they achieved, and the trials they endured by faith (Heb. 12:1). They are all commended because their faith had substance and was evident in all they did. They looked beyond the convenient, self-satisfying evil of their times; unknown destinations; the power of the grave; the sacrifices demanded of them; the lure of power, fame, and treasure; the dangers to be faced and the formidable walls to be pulled down; the threats of giants; and the prospect of being mocked, flogged, stoned, chained, or

---

19. Quoted in Shea, *Spiritual Autobiography in Early America*, 157.

put to death in horrible ways. Their faith was fixed upon a faithful God and fueled by the promises of a greater life, a better country, and a final dwelling place.

What challenges do you face today as a pastor? Perhaps a more appropriate question to ask, is, "What are you reading, watching, and listening to on a regular basis?" How are you nurturing the life of your soul? Pastors who either fear being "too heavenly minded to be of any earthly good" or who think they need to be completely immersed in the swamp of modern life to be useful, miss the lessons of Hebrews 11 and 12 and of the Puritan pastors, who believed that until someone truly becomes heavenly minded, he will be of no earthly good to God or to his fellow men.

So, what are you reading that raises your eyes above a broken world and points you to the skies? Cease from spending so much time sifting through the wreckage of contemporary culture or studying the ills of modern life. Feast your eyes on accounts of how the nations have been brought subject to Christ, and how persons sick with sin have found a sovereign remedy in Christ and His gospel. Read Christian biographies, particularly of the Puritan divines.

PART FIVE

Dignity

A true minister, one who is a genuine angel and a true interpreter is no common or ordinary man. Such men are thin on
the ground, one of many—indeed, one of a thousand.

—WILLIAM PERKINS

CHAPTER 12

"One among a Thousand"

Today's discouraged ministers need to rediscover God's perspective on who we are, both as Christians and as servants of Christ, and to be reminded of the dignity and importance of what He has called us to do. All too often, our self-worth as pastors is determined by the world's values or by our personal need to prove that we are important. These mistaken and unreliable indicators drive ministers to define their worth by tangible accomplishments such as the number of members in their church, the size of the church building, the scale of church finances, or their personal influence in the larger community.

The Puritans learned to value the ministry by another standard. They said man was blessed by God, "if there be a messenger with him, an interpreter, one among a thousand, to shew unto man his uprightness" (Job 33:23). Matthew Poole (1624–1679) said that "one among a thousand" was an able and faithful minister of the Word, "a person rightly qualified for this great and hard work [of declaring the mind of God], such as there are but very few, scarce *one of a thousand*."[1]

Challenges Faced by Puritan Pastors

Sometimes pastors are discouraged because people undermine their authority. Some people question a pastor's decisions or teachings. Some question our very authority to lead the church. The most serious challenge to the legitimacy of a Puritan pastor's authority came

---

1. Matthew Poole, *A Commentary on the Holy Bible* (1685; repr., London: Banner of Truth, 1962), 1:1005.

via government persecution. Ministers in England who refused to comply with the Act of Uniformity in 1662 were ejected from their posts in the Church of England. This act implied that ministers who were not ordained and licensed by the bishops of the national church were false prophets and were leading people astray.

The legislation resulted in the imprisonment of Puritans who continued to preach, especially those who had separated themselves from the Church of England. When John Bunyan stood before the judges that were about to send him to jail, his wife, Elizabeth, made an impassioned statement that probably infuriated the judges. She said, "Because he is a tinker and a poor man, therefore he is despised and cannot have justice."[2] Bunyan spent more than twelve years in jail. Other ministers managed to avoid imprisonment, but they still suffered harassment and often had to pay heavy fines.

Puritan ministers also faced a rising tide of lawless spirituality. Tension was increasing between the Puritans and groups such as the Society of Friends, or Quakers, the Familists,[3] and antinomians such as Ann Hutchinson. These groups sought to replace the preaching of the Word by ordained ministers with lay ministry and revelations announced by those who claimed to have "inward light." From June 1636 through May 1640, Thomas Shepard delivered a series of lectures on the parable of the ten virgins because of "a leaven of Antinomian and Familistical opinions stirring in the country."[4] In his lectures he defended the importance of listening to sound sermons from preachers who were led by the Spirit to preach the Word. He said,

> Of confutation of those that think there is not that necessity of the ministry to convey the Spirit; but…think good books may do the deed, and hence can profit as much at home as thereby; but these virgins are not directed to books, but persons…. They

---

2. John Bunyan, "Grace Abounding," in *Works*, 1:126. By contrast, ministers of the Church of England often belonged to the gentry, being from landowning, wealthy, or aristocratic families.

3. The Familists, or "Family of Love," was a movement founded in Europe by Henry Nicholas (1501–1580), who taught a mystical, pantheistic union of the soul with the divine based on visions Nicholas claimed to have had. It spread to England and later appears to have merged into the Quaker movement.

4. Thomas Shepard, "The Parable of the Ten Virgins," in *Works*, 2:8.

would have it by immediate revelation, by elevations of the soul to God.... If indeed we had only souls, and no bodies, then we might lay aside our Bibles; but seeing it is not so, look to the word thus dispensed; hence the Lord saith, "Hear, and your souls shall live."[5]

Along with these movements that rejected the Puritan pastor's authority, the Puritans were scorned for their plain preaching and Reformed theology. As in all ages, the gospel offends some people when it is faithfully preached in the name of Christ and in the power of the Spirit. The gospel will always be foolishness to the so-called wise people of this world, and a stumbling block to those who live by the law and its traditions. Flavel warned people of God's judgment against those who would not listen to His servants who faithfully preached the Word:

> Such a judgment the Lord threatens in Amos 8:11. "Behold the day is come, saith the Lord, that I will send a famine in the land, not a famine of bread, nor a thirst for water, but of hearing the word of the Lord." The meaning is, I will send a more fearful judgment than that of the famine of bread.... And we find both in human and sacred histories, that when God hath shut up the spiritual clouds, removing or silencing his minister, sensible Christians have ever been deeply affected with it, and reckoned it a most tremendous judgment. Thus the Christians of Antioch, when Chrysostom their minister was banished, they judged it better to lose the sun out of the firmament, than lose that, their minister.... Oh the loss of a gospel-ministry is an inestimable loss, not to be repaired but by its own return, or by heaven.[6]

In the midst of those challenges and the ordinary difficulties of ministry, the Puritans dug deep into Scripture to confirm the worth and dignity of the pastoral office. This helped them defy the enactments of the king, turn deaf ears to the slander of critics, resolutely oppose the sects, and heed only the voice of the Head of the church who commissioned and commended their service to Him.

---

5. Shepard, "The Parable of the Ten Virgins," in *Works*, 2:500–501.
6. John Flavel, "The Heavenly Use of Earthly Things," in *Works*, 5:82.

A Special Calling from God

The Puritans defined their calling and ordination by carefully studying the Scriptures. Like a surgeon, John Owen dissected the Roman Catholic idea of the ministry as a priesthood in *The Duty of Pastors and People Distinguished*. He wrote,

> That the name of priests is nowhere in the Scripture attributed *peculiarly* and *distinctively to the ministers of the gospel as such.* Let any produce an instance to the contrary, and this controversy is at an end. Yea, that which puts a difference between them and the rest of the people of God's holiness seems to be a more immediate participation of Christ's prophetical office, to teach, instruct, and declare the will of God unto men; and not of his sacerdotal [office], to offer sacrifices for men unto God…. And yet, when Christ ascended on high, he gave some to be prophets, for the edification of his body, Eph. 4:11; none as we find, to be priests.[7]

In other words, after Pentecost, no office in the church corresponds to the Aaronic or Levitical priesthood of the Old Testament. However, Owen affirmed that ministers do have a special calling from God. He said that, according to Scripture, the following is required of a man to be duly ordained as pastor or teacher of the church. He must be:

- Furnished with gifts of the Holy Spirit for the edification of the church, and the work of the ministry (Eph. 4:7, 8, 11–13);

- Blameless, temperate, and exemplary in his manner of life (Titus 1:7–9; 1 Tim. 3:2–7);

- Willing to give himself to the work of the ministry (1 Peter 5:1–3);

- Called and chosen [elected] by the suffrage and consent of the church (Acts 14:23 [cf. Acts 6:2–5]);

- Solemnly ordained or set apart, by fasting and prayer, and the laying on of hands, to the ministry of the Word (Acts 13:2, 3; 1 Tim. 4:14, 5:22).[8]

---

7. John Owen, "The Duty of Pastors and People Distinguished," in *Works*, 13:26.

8. Owen, "A Brief Instruction in the Worship of God and Discipline of the Churches of the New Testament," in *Works*, 15:493. This came to be known as the "Independents' Catechism."

Christ alone is the head of His church, but He delegates authority to His servants, as defined in the Scriptures. Such ministers act
"not in the name or authority of the church by which their power is
derived unto them... but in the name and authority of Jesus Christ."[9]

Therefore the church must honor faithful ministers of the Word
(1 Thess. 5:12–13; 1 Tim. 5:17), conscientiously obeying them because
they speak in the name of the Lord (Heb. 13:7, 17; 1 Cor. 16:16); earnestly praying for them and, if necessary, exhorting them to fulfill their
ministry (Eph. 6:18, 19; Col. 4:3; 2 Thess. 3:1; Col. 4:17); sharing goods
with them to supply their physical and temporal needs and enabling
them to be generous to others (Gal. 6:6; 1 Cor. 9:14); and standing by
them in their suffering for the gospel (2 Tim. 1:16–18; 4:16).

George Gillespie, a Scottish Presbyterian and delegate to the
Westminster Assembly, also had a high view of the ministerial calling, arguing that men who were not called by the church should be
barred from the ministry. He wrote:

> It is not lawful for any man, how fit soever and how much soever
> enriched or beautified with excellent gifts, to undertake the
> administration either of the word or sacraments by the will of
> private persons, or others who have not power and right to call,
> much less it is lawful by their own judgment to assume and arro-
> gate the same to themselves. But before it be lawful to undergo
> that sacred ministry in churches constituted, a special calling, yea
> beside, a lawful election (which alone is not sufficient), a mission
> or sending, or (as commonly it is termed) ordination, is necessar-
> ily required, and that both for the avoiding of confusion, and to
> bar out or shut the door (so far as in us lieth) upon imposters;
> as also by reason of divine institution delivered to us in the Holy
> Scripture, Rom. 10:15; Heb. 5:4; Titus 1:5; 1 Tim. 2:7.[10]

Ministers must guard against pride and clothe themselves in
humility (1 Peter 5:3, 5), but they must not despise their office nor
permit others to despise it (1 Tim. 4:12). Thomas Goodwin said,
"Despise not the ministry nor the work of it. It is to convert souls, and

---

9. Owen, "The Worship of God and Discipline of the Churches," in *Works,* 15:499.
10. George Gillespie, "Propositions Concerning the Ministry and Government
of the Church," in *Works,* 1:5.

therefore it is the best calling in the world: 1 Tim. 1:12, 'And I thank Jesus our Lord, who hath enabled me, for that he counted me faithful, putting me into the ministry.'"[11]

Baxter wrote, "Consider that you have the honor, to encourage you to the labor. And a great honor it is to be the ambassadors of God, and the instruments of men's conversion, to 'save their souls from death, and to cover a multitude of sins.'" It is a great honor for pastors to be supported by the church so they may give themselves wholly to the work of the ministry. It is a great privilege to train for the ministry, to mine the riches of Scripture, to explore the great system of Christian doctrine, and to journey with others through church history. Baxter thus asked,

> Is it nothing to be brought up to learning, when others are brought up to the cart and plough; and to be furnished with so much delightful knowledge, when the world lieth in ignorance?… [W]hat an excellent privilege is it, to live in studying and preaching Christ—to be continually searching into his mysteries, or feeding on them—to be daily employed in the consideration of the blessed nature, works, and ways of God.… We may do almost nothing else but study and talk of God and glory, and engage in acts of prayer and praise, and drink in his sacred, saving truths.[12]

Even so, the chief dignity of the pastoral calling is its origin in the will of Christ and its institution in the Word of God. Perkins thus said ministers are "the high commissioners of God." Governments appoint men to exercise power in doing great things, and fathers count it an honor for their sons to receive such a position. Yet Perkins wrote, "But here is a higher commission—a commission from God to redeem souls from the power of hell and from the grip of the devil. This is a true high commission; so high that it was never granted from the court of heaven to any creature, except ministers."[13]

Biblical Descriptions of Ministers of the Word

Puritan pastors were encouraged to lift their heads up (Ps. 3:3) to see God's perspective on their office and work. The dignity of their office

---

11. Goodwin, "The Work of the Holy Ghost in Our Salvation," in *Works,* 6:415.
12. Baxter, *The Reformed Pastor,* 190–92.
13. Perkins, *The Art of Prophesying,* 118.

shines through many word pictures in the Bible. Here are some of the ways God's Word describes ministers of the Word.

1. Stewards in Christ's house. Flavel said, "To them he hath committed the dispensations of the word and sacraments, which contain the great mysteries of the Kingdom of God."[14] Goodwin wrote,

> When James and Paul, and other apostles, style themselves servants of Christ, they intend it not in that sense wherein all Christians are servants of Christ, but they intend their being as [domestic][15] household servants, that have a proper constant work every day assigned to them. As officers and courtiers write themselves servants to the king in a special manner, and not as other subjects; therefore a minister is styled by this, as a name more proper to him, 'the servant of God,' 2 Timothy 2:4.[16]

2. Christ's ambassadors on earth. Herbert said, "A pastor is a deputy of Christ for the reducing and bringing back from error of man to the obedience of God."[17] Flavel said, "Ambassadors represent and personate the prince that sends them; and the honours or contempts done to them, reflect upon, and are reckoned to the person of their master, Luke 10:16. 'He that heareth you, heareth me;' 'and he that despiseth you, despiseth me.'"[18]

3. Watchmen over the city of God. Foxcroft wrote, "The faithful watchman walks his rounds and inspects the whole town, not confining his care to this or that particular house. So they who keep the watch of the Lord at the gates of the temple must walk circumspectly, watch in all things, and tend to every house."[19] Matthew Henry said,

> They watch for the souls for the people, not to ensnare them, but to save them; to gain them, not to themselves, but to Christ;

---

14. Flavel, "The Character of a True Evangelical Pastor," in *Works,* 6:567.

15. The original reads "menial" but appears to do so in the old sense of "familial" or "domestic." The context does not well suit the modern sense of "menial," that is, slavish, degrading, not requiring skill, nor having honor. Rather, Goodwin compared ministers to "domestic" servants entrusted with specific responsibilities in the household of a nobleman.

16. Thomas Goodwin, "The Churches of Christ," in *Works,* 4:369.

17. Herbert, *The Country Parson,* 55.

18. John Flavel, "The Method of Grace," in *Works,* 2:52–53.

19. Foxcroft, *The Gospel Ministry,* 18.

to build them up in knowledge, faith, and holiness. They are to watch against every thing that may be hurtful to the souls of men, and to give them warning of dangerous errors, of the devices of Satan, of approaching judgments; they are to watch for all opportunities of helping the souls of men forward in the way to heaven.[20]

4. Fishers of men. Foxcroft wrote, "Ministers are called 'fishers of men' (e.g. Mark 1:17). Now the net of the gospel (to allude to what one has faithfully and wisely observed concerning human laws) is not to be like a spider's web, which catches small flies and lets the oxen escape."[21] As preachers, we fish with the glorious nets of the Word of God.

5. Shepherds of Christ's blood-bought flock. Matthew Henry said, "The world is God's by right of creation, but the church is his by right of redemption, and therefore it ought to be dear to us, for it was dear to him, because it cost him dear.... Did Christ lay down his life to purchase it, and shall his ministers be wanting in any care and pains to feed it?"[22] What a high and noble calling ministers have as shepherds of the precious lambs whom Christ has entrusted to them!

6. Builders of God's temple. Burgess said that by preaching Christ, pastors "lay a good and sure foundation in the hearts of their hearers."[23] When we teach people the truths of the Bible in a faithful, plain, and spiritual way, we build on that foundation with precious and excellent materials, for, "The truths of Christ preached in a pure and sincere manner, this is gold, silver, and precious stones."[24]

7. God's co-laborers. Burgess said, "The ministers of the gospel are workers with God, for the conversion of men's souls...not by immediate producing of any spiritual effects, but by the external application of the ministry to the people."[25] Thus when God so wills, the ministry of weak men can produce almighty effects: "the blind see, the poor

---

20. Matthew Henry, *Matthew Henry's Commentary on the Whole Bible* (Peabody, Mass.: Hendrickson, 2003), 6:777 [on Heb. 13:1–17].

21. Foxcroft, *The Gospel Ministry,* 17.

22. Henry's *Commentary,* 6:215 [Acts 20:28].

23. Burgess, *Scripture Directory,* 125.

24. Burgess, *Scripture Directory,* 157.

25. Burgess, *Scripture Directory,* 110.

are humbled, and lofty cast down, and men's hearts changed, for God worketh with it."[26]

Conclusion

Sometimes we think it is prideful to contemplate the honor that God has bestowed upon us as ministers of the Word. However, denigrating God's gifts and calling is a kind of false humility. Yes, we are unworthy servants, debtors to grace alone, and the chief of sinners. We must be cleansed with the blood of Christ every day of our lives. However, the office we hold is "a good work" (1 Tim. 3:1). It is a high calling to a great task. As the founders of the Presbyterian Church in the U.S.A. declared, "The pastoral office is the first in the church, both for dignity and usefulness."[27]

When you are discouraged, remind yourself, first, of the new identity God gave you as a child of God through faith in Jesus Christ, and second, of the dignity of the office to which God has called you as a minister of the Word. Then, when the world sneers at you (as it did at Christ), say to yourself, "I am a steward in Christ's household, an ambassador of heaven on earth, a watchman over the city of God, a fisher of men, a shepherd of Christ's blood-bought flock, a builder of God's holy temple, and, wonder of wonders, a co-laborer with God in the extension of His kingdom."

---

26. Burgess, *Scripture Directory,* 113.

27. "Form of Government," *The Constitution of the Presbyterian Church in the U.S.A.* (Philadelphia: Presbyterian Board of Publication, 1839), 408.

CHAPTER 13

Doing the Work of Angels

Pastors can be demoralized by the seeming glory of our secular, materialistic culture. Gordon MacDonald questioned the importance of his work as a pastor while serving a church near Boston. He writes:

> I have felt the feelings of intimidation as I have driven Storrow Drive into Boston. To the left as one drives along the Charles River are the beautiful buildings of Harvard, and to the right are the more austere dwelling places of the Harvard Business school. Further down Storrow Drive, again to the left, is the campus of the Massachusetts Institute of Technology (MIT), many of the buildings roofed with antennas, satellite dishes, and other strange looking objects that suggest to the uninitiated that mysterious things go on there, that people are talking to the stars. Ahead are the buildings of Boston's downtown where many multinational corporations have their headquarters. It is a temptation to allow all of that to rebalance the mind and spirit, to permit oneself to think that in places such as these offices, labs, and classrooms the real power to change and control history is being generated and discharged. Spiritual passion can quickly dissipate when one compares these concrete symbols of human power to the abstract gospel of Jesus Christ, and it is tempting to say with the disciple who was disheartened over the inadequacy of the lunch to feed thousands, "But what is the gospel among so many."[1]

1. Gordon MacDonald, *Restoring Your Spiritual Passion* (Nashville: Oliver-Nelson Books, 1986), 67.

MacDonald nonetheless concludes that there are greater forces in the universe than human technological expertise or the power of corporate wealth and enterprise. Only the power of Christ's gospel gives meaning to history. Only Christ's gospel can change the human heart. The gospel is the wisdom of God (1 Cor. 2:7) and the power of God (Rom. 1:16).

We as pastors have been given a heavenly work to do. If we could see the palace of our King, the glorious temple in heaven, and the mighty spirits residing there, the towering skylines of our cities would seem like anthills, and the enterprises of men would be no more impressive than the games children play at recess. We would realize that "they that be with us are more than they that be with them," indeed, that round about us are "horses and chariots of fire" (2 Kings 6:16–17). We would say with Richard Sibbes: "In Christ we have the attendance of angels.... We have Elisha's guard about us continually, but we see them not.... A Christian is a king; he is never without his guard, that invisible guard of angels."[2]

Ministers and Angels
Quite surprisingly, the topic of angels and their work is a recurring theme in Puritan literature. Although the Puritans affirmed that the angels are subordinate to Christ, they drew comfort from the scriptural promises of angelic protection. They did not single out pastors as if they alone were the objects of angelic concern, but applied the general promise that the Lord commands His angels to guard those who trust in Him (Pss. 34:7; 91:9–10; Heb. 1:13–14).

Thomas Goodwin, noting that Scripture calls angels "the heavenly host,"[3] said angels are "the men of war, they are the militia of heaven." These fierce, supernatural soldiers are the mortal enemies of sinners, for we are told that angels will cast sinners into the fires of hell at the command of the Son of man (Matt. 13:41–42). But

2. Sibbes, *Works*, 5:499–500.

3. "Host" means a multitude, whether of stars, angels, or warriors; a fighting host, whether composed of angels or men, is an army. Israel's God is *Jehovah Sabaoth*, "the Lord of Hosts," meaning that He can summon an army of armies, as fighting forces under His command (cf. Matt. 26:53).

Goodwin also reminds us that Christ made peace with His blood, so that if we are in Christ, the angels are our friends who fight for the gospel and for the church.[4]

William Perkins believed the angels provide special help to ministers of the Word. He observed how God used angels to care for his prophets in passages such as Isaiah 6:6 and 2 Kings 6:16. He wrote, "Angels are sent out to help and serve the elect, especially God's ministers.... Even today, their protection and strengthening ministry is no less a reality to the godly ministers of the New Testament, even if it comes to us without the same signs or visible manner as in the Old."[5] That is a great comfort, for though men may despise gospel ministers, angels still care for them.[6]

The Puritans rejoiced that God sends angels to care for the heirs of salvation (Heb. 1:14). The verb rendered "to minister" in Hebrews 1:14 is a prepositional phrase in Greek, *eis diakonia,* meaning "to serve as deacons" for salvation's heirs, just as the deacons were tasked with assisting the needy and caring for the church's temporal concerns. Thomas Manton clarified this truth, saying, "They are not ministers of conversion and sanctification: to this ministry Christ hath called men, not angels; but in preserving the converted the angels have a hand...they guard the bodily life chiefly."[7] Perkins also denied that the angels do the work of gospel ministry with us or for us.[8] But they do care for ministers. He wrote, "They also often minister bodily strength and assistance and many comforts to them in their troublesome travels.... What if you have influential men of this world against you, when you have angels for you?"[9]

God's angels also observe our preaching of the gospel and rejoice at the repentance of each sinner (Luke 15:10).[10] As Manton said, angels delight in the gospel, closely watch ministers and churches, and learn

---

4. Goodwin, *Works,* 1:189.

5. William Perkins, "The Calling of the Ministry," in *The Art of Prophesying,* 160.

6. Perkins, "The Calling of the Ministry," 161.

7. Manton, *Works,* 1:284–85.

8. Perkins, "The Calling of the Ministry," 161.

9. Perkins, "The Calling of the Ministry," 161.

10. Perkins, "The Calling of the Ministry," 163.

more of God's wisdom through us (1 Cor. 4:9; 11:10; Eph. 3:10; 1 Tim. 5:21; 1 Peter 1:12).[11]

Angels are also called "ministers" or "servants" of the Lord (Ps. 103:20–21). Perkins, like other Puritans, warned us not to pray to angels or worship them. Prayer is offered to God alone, because God alone can hear and answer our prayers. Likewise worship belongs to God alone, as the One who is truly worthy of it. An angel is a minister's "fellow servant" (Rev. 19:10; 22:8–9),[12] which the Puritans viewed as an honor for the pastor. Perkins said that angels and ministers are "fellow-labourers" as God's ambassadors and officers; in a special way "they share titles in common, angels being called ministers, and ministers, angels."[13] That leads to our next section.

Ministers as Inferior Angels

The Puritans clearly distinguished angels as incorporeal heavenly spirits from human beings, composed of both spirit and body. They knew that no son of Adam could attain angelic purity here on earth. Nevertheless they saw parallels between the work of angels and the calling of a gospel preacher.[14] James Janeway writes, "His ministers are sent to do the work of inferior angels, to preach glad tidings of great joy."[15] Cotton Mather said that if you bring the gospel to those in the shadow of death, your ministry "will do the work, and give you the welcome, of a good angel unto them."[16] In this he was echoing the apostle Paul's statement that the Galatians once welcomed him "as an angel of God, even as Christ Jesus" (Gal. 4:14).

These writers are referring to the basic meaning of the Hebrew and Greek words. This analogy between angels and ministers is linked to the title of Christ, who is our chief Prophet as the "Angel of

---

11. Manton, *Works,* 1:334–35.

12. Perkins, "The Calling of the Ministry," 163.

13. Perkins, "The Calling of the Ministry," 162.

14. This analogy is older than the Puritans, going back at least to Thomas Aquinas's commentary on Revelation. See John Mayer, *Ecclesiastica Interpretatio; or the Expositions upon the Difficult and Doubtful Passages of the Seven Epistles called Catholike and the Revelation* (London: John Haviland for John Grismand, 1627), 260.

15. Janeway, *The Saints' Encouragement,* 43.

16. Mather, *Bonifacius: An Essay Upon the Good,* 74.

the Covenant" (Mal. 3:1).[17] The Puritans understood that the Hebrew word, *malak,* and the Greek, *angelos,* usually translated as "angel" in the English Bible, both mean "messenger." Thus the Old Testament priest in his role as a teacher of God's Word was called "the messenger [literally, angel] of the LORD of hosts" (Mal. 2:7).[18]

Arthur Dent (1553–1607) said, "But by the word *angel,* he meaneth the minister or pastor of every church: which therefore is called an angel, because he is the minister of God, as the word signifieth: as also because every faithful minister ought to be received and regarded as an angel of God, as the apostle witnesseth to the Galatians" (Gal. 4:14).[19]

The Puritans also found evidence of the angelic nature of a pastor's calling in Christ's letters to the churches in Revelation. These letters are addressed to "the angel" of each of the seven churches (Rev. 2:1, 8, etc.).[20] Fenner reasoned that these angels could not be the angels in heaven because they are sometimes rebuked for faults. They could not be fallen angels, either, because they are sometimes commended. He said, "It remains then, that a metaphorical angel is here understood, and that is the minister of the church."[21]

Other Puritans confirmed this interpretation by citing Revelation 14:6, in which an angel in heaven preaches "the everlasting gospel" to "every nation." James Durham (1622–1658) commented, "The angels are ministering spirits, sent forth to minister for them that are heirs of salvation (Heb. 1:14) but they do not have the everlasting gospel to preach. This treasure is put in earthen vessels, that the excellency

---

17. Manton, *Works,* 10:468.

18. James Durham, *Commentary upon the Book of the Revelation* (Willow Street, Pa.: Old Paths, 2000), 63.

19. Arthur Dent, *Exposition upon the whole Revelation* (London: by N. O. for Simon Waterson, 1633), 35–36.

20. Matthew Poole, *A Commentary on the Whole Bible* (Peabody, Mass.: Hendrickson, n.d.), 3:952.

21. Fenner, *Christ's Alarm to Drowsie Saints,* 6. Fenner realized that at least some of these churches had more than one elder (Acts 20:17). He interpreted the singular "angel" to refer to the ministers collectively, implying that they should stand together in unity (p. 19). So also Durham, "By *angels* we understand all the bishops and presbyters that were over those churches.... Therefore take we the style *angel,* to be collective... *ministers* of such a church" (*Commentary upon the Book of the Revelation,* 63–64).

of the power may be of God (2 Cor. 4:7)…the ministers are called angels, because they are God's messengers, entrusted by Him with a high and heavenly employment."[22] Matthew Poole wrote, "This angel seems to me to represent faithful ministers' speed and diligence to preach the gospel in all parts of the world."[23]

How are ministers like the angels in heaven? Puritan expositors found several points of likeness between these two orders of the servants of God, highlighting the dignity and honor of the pastoral office:

1. They are both heavenly. The angels are pure spirits. Fenner said that although ministers are embodied spirits, they are called to be spiritual men, "holding forth the fruits of the Spirit," and laboring to lead men into a "relish of all the things of the Spirit of God."[24] Angels are "creatures of another world," i.e., heaven (Matt. 24:36), who come to earth only to do God's errands. All children of God are heavenly creatures because they are "born from above" (John 3:3, KJV margin, n. 1), but the minister especially so, for he must preach the gospel of the kingdom of heaven and care little for earthly wealth and earthly wisdom.[25] He must be holy, for he knows that "angels are holy."[26]

2. They both study God's mysteries. Benjamin Keach (1640–1704) wrote, "Angels desire to pry into the mysteries of grace and mercy in Jesus Christ (1 Peter 1:12). Christ's true ministers also make it their business to dig into the hidden mysteries."[27]

3. They are both God's servants. Angels do not come to men unless they are sent by God, Fenner said. Likewise ministers must not serve unless they are sent by God (John 1:6, Rom 10:15).[28] As angels fly

---

22. Durham, *Commentary upon the Book of the Revelation,* 736. In Durham's historicist interpretation, the angels of Revelation 14 represent the preaching of the gospel and shaking of the kingdom of the Roman Babylon, that is, the Roman Catholic Church, by the Reformers like Luther. See also Thomas Goodwin, "An Exposition of Revelation," in *Works,* 3:86–88.

23. Poole, *Commentary on the Whole Bible,* 987. See also Dent, *An Exposition upon the whole Revelation,* 271.

24. Fenner, *Christ's Alarm to Drowsie Saints,* 7–8.

25. Fenner, *Christ's Alarm to Drowsie Saints,* 9.

26. Fenner, *Christ's Alarm to Drowsie Saints,* 11.

27. Benjamin Keach, *Preaching from the Types and Metaphors of the Bible* (Grand Rapids: Kregel, 1972), 828.

28. Fenner, *Christ's Alarm to Drowsie Saints,* 9.

quickly to do God's will (Isa. 6:6), ministers must heed the command to bring in the harvest (John 4:38).[29] Keach wrote, "Angels are very obedient to God, they do his commands, and wait for his word. The faithful preachers of the gospel are very ready to obey God's commands, though they are thereby exposed to great danger, if God bid them go, they go (Rom. 1:15)."[30]

4. *They are both servants to the church.* God sends out angels as ministering spirits for the heirs of salvation (Heb. 1:14). Fenner said ministers likewise exist for the good of the church of Jesus Christ (1 Cor. 3:22).[31] They are here mainly for God's elect.[32] Keach said angels "do not think it below them" to serve the saints; thus faithful preachers must also serve the members of the church willingly even though the preacher might "far excel" them in gifts and abilities.[33]

5. *They both are ministers of the Word, declaring God's will to men.* Angels proclaimed God's good news at Christ's birth (Luke 2:8–14). Pastors have the same office: to proclaim to sinners the knowledge of salvation and forgiveness of sins (Luke 1:76–77).[34] John Mayer (1583–1664) said of pastoral ministry, "The will of God is, as it were, by angels from heaven declared."[35]

6. *They both comfort the downcast.* Keach wrote, "Angels are often sent to comfort the saints when cast down, as they ministered to Christ in his agony. So are gospel preachers sent to comfort the feeble-minded[36] [those given to doubt and indecision], and support the weak; they know how to comfort others with the same comfort whereby they themselves are comforted of God (2 Cor. 1:4)."[37]

---

29. Fenner, *Christ's Alarm to Drowsie Saints,* 12–13.
30. Keach, *Types and Metaphors,* 828.
31. Fenner, *Christ's Alarm to Drowsie Saints,* 9.
32. Fenner, *Christ's Alarm to Drowsie Saints,* 16.
33. Keach, *Types and Metaphors,* 829.
34. Fenner, *Christ's Alarm to Drowsie Saints,* 10.
35. Mayer, *Ecclesiastica Interpretatio,* 260.
36. See 1 Thessalonians 5:14; W. E. Vine prefers the translation "fainthearted." See *An Expository Dictionary of New Testament Words* (Old Tappan, N.J.: Fleming H. Revell, 1940), 70.
37. Keach, *Types and Metaphors,* 829.

Conclusion

God has willed that the treasure of the gospel be entrusted to ministers who are mere "earthen vessels" so that, as Charles Hodge says, "the exceeding great power, the wonderful efficiency of the gospel… may be known and acknowledged to be of God, i.e., to flow from him as its source, and not from us" (cf. 2 Cor. 4:7).[38] Even so, it pleases God by the ministry of men to gather a church to Himself unto life eternal, from among the lost children of men.[39] Pastors have a high calling. We are stewards of the mysteries of God (1 Cor. 4:1), ambassadors for Christ (2 Cor. 5:20), and workers together with Him (2 Cor. 6:1). Let us thus never be ashamed to be ministers of the gospel. The very angels of God serve us as we serve the church bought with Christ's blood.

God has granted ministers of the Word the same title as His heavenly servants, for both are "messengers of the LORD of hosts" (Mal. 2:7). God wills that a church receive its pastor as "an angel of God, even as Christ Jesus" (Gal. 4:14), and pastors should strive to be worthy of such honor. Durham said, "Ministers are called angels, because they are God's messengers, entrusted by Him with a high and heavenly employment; and it is a title that should put ministers in mind of their duty, to do God's will on earth as the angels do it in heaven, in a spiritual and heavenly way, cheerfully, willingly and readily; and it should put people in mind of their duty, to take this word off [from] minister's hands, as from angels."[40] "That is the dignity due to them."[41]

Fenner concludes by saying that the ministry is no base office, for ministers are "angels of God."[42] Men should thus receive their ministers "even as an angel of God" (Gal. 4:14), with reverence for the Word they preach and the office they bear, even though they see "nothing

---

38. Charles Hodge, *An Exposition of the Second Epistle to the Corinthians* (Grand Rapids: Eerdmans, 1973), 92.

39. Form of Ordination of the Ministers of the Word, "Doctrinal Standards, Liturgy, and Church Order," in *The Psalter* (Grand Rapids: Reformation Heritage Books, 1999), 144.

40. Durham, *Commentary upon the Book of the Revelation*, 736.

41. Durham, *Commentary upon the Book of the Revelation*, 63.

42. Fenner, *Christ's Alarm to Drowsie Saints*, 9.

but a poor mortal man there."[43] Keach wrote, "This may inform us, what glory and dignity God hath conferred upon his servants who labour in the ministry; they have a glorious name, and are greatly honored by the Lord, and therefore should be received with all due respect, and esteemed very highly for their work's sake."[44]

So lift up your heads, brothers. It is false humility to act as though the ministerial office has no dignity. The work of your office is a high calling, for it is an angelic calling. Though "we preach not ourselves" (2 Cor. 4:5), we should magnify our office (Rom. 11:13) by our faithfulness, diligence, and godliness of life. Yet in all our consideration of what the Bible says about angels, we must remember that like the most glorious of the angels, we are only the servants of the Lord and ministers of His Word. Isaac Ambrose (1604–1664) wrote, "We have far less written in God's word of the nature of angels, than of God himself; because the knowledge of God is far more practical, and less controversial, and more necessary to salvation."[45] He thus advised, "O then let us eye God, and eye Jesus Christ, in all, above all, and beyond all angel-ministration."[46]

---

43. Fenner, *Christ's Alarm to Drowsie Saints*, 18.

44. Keach, *Types and Metaphors*, 829.

45. Isaac Ambrose, "The Ministration of and Communion with Angels," in *Works of Isaac Ambrose* (London: Henry Fisher, 1823), 480.

46. Ambrose, "Angels," in *Works*, 537.

CHAPTER 14

The Urgency and Importance
of Preaching the Word

Richard Baxter said he preached "as never sure to preach again, as a dying man to dying men." The uncertainty of life and his own mortality filled him with a sense of urgency whenever he entered the pulpit.

Baxter wasn't the only Puritan to express this sense of urgency in the ministry. Increase Mather wrote:

> There is no work in the grave whither we are all a going apace; we have but a short age to be working in, our days are but an hands breadth, and our age is as nothing. The thought of it should make us do all the good we can, the little time that we have to live: It concerns us to work whilst the day of life last, for the night of death is hastening, when no man can work.[1]

The Puritans reckoned with the reality of impending death—their own and that of the people they served. Life expectancy was much shorter in that time. Death often came swiftly and suddenly.

In the twenty-first century we have lost much of this sense of urgency because life expectancy in Western countries has dramatically increased over the past century. In 1900, life expectancy in the United States was 49.2 years; in 1950, 68.1 years; and in 2007, 77.9 years.[2] On average we live thirty years longer than our ancestors did a century ago. For this blessing we thank God.

---

1. Mather, "David Serving His Generation," in *Jeremiads,* 30.
2. Elizabeth Arias, "United States Life Tables, 2007," *National Vital Statistic Reports* 59, no. 9 (September 28, 2011), 48, http://www.cdc.gov/nchs/data/nvsr/nvsr59/nvsr59_09.pdf (accessed December 16, 2011).

The problem of a longer life span, however, is that many of us assume that we have many years left so we lose the sense of urgency in our work. In *The Screwtape Letters,* C. S. Lewis records a dialogue between Uncle Screwtape and Wormwood, his young demon apprentice. Uncle Screwtape says it is far better for the "demon business" that people die of old age in nursing homes than for men to die in war. He explains, "How disastrous for us is the continual remembrance of death which war enforces. One of our best weapons, contented worldliness, is rendered useless."[3] So, too, pastors in congregations with a disproportionate number of young families and children may not face the reality of death and dying as often as pastors of congregations with a more balanced mix of young families and senior members.

In addition, our fast-paced, forward-looking culture doesn't want to spend too much time grieving. A funeral director recently said that in Bible times people would grieve for forty days. Even fifty years ago, people allowed themselves more time to grieve. This grief was shared by a caring community, particularly fellow church members. By contrast, people today only want to grieve forty minutes so they can "get on with their lives," said the funeral director. He went on to say that it isn't any wonder that people have emotional problems long after a death because they haven't grieved long enough over their losses and come to terms with their own mortality.

The Puritan pastors had an advantage in this regard. They and their congregations knew what it was to grieve, and they grieved often. They knew the truth of Ecclesiastes 7:2, which says, "It is better to go to the house of mourning, than to go to the house of feasting: for that is the end of all men; and the living will lay it to his heart." In the wake of a death in the congregation or the wider community, Puritan preachers called on people to examine themselves as to whether they belonged to Christ and were prepared to meet God.

Matthew Henry took part in the funeral service for Samuel Benion, a thirty-five-year-old pastor who had served his congregation for only two years. Henry's words attest to the Puritan sense of the brevity of life:

---

3. C. S. Lewis, *The Screwtape Letters: Special Illustrated Edition* (New York: HarperCollins, 1979), 30.

Here was one who did indeed live fast, did spend and was spent in the business of life, and gave this reason why he took so much pains in his work, because he thought he had but a little time to be working in. His heart seemed to be set on that scripture, and it is not long since he preached upon it on occasion of the death of a worthy good friend of his at Whitchurch, "I must work the work of him that sent me while it is day; the night comes when no man can work."[4]

Ministers today who do not regularly ponder the brevity of life and their own mortality should consider the wisdom of Joseph Alleine's words given in an earnest letter to his congregation, warning them not to set their hearts and minds on things below that rust, rot, and die. That challenge is especially fitting for pastors who are called by God to speak to people about eternal matters. Alleine wrote:

Set your enemies one against the other; death against the world; no such way to get above the world, as to put yourselves into the possession of death. Look often upon your dust that you shall be reduced to, and imagine you saw your bones tumbled out of your graves as they are like shortly to be, and men handling your skulls, and inquiring "Whose is this?" Tell me of what account will the world be then; what good will it do you? Put yourselves often into your graves, and look out from thence upon the world, and see what judgment you have of it then. Must not you be shortly forgot among the dead? Your places will know you no more, and your memory will be no more among men, and then what will it profit you to have lived in fashion and repute, and to have been men of esteem? "One serious walk over a church-yard," as one speaks, "might make a man mortified to the world."[5]

The Primacy of Preaching the Word for Salvation

Perhaps you wonder why seventeenth-century pastors were so urgent about ministry, especially about preaching the gospel. Were they not all Calvinists in theology, which teaches that God has already chosen

---

4. John 9:4. See Matthew Henry, *The Miscellaneous Works of the Rev. Matthew Henry*, (London: J. O. Robinson, 1833), 2:1013.

5. Alleine, *Life and Letters of Joseph Alleine*, 158.

His elect souls and will surely bring them to a saving relationship, with or without our efforts? Will not God bring about His desired results in His own time and in His own way, without our help?

Thomas Goodwin answered those questions by saying that the preaching of the Word is the principal way Christ gathers His church (Deut. 32:2; Isa. 55:10–11; Luke 4:4; John 17:19–20; Acts 10:44; Rom. 10:17; 1 Cor. 2:4; Eph. 1:13).[6] Goodwin said that each person of the Trinity is engaged in employing the preaching of the Word to save the elect: "As God the Father appointed it, and God the Son prayed for it, so God the Holy Spirit is by promise and covenant engaged to accompany it with his blessing unto the seed of Christ forever."[7]

He went on to explain why God just doesn't snap His fingers or use angels or some other means to bring people into a saving relationship with Himself. First, in answering why God chooses to work through means instead of by a direct exercise of His power, Goodwin cites two reasons:

1. God loves variety and diversity in the means of accomplishing His plans. "At the first creation he used no means…yet now in this new creation he is pleased to shew his diverse ways of working, and takes creatures to work by, whom therefore he calls co-workers with him (1 Cor. 3:9)."[8]

2. God has chosen to hide His saving power in means that are "so small and so unlikely" that the world despises them and so seals its own doom. In the same way God "did befool the devil and the world in sending the Prince of glory, clad and concealed in infirmities, to be crucified, and so to bring about God's greatest work (1 Cor. 2:6–8)!"[9]

Second, Goodwin explained why God, of all things, chose the preaching of His Word to save sinners, offering, once more, two biblical reasons:

---

6. Thomas Goodwin, "The Constitution, Right Order and Government of the Churches," in *Works,* 11:360.

7. Goodwin, "The Constitution, Right Order and Government of the Churches," in *Works,* 11:361.

8. Goodwin, "The Constitution, Right Order and Government of the Churches," in *Works,* 11:361.

9. Goodwin, "The Constitution, Right Order and Government of the Churches," in *Works,* 11:361–62.

1. God chose preaching because it is the weakest of all means: "Now to manifest his power the more, he will take the voice of a frail man speaking his word for him; and what is weaker than a man's breath?" Goodwin asked. "He sent his apostles forth, a company of poor fishermen; and were they likely men to conquer the world by commanding living men to believe on one crucified, especially when the conditions were such as these, that men rich, and learned, and great, should wholly deny themselves and their own wisdom, and become fools; was this ever likely?" So when men fall down before Christ, God alone is glorified for their conversion.[10]

2. God chose preaching because our corrupt nature tends to seize upon visible representations and make them into idols. God reveals Himself in creation, but men worship the creation rather than the Creator (Rom. 1:19-25). God gave the church the sacraments as "visible signs," the Word preached to the eye, so to speak. Even though God chose the most common elements of bread and wine, men still try to make them into idols. But words are "the most naked and simple representation" God can make of Himself "to reasonable creatures."[11]

Third, Goodwin explained why God chose the public hearing of the Word rather than the private reading of it, citing two reasons:

1. God intended to "confound Satan" in the same manner in which Satan took mankind captive. "Our first parents took their infidelity in by the ear, and therefore God thought good to let faith in the same way."[12]

2. God planned to call "many simple people" for whom reading would be difficult. Uneducated people can hear with understanding, so the preaching of the gospel may reach even the poor and the unlearned.[13]

Fourth, God chose the Word as preached or expounded, not only by reading it in public worship, for three reasons:

---

10. Goodwin, "The Constitution, Right Order and Government of the Churches," in *Works,* 11:362.

11. Goodwin, "The Constitution, Right Order and Government of the Churches," in *Works,* 11:362–63.

12. Goodwin, "The Constitution, Right Order and Government of the Churches," in *Works,* 11:363.

13. Goodwin, "The Constitution, Right Order and Government of the Churches," in *Works,* 11:363.

1. God chose the preached Word because people often need help in understanding it and applying it to their lives. In Acts 8:30–31, Philip asked the eunuch who was reading Isaiah's prophecy, "Understandest thou what thou readest?" The eunuch responded, "How can I, except some man should guide me?" Therefore the church needs men who will devote themselves to study the Word and to explain it to others (Ezra 7:10).[14]

2. After Christ ascended to heaven, He "gave gifts unto men" (Eph. 4:8). Some of His best gifts are given to ministers of the Word (1 Cor. 3:22), who can expound the treasures of wisdom and knowledge in Christ (Col. 2:3).[15]

3. Ordinarily God does not convert people by the letter of the Word but by the "spiritual meaning of it, as revealed and expounded." The preacher opens the husk of a Scripture passage and finds the kernel. The devil can twist the letters of Scripture to his own purposes, but faithful ministers open its meaning and apply it to the soul as a physician applies medicine.[16]

Fifth, God choose to have His Word preached by men, not by angels or by His own voice for the following two reasons:

1. God's voice terrified the people of Israel, whereas human preachers are more familiar to us by matching our nature and situation (Deut. 5:25–27).

2. Angels also cause people to tremble. We are also "apt to worship them, as John would have done (Rev. 22:8)." So God saw fit to appoint men as the interpreters and preachers of His saving Word.[17]

The Puritans believed that the faithful preaching of the Word is the chief means by which Christ draws sinners to Himself to save them. To preach the gospel, Puritan pastors were willing to suffer great hardship, defy opposition, and face death because God had

---

14. Goodwin, "The Constitution, Right Order and Government of the Churches," in *Works,* 11:363.

15. Goodwin, "The Constitution, Right Order and Government of the Churches," in *Works,* 11:363.

16. Goodwin, "The Constitution, Right Order and Government of the Churches," in *Works,* 11:364.

17. Goodwin, "The Constitution, Right Order and Government of the Churches," in *Works,* 11:364.

called them to this vitally important task. Central to their calling was their belief in the importance of the human soul.

The Importance of the Human Soul

In the twenty-first century, some ministers are embarrassed by their calling, especially when dealing with people who have advanced degrees or who are on the cutting edge of science, medicine, law, or finance. As we saw in the last chapter, Gordon MacDonald expressed the feeling of many pastors when he was intimidated by the magnificence and scientific know-how of the culture around us.

The apparent glory of this world rests upon the false assumptions of materialism, however. Human life does not consist of the pleasures of the body, possessions bought with money, and pride in our earthly accomplishments. When we come to see our fellow human beings as people with immortal souls headed for an unknown eternity, we will cease to measure them by the world's standards. With the right perspective, we will see the gospel ministry as the greatest and most noble work of all.

Seventeenth-century Puritan pastors highly valued their calling because they had a high view of the human soul. Henry Scougal (1650–1678) wrote, "We have to do with rational and immortal souls, those most noble and divine substances which proceed from God, and are capable of being united to Him eternally, but withal in hazard of being eternally separated from Him."[18]

Flavel reminds us that God is concerned about the souls of mankind, and ministers will be held accountable for the souls of those entrusted to their care: "The precious and immortal souls of men are committed to us; souls, about which God hath concerned his thoughts from eternity; for the purchase of which Christ hath shed his own blood; for the winning and espousing of which to himself, he hath put you into this office; at whose hands he will also require an account of them in that great day."[19]

---

18. Henry Scougal, *The Works of the Rev. Henry Scougal* (Morgan, Pa.: Soli Deo Gloria, 2002), 214.

19. Flavel, "The Character of a True Evangelical Pastor," in *Works*, 6:584.

Thomas Goodwin reminds us that "all heaven, all hell and often-times earth" are concerned about the conversion of each human soul. He wrote:

> The converting and drawing of a soul to believe is a business of infinite moment; and why? Because all heaven, and all hell, and often times earth, or much on earth, are stirred about it, even as they use [are accustomed] to be at great transactions. What a stir there is in the spirits of men when a great transaction falls out in state affairs! There is much more in this. All in heaven are stirred, for you have seen that the three persons move in it; and Christ tells us there is joy in heaven even amongst the angels when a soul is turned to God. And all in hell are stirred about it too, for all the devils rage and come forth, and are all in arms. The strong man, when he is bound and cast out, is in a rage, and therefore pours forth all the floods of persecutions and disgraces, and temptations, and violence upon the soul.[20]

Watson gave two final reasons why pastors (and all Christians) should value the human soul and desire to lead others to Christ: all living things propagate, and every member added to Christ's body is a jewel added to His crown. He explained that a minister of the Word

> is not content to go to heaven alone but wants to take others there. Spiders work only for themselves, but bees work for others. A godly man is both a diamond and a lodestone—a diamond for the sparkling luster of grace and a lodestone for his attractiveness. He is always drawing others to embrace piety. Living things have a propagating virtue…. It is glory to Christ when multitudes are born to him. Every star adds a luster to the sky; every convert is a member added to Christ's body and a jewel adorning his crown. Though Christ's glory cannot be increased, as he is God, yet as he is mediator, it may.[21]

Mercy for Souls Facing Hell

The Puritans were spurred to preach on hell by the thought of human souls departing this life without Christ to spend eternity in hell, to

---

20. Thomas Goodwin, "Of Justifying Faith," in *Works*, 8:150.
21. Watson, *The Godly Man's Picture*, 184–85.

live forever in darkness and torment, cut off from God. Compassion for souls heading to hell should spur all Christians into action. Sadly, in the twenty-first century, little is said about hell in sermons or in popular Christian literature. What was a major evangelistic emphasis in the past has been expunged from the mouths of today's preachers. Well-meaning evangelicals today either ignore the subject altogether or propose that people will have a second chance to accept Christ after death. Or they embrace the heresy of soul-annihilation at death or when Christ comes again and perhaps even flirt with the idea of universal salvation.

Modern pastors who do not preach on hell may fear the consequences of preaching on such an offensive topic on a Sunday morning. Vocal critics might fault a minister for being too negative. Visitors shopping for a church might find the topic a colossal turn-off. Regardless, God has called us to declare "all the counsel of God" (Acts 20:27) concerning the way of salvation. From the attention that Jesus devoted to the topic of hell in His preaching, it is clear that He regarded it as a vital part of preaching the gospel.

Hell was very real to Puritan pastors. They thus preached and taught a great deal about it, but not without compassion for the lost. In reading through some of their sermons and writings, one can almost see the tear stains on each page that refers to eternal damnation. Solomon Stoddard was deeply concerned about people in his day who did not grasp the nature of hell and its eternal severity. He wrote,

> Many men are not aware what a terrible thing it is to be damned. They have a deeper sense of poverty and reproach than they have of damnation. They look upon hell as an uncomfortable place; they think that if it must be their portion to go to hell they shall bear it as well as others; they are not likely to go there alone. They seldom think of it. They look upon it as a remote thing at a great distance, and it doesn't terrify them.[22]

Almost every Puritan writer addressed the topic of hell, but a few works stand out for our consideration. Thomas Vincent (1634–1678)

---

22. Solomon Stoddard, "Preaching the Gospel to the Poor in Spirit," in *Puritan Pulpit*, 230.

wrote an entire book on the subject, *Fire and Brimstone,* in which he compared the "everlasting burnings" of hell with the sulfuric fire that destroyed Sodom and to the volcanic fire of Mount Etna, which had erupted in 1537. Vincent's goal in these comparisons was to show that hell is closer than people think, and its fires will never be extinguished. He wrote:

> When you hear of Sodom and Gomorrah's burning, you might think this was done long ago and be unconcerned. When you hear of Etna's burning, you might think this was far away and be unconcerned. But when we come to discourse of hell's burnings, here you are all concerned. Those burnings are past; these are burnings to come. Those burnings were for a while; these burnings will be forever. The greatest part of the children of men will be cast into these burnings, and very few comparatively will escape. Oh, what a vast number of all kindreds, nations and languages will there be tormented in hell forever! What a vast number of professing Christians, yea, of professors of the gospel! You need to look to it that none of you are found in that number.[23]

Vincent urged readers to ponder the endless duration of suffering in hell. He warned,

> When you have been the space of as many years in hell as there are stars in the firmament, as there are drops of dew upon the earth in the morning, as there are spires of grass which spring out of the earth, as there are drops of water in the ocean, as there are sands upon the seashore, your torments will be as far from being assuaged, and as far from being ended, as at the first minute of your entrance into this dreadful place.[24]

Robert Bolton also wrote about hell and eternal judgment. He summarized the two parts of hellish torment as privation and pain. He said that the privation of all good is the most horrible part because,

> [The loss] of a taste of those overflowing rivers of pleasure... one hour's company with all the crowned saints and glorious

---

23. Thomas Vincent, *Fire and Brimstone* (Morgan, Pa.: Soli Deo Gloria, 1999), 122.
24. Vincent, *Fire and Brimstone,* 148.

inhabitants of that happy place; but of one glance at the glorified body of Jesus Christ; but of one glimpse of that unapproachable light, and Jehovah's face in glory—I say, the loss but of any one of these would be a far dearer and more invaluable loss than that of ten thousand worlds, were they all composed of purest gold, and brim-full with richest jewels.[25]

When addressing fellow colleagues in ministry, the Puritans didn't spare words, either. Pastors such as Bunyan and Baxter challenged ministers to examine their own souls in view of the value of human souls and the horrors of hell. Baxter wrote:

Must I turn to my Bible to show a preacher where it is written that a man's soul is worth more than a world—much more, therefore, than a hundred pounds a year? Or that both we and all that we have are God's, and should be employed to the utmost for his service? Or that it is inhuman cruelty to let souls go to hell, for fear my wife and children should fare somewhat the harder, or live at lower rates; when, according to God's ordinary way of working by means, I might do much to prevent their misery, if I would but a little displease my flesh, which all who are Christ's have crucified with its lusts?[26]

Bunyan was even bolder. He asked, "Will it grieve thee to see thy whole parish come bellowing after thee to hell, crying out, 'This we may thank thee for; thou didst not teach us the truth; thou didst lead us away with fables thou wast afraid to tell us of our sins, lest we should not put meat fast enough into thy mouth?'"[27]

Flavel challenges today's pastors to compare the torments of hell with the costs of ministry on earth. Should not knowledge of those torments compel us to make the most of every opportunity God gives us to be merciful to people's souls by warning them of the judgment to come? "Would you think any care, any pains, any self-denial too much, to save and redeem one of these opportunities?"[28]

---

25. Robert Bolton, *The Four Last Things,* 83.

26. Baxter, *The Reformed Pastor,* 142–43.

27. Bunyan, *The Riches of John Bunyan,* 390.

28. John Flavel, "A Treatise of the Soul of Man," in *Works,* 2:233.

The Spiritual Battle

Along with recognizing that God saves souls through the preaching of the gospel, that human souls are precious, and that hell is real, the Puritans also understood that following Christ involves us in a massive though unseen war. An enemy seeks to destroy us and the sheep God has placed under our care. His goal is to rob our Lord of the glory due His name. Preaching the gospel is a key part of "fighting the good fight" to obtain victory over this deadly foe.

Puritan pastors often preached and wrote about the spiritual battle Christians face daily against Satan, who is a ravening wolf, and other false teachers who come to us in sheep's clothing. They offer most helpful teaching on how to live the Christian life when under attack.[29] John Bunyan's allegorical work, *The Holy War,* is particularly relevant. So is *Precious Remedies against Satan's Devices,* a book by Thomas Brooks, which is a virtual encyclopedia on spiritual warfare. Brooks documents every type of scheme, temptation, and allurement that Satan regularly uses to defeat Christians and divide the church. He also provides helpful and practical "remedies" or weapons to defeat Satan's schemes.[30]

Richard Alleine (1611–1681) published *The World Conquered by the Faithful Christian* to encourage Christians to keep striving for victory because, "A true Christian has his enemies under his feet even while he is in the fight. He is a soldier as soon as he is a saint, and he is

---

29. In addition to the works mentioned in this section, see Isaac Ambrose, *War with Devils; Ministration of, and Communion with Angels* (Glasgow: Joseph Galbraith and Co., 1769); Benjamin Colman, *The Case of Satan's Fiery Dart* (Boston: Rogers and Fowle, for J. Edwards, 1744); John Downame, *The Christian Warfare against the Devil, World, and Flesh* (1604; facsimile repr., Vestavia Hills, Ala.: Solid Ground Christian Books, 2009); Richard Gilpin, *Daemonologia Sacra, or, A Treatise on Satan's Temptations* (1677; repr., Morgan, Pa.: Soli Deo Gloria, 2000); William Gouge, *The Whole-Armour of God* (London: John Beale, 1616); William Gurnall, *The Christian in Complete Armour: A Treatise of the Saints' War Against the Devil,* two volumes in one (1662–1665; repr., Edinburgh: Banner of Truth, 2002); Benjamin Keach, *War with the Devil* (Coventry: T. Luckman, [1763]); William Spurstowe, *The Wiles of Satan* (1666; Morgan, Pa.: Soli Deo Gloria, 2004); Samuel Willard, *The Christian's Exercise by Satan's Temptations* (Boston: B. Green and J. Allen for Benjamin Eliot, 1701).

30. Thomas Brooks, *Precious Remedies against Satan's Devices* (Edinburgh: Banner of Truth, 2000).

a conqueror as soon as he is a soldier. His very taking up arms ensures his victory."[31] On the other hand, the world and the devil are formidable enemies who darken and deaden the minds of men to spiritual truths and stir them up to evil.[32] Alleine proposed sixteen measures, offensive and defensive, to win victory over the world and Satan.

Isaac Ambrose, in his book *The Christian Warrior,* reminded Christians of the cruel ways in which Satan tries to deceive, afflict, and destroy people who are about to die:

> There can be no doubt that such a subtle enemy as the devil has an endless variety of temptations for dying men.... Some he drives to unfounded confidence, others to distrust. Some he fills with spiritual pride, others with dejection. He persuades some that they are rich and have need of nothing, and tells others that they have no grace at all. Some he fills with too confident assurance of their election, others with fear that they are reprobates. Some he fills with overmuch sorrow through fear of eternal death, others he stupefies that they mind neither death nor judgment.[33]

Therefore, fellow pastors, take heart. We are engaged in a battle for the everlasting souls of men. Is it any wonder that Satan uses everything at his disposal to discourage, tempt, and overthrow us as faithful ministers? Indeed, the discouragements you face, the dangers that beset you, and even depression itself are weapons in Satan's arsenal, forged in wickedness and raised against you to destroy you.

The Puritans were very much aware that ministers of the Word are prime targets for Satan's deadliest schemes and assaults. They found encouragement in the midst of battle by keeping two important truths in mind. First, if Satan is attacking you, you must be doing something that he doesn't like. Baxter warned pastors, "If you will be leaders against the prince of darkness, he will spare you no further than God restraineth him. He beareth the greatest malice to those that are engaged to do him the greatest mischief."[34] The preacher of the

---

31. Richard Alleine, *The World Conquered by the Faithful Christian* (Morgan, Pa.: Soli Deo Gloria, 1995), 2.

32. Alleine, *The World Conquered,* 11–41.

33. Isaac Ambrose, *The Christian Warrior* (Morgan, Pa.: Soli Deo Gloria, 1997), 138.

34. Baxter, *The Reformed Pastor,* 117.

gospel is a holy invader pressing into the territory of the devil. We must therefore not be slack in our efforts, shirk our duty, or shrink back from danger.

Second, we should not be surprised by bitter opposition or persistent attacks against us. The ancient murderer knows that his time is short. He wars against the Lamb of God, but the Lamb will yet overcome him, for He is the Lord of lords and King of kings. We who stand with this Lamb are "called, and chosen, and faithful" (Rev. 17:14). Thus, encourage yourself with the words of comfort that Flavel offers:

> But whenever the gospel comes with Spirit and power, laying the axe to the root, shewing men the vanity of their ungrounded hopes, pressing the necessity of regeneration and faith, this preaching quickly gives an alarm to hell, and raises all manner of opposition against it.... No prince on earth is more jealous of the revolt of his subjects than he; and it is time for him to bestir himself, when the gospel comes to dethrone him, as it doth in the faithful preaching of it.... O what showers of calumnies, and storms of persecution doth he pour upon the names and persons of Christ's faithful ambassadors! Certainly, he owes Christ's ministers a spite, and they shall know and feel it, if ever he get them within the compass of his chain. But let this discourage none employed in this glorious design; the Lord is with them to protect their persons and reward their diligence.[35]

35. John Flavel, "England's Duty," in *Works*, 4:204.

PART SIX

Eternity

We may say of our work, with reason, what the painter vainly boasted of: "The impressions we make shall last forever."

— HENRY SCOUGAL

❦

CHAPTER 15

The Reward of Grace

The hope of glory (Rom. 5:2) and the promise of a reward for our toil is the final catalyst for encouraging us as pastors.[1] Our work is an immortal work. We will see in this chapter how seventeenth-century pastors were blessed by considering the temporal and eternal rewards that Christ promises to His servants. Let us begin by viewing in general what the Puritan pastors thought about these rewards, then look at three specific rewards mentioned by Puritan authors.

The Nature of the Promised Rewards

From the beginning of our study on Puritan pastors, we have seen that the greatest motivation for their work was to honor Christ's name. The greatest reward for them, as it is for all Christians, was to know Christ and have communion with Him. When the seventy disciples returned to Jesus and joyfully reported that even the devils were subject to them in His name, Jesus replied, "Rejoice not, that the spirits are subject unto you; but rather rejoice, because your names are written in heaven" (Luke 10:20). Jesus was teaching them and all His servants that our greatest joy and reward is the love of Christ and the inheritance laid up for us in heaven. Johann Franck thus wrote:

> Hence with earthly treasure!
> Thou art all my pleasure,
> Jesus all my choice.

---

1. "This reward is not of merit, but of grace" (Heidelberg Catechism, Q. 63).

Hence, thou empty glory!
Naught to me thy story,
    Told with tempting voice.
Pain or loss or shame or cross
    Shall not from my Savior move me,
    Since He deigns to love me.[2]

The Puritans were not averse to looking at the gracious rewards promised to God's servants in Scripture. Henry Scougal wrote, "If your work is great, your reward is infinitely greater, and you have omnipotence engaged in your assistance."[3] Increase Mather, a New England pastor, encouraged ministers to consider the rewards promised to them, saying:

> And let us consider, that our service will be rewarded, though it may be not by men. We may do the most generous and general service for our people, and be ill rewarded by an ungrateful world. But we serve a better master than is the generation whom we serve, we serve the Lord Jesus Christ; and he will be sure to reward whatever service we have done according to the will of God.... If he that has given a cup of cold water to a disciple shall be rewarded, what a glorious reward shall that man have, who has been influential to the conversion and salvation of many souls.[4]

Puritan pastors also cherished the promises in passages such as Matthew 6:4, 6, 18 and Hebrews 6:10, which remind God's faithful servants that He sees what is done in secret, and the work that His servants do will never be forgotten. Flavel also assured Christ's servants that God does not forget anything done in His name:

> But far beyond this; what will it be to hear Christ, the prince of pastors, say in that day, "Well done good and faithful servant; thou hast been faithful over a few things, I will make thee ruler over many things: enter thou into the joy of thy Lord" (Matt. 25:21). O sirs! We serve a good master, who is not unrighteous

---

2. Johann Frank, "Jesus, Priceless Treasure" (1653; Eng. trans. Catherine Winkworth, 1863), *Psalter Hymnal* (Grand Rapids: Publication Committee of the Christian Reformed Church, 1959), 441.

3. Scougal, *Works,* 249. (The quote introducing part 6 is found on p. 233.)

4. Increase Mather, "David and His Generation," in *Jeremiads,* 30.

to forget our work, and labour of love for his name-sake. He keeps an exact account of all your fervent prayers, of all your instructive and persuasive sermons; and all your sighs, groans, and pantings, with every tear and drop of sweat, are placed like marginal notes against your labours in his book, in order to a full reward.[5]

Foxcroft warned pastors not to apply the world's standards of success (immediate, tangible results) when evaluating their work. He wrote: "Their acceptance and reward is in proportion to the degree of their care and pains, and not to the event and success; it is measured by their fidelity, not by the efficacy of their labors—for this is wholly of the Lord, and their sufficiency is from God."[6]

Nonetheless, pastors today should read 1 Corinthians 3:12–15 concerning the building materials they use in their ministries. Paul warns us that our work will be tried by fire, "If any man's work abide which he hath built...he shall receive a reward" (v. 14). Gillespie said the fires of God's kiln are already at work, testing the quality of the materials used. He wrote:

There is a fire which will prove every man's work, even an accurate trial and strict examination thereof, according to the rule of Christ; a narrow inquiry into, and exact discovery of every man's work...whether this fiery trial be made by the searching and discovering light of the word in a time of reformation, or by affliction, or in a man's own conscience at the hour of death. If by some or all of these trials, a minister's work be found to be what it ought to be, he shall receive a special reward and praise; but if he have built wood, hay, and stubble, he shall be like a man whose house is set on fire about his ears; that is, he shall suffer loss, and his work shall be burnt, yet himself shall escape.[7]

A gracious character is another aspect of the rewards that Scripture and the Puritan pastors write about. The Lord promises to reward His servants for their faithfulness and according to the materials used, but in the end, His reward will surpass the value of all

---

5. Flavel, "The Character of a True Evangelical Pastor," in *Works*, 6:580.
6. Foxcroft, *The Gospel Ministry*, 73.
7. George Gillespie, "Sermon Preached to the House of Lords (1645)," in *Works*, 10.

our work. Gurnall said this reward is hardly equal to the labors that secure it. He wrote:

> The Christian's labor here bears no proportion at all to his reward hereafter; and therefore the apostle says that it is not worthy to be compared with the glory that shall be revealed. His labor is finite, but his reward is infinite; and there is no proportion between finite and infinite. There is but little proportion, you will admit, betwixt a drop of water and the sea; yet there is some, because, though vastly greater, yet not infinitely greater. But between finite and infinite, there is none at all…. The Christian's reward is infinite in its duration. Their reward is an everlasting life; but their work and labor for the Lord is so short… The Christian is a few hours in the field at his work and then is called into an everlasting rest in the Father's house.[8]

Spiritual Children

One specific reward of ministry is the joy of begetting spiritual children in Christ. Spiritual children include not only our own "covenant children" by birth or adoption, but also the believers we have evangelized, mentored to follow Him, and even instructed to preach in the name of Christ. Bunyan illustrates this thought beautifully in *Pilgrim's Progress*. Christian is led into a small room by Interpreter where he sees a picture of a grave-looking man whose eyes are lifted up to heaven, with the world to his back, books in his hands, and a crown of gold on his head. When Christian asks Interpreter the meaning of the picture, he is told:

> The man whose picture this is, is one of a thousand; he can beget children, 1 Cor. 4:15, travail in birth with children, Gal. 4:19, and nurse them himself when they are born. And whereas thou seest him with eyes lifted up to heaven, the best of books in his hand, and the law of truth written on his lips; it is to show thee that his work is to know and to unfold dark things to sinners; even as also thou seest him stand as if pleaded with men. And whereas thou seest the world as cast behind him, and that

---

8. William Gurnall, *The Christian's Labor and Reward* (Morgan, Pa.: Soli Deo Gloria, 2004), 41.

a crown hangs over his head; that is to show thee that, slighting and despising the things that are present for the love that he hath to his Master's service, he is sure, in the world that comes next, to have glory for his reward.[9]

The apostle Paul tells Thessalonian believers that when Christ comes again, they will be Paul's joy and crown of rejoicing (1 Thess. 2:19–20). And he reminds Corinthian believers that "though ye have ten thousand instructors in Christ, yet have ye not many fathers: for in Christ Jesus I have begotten you through the gospel" (1 Cor. 4:15). But Paul also begat other spiritual children: Timothy, "my own son in the faith" (1 Tim. 1:2), noting that "as a son with the father, he hath served with me in the gospel" (Phil. 2:22); Titus, "mine own son after the common faith" (Titus 1:4); Onesimus, "my son…whom I have begotten in my bonds" (Philemon 10); and doubtless many others. Paul guided these men into the way of Christ, taught them the fundamentals of the faith, and trained them for the ministry.

Many Puritan pastors knew the frustration of working hard but seeing few spiritual children as a result. They were helped by cultivating a long-term view of their work. John Cotton reminded pastors to consider that God often works in hidden ways: "But if a minister complain (as you say) of not converting one soul in forty years. First consider he might convert some and never know it; as Elijah turned many to righteousness who knew not one."[10]

Another New England pastor, Solomon Stoddard, was uplifted by realizing that the lessons and sermons he taught now could be used in the future as the Spirit enabled a person to recall the truths learned as a youth:

> If men hear the gospel and don't make a right use of it now, yet they will retain the knowledge of it, and it may do them service afterwards…. It may be, when they have no opportunity to hear the gospel, they will call to mind what they have heard some years before, and ponder on what has been preached to them formerly…. They may be made poor in spirit when they lie upon

---

9. Bunyan, "Pilgrim's Progress," in *Works*, 3:98.

10. See 1 Kings 19:14, 18. John Cotton, "A Letter to Herbert Palmer (1626)," in *The Correspondence of John Cotton*, 117.

a sick bed and cannot hear the word preached; and when what they formerly heard may work effectually on them.[11]

Ministers today may be discouraged by a lack of spiritual fruit upon their work. Sometimes we are disheartened by a lack of response to our evangelistic work. We may become reluctant to scatter the seed of the Word unless we have some guarantee that it will numerically "grow our church." Churches and even pastors may then discourage missionary work or offerings for missions, opting to keep their members' money and talents at home where results are more visible and immediate. Churches with budgets and ministries that reflect this near-sighted perspective should think in larger and longer terms. Ministers who are jealous of money and talents sent to faithful servants of God on the mission field should examine their own hearts and ask God for a new vision for ministry that is crafted with the day of judgment in mind.

Spiritual Legacies

The covenant of grace teaches us to think of people who will come after us and the legacy we should leave to them. God says in Genesis 17:7, "I will establish my covenant between me and thee and thy seed after thee in their generations for an everlasting covenant." Raising spiritual children is a way to amass a wonderful legacy. Another is to produce writings, testimonies, and songs that may be read or sung now and passed down to future generations. The hymn that Horatio Spafford wrote after losing his children in the Atlantic Ocean continues to bring comfort to believers in extreme sorrow. The words of "It Is Well with My Soul" have eased the suffering of countless saints. One of the joys in heaven may be the testimonies of people who have been comforted by his song.

Another legacy that we pass to others is due to the hard work and costly battles fought by earlier generations so that people today may have the gospel message and hear it preached. While we may see few results of our labors today, we should remain faithful to our

---

11. Stoddard, "Preaching the Gospel to the Poor in Spirit," in *The Puritan Pulpit*, 226.

task, knowing that we thereby become part of the holy succession of faithful witnesses who have earnestly contended for the faith through the ages. Flavel wrote:

> How dear hath this inheritance of truth cost some Christians? How little hath it cost us? We are entered into their labours; we reap in peace what they sowed in tears, yea, in blood. O the grievous sufferings that they chose to endure! Rather than to deprive us of such an inheritance, those noble souls, heated with the love of Christ, and care for our souls, made many bold and brave adventures for it; and yet at what a low rate do we value what cost them so dear? Like young heirs that never knew the getting of an estate, we spend it freely. Lord, help us thankfully and diligently to improve thy truths, while we are in quiet possession of them. Such intervals of peace and rest are usually of no long continuance with thy people.[12]

Another spiritual legacy is revival in churches and in nations. The Spirit of God has caused revivals in answer to much earnest prayer. He has used the sermons of God's faithful servants to accomplish extraordinary things. The New England Puritans, beginning with John Winthrop, prayed earnestly, worked diligently, and sacrificed dearly to make their colony a model of a Christian community as "a city upon a hill," doing justly, loving mercy, and walking humbly with God (Micah 6:8); practicing self-denial, assisting the needy, loving one's neighbors, and promoting a concern for the common good.[13] They wanted the world to see God's righteousness unfolding in the lives of His people to His ultimate praise and glory.

Later, when the founders' vision began to fade, Jonathan Edwards prayed for revival in the churches of New England and throughout the world. Solomon Stoddard, who documented many smaller revivals in his own congregation in Northampton, also prayed for revival on a large scale. He preached a sermon titled, "The Way for a People to Live Long in the Land That God Has Given Them," in which he said,

---

12. Flavel, "The Heavenly Use of Earthly Things," *Works*, 5:176–77.
13. John Winthrop's *City upon a Hill*, 1630, http://www.mtholyoke.edu/acad/intrel/winthrop.htm (accessed January 10, 2011).

To ministers I say, labor after the saving conversion of men. The people among whom we live are already converted to the profession of the Gospel; labor after their sincere conversion.... If there is not a great deal of real piety in the land, neither regard to reputation nor the safety of their souls will make them carry well; if the country should have many judgments, that would not bring an unconverted people to reformation. Judgments will sooner destroy the bodies of men and the estates of men than their lusts; it is an easier matter to break the bones of men than the hearts of men.[14]

Stoddard's grandson lived to see the Great Awakening both abroad and at home, especially in Stoddard's church in Northampton under Edwards's ministry. In this massive revival God used the faithful preaching of the doctrines of grace passed on by Puritan ministers of a bygone age. The foundation for revival was laid by earlier Puritans who had labored so hard for the good of succeeding generations.

If you are discouraged in ministry today, perhaps you ought to take a step back from your work and consider the questions below. Hopefully the answers to these questions will spur you to think ahead and aim at long-term results in your ministry.

1. How has the Lord used the labors of faithful men in the past to lay a foundation for your Christian life and work today?

2. Has the Lord ever used you to mentor a future pastor, missionary, teacher, or other full-time Christian worker?

3. How has the Lord used you in ministry outside your congregation?

4. Has the Lord given you the gift of writing to produce a written legacy of faith and devotion for others?

5. Has the Lord given you the opportunity to sit beside a dying member of your church and hear the person's testimony that included gratitude for your ministry?

---

14. Solomon Stoddard, "The Way for a People to Live Long in the Land," in *The Puritan Pulpit*, 183.

6. Can you think of people whose faith has been strengthened under your ministry?

7. Consider the most difficult time you have experienced in ministry. How was God's name exalted or His purpose accomplished as a result of that experience?

Vindication

Another reward that may seem out of place, especially with the Puritans, is vindication for God's children. This vindication is not getting even, taking vengeance on someone, or gloating after a major victory. Vindication, in the mind of the Puritan pastors, is the manifestation of God's righteousness in establishing the righteousness of His faithful servants: "And he shall bring forth thy righteousness as the light, and thy judgment as the noonday" (Ps. 37:6). "No weapon that is formed against thee shall prosper; and every tongue that shall rise against thee in judgment thou shalt condemn. This is the heritage of the servants of the LORD, and their righteousness is of me, saith the LORD" (Isa. 54:17). Those who walk by faith, and with joy and delight seek to live according to the will of God in all good works, can expect to be vindicated, if not in this life, surely at the last day and in the life to come. The apostle Paul sees Christ's second coming as a day of vindication when the knees of all mankind will bow, and the tongues of all will confess that Jesus is Lord (Phil. 2:10–11).

Pastors may surely find this type of vindication a reward for their faithful service, long hours, bitter tears, and sore trials. Those who have been reviled because of their faith in Christ, even martyred for the cause of Christ, will be rewarded at the end with unending joy. The sufferings they endure and the time, talents, and gifts they give are not in vain. They will be vindicated on the last day, but even before that, in their hour of death. Robert Bolton wrote of this triumph that saints enjoy the moment they die:

> But that happy man, who, in the short summer's day of his miserable and mortal life, gathers grace with a holy greediness, plies the noble trade of Christianity with resolution and undauntedness of spirit, against the boisterous current and corruptions of the times.... I say that man, though ever so contemptible

in the eyes of the worldly wise, though ever so scornfully trod upon and overflown by the tyranny and swelling pride of those ambitious self-flattering giants, who, like mighty winds when they have blustered a while, breathe out into nought, shall most certainly, upon his dying-bed, meet with a glorious troop of blessed angels; ready and rejoicing to guard and conduct his departing soul into his Master's joy.[15]

Conclusion: All of Grace

Jesus teaches us powerfully that all of these rewards accrue to us from God's grace. In ourselves, we are but unprofitable servants who deserve no rewards. Jesus says in Luke 17:10, "So likewise ye, when ye shall have done all those things which are commanded you, say, We are unprofitable servants: we have done that which was our duty to do."

It is God's grace to be granted to do a good work and God's grace to be rewarded for a good work done. As A. A. Hodge quipped: "It is all *of grace*—a grace called a reward added to a grace called a work." Perhaps the Belgic Confession says it best: "We are beholden [obliged] to God for the good works that we do, and not He to us, for it is God that worketh in us both to will and to do of His own good pleasure" (art. 24).

As gospel ministers, let us keep our hand on the plow, not looking back, for whoever looks back is not fit for the kingdom of God (Luke 9:62). Let us persevere in the work of the Lord, aiming for His glory and the heralding of His gospel message, even as we trust that we shall be the recipients of the triune God's gracious rewards forever.

---

15. Bolton, *Four Last Things,* 9.

CHAPTER 16

The Glories of Heaven

Our encouragement of today's pastors through the study of seventeenth-century writers will conclude with a literary tour of the glories of heaven. We will begin with the book *Visions of Heaven and Hell*, which itself has been on a journey. Though the book is listed under the authorship of John Bunyan and has been sold under his name for centuries, Bunyan did not write the book.

George Larkin[1] wrote the book, which was first published as *The World to Come, the glories of heaven and the terrors of hell* (1699). After Larkin's death in 1725, Edward Midwinter reprinted the book under John Bunyan's name, with the title *The Visions of John Bunyan; being his last remains, giving an account of the Glories of Heaven*

---

1. George Larkin (c. 1642–1707) was a printer and writer who associated with both political and religious dissenters against the establishment. He printed the first edition of Bunyan's *Grace Abounding* (1666), as well as works by Particular Baptists such as William Kiffin and Benjamin Keach. He also printed satires by Ralph Wallis and Andrew Marvell. His publications regularly landed him in hot water with the authorities. He was imprisoned at various times under the reigns of Charles II, James I, and William and Mary. In 1684 he was sentenced to a fine and to stand in the pillory for "printing a seditious paper" titled "Shall I, Shall I, No, No," urging readers not to conform to the Church of England. See Martin Dzelzainis, "George Larkin and the London literary underground 1666–1690," March 2006 Conference on "'This Persecuted Means': Radicalism and the Book, 1600–1870" (Princeton University, March 2–4, 2006), http://www.princeton.edu/csb/conferences/march_2006/papers/dzelzainis.pdf (accessed December 20, 2011). This paper is part of a forthcoming book by Martin Dzelzainis, *The Flower in the Panther: Truth Telling, Print, and Censorship in England, 1662–1695*.

and the Terrors of Hell, and of the World to Come. Perhaps Midwinter thought the book would sell better under Bunyan's name.[2]

The book tells the tale of Epenetus (cf. Rom. 16:5), a pastor who tries to witness to an atheist. The atheist, like infidels of every era, argues that God, Satan, heaven, and hell are not real. In trying to persuade the atheist that he is wrong, the pastor starts to doubt his own faith. His doubts eventually so overwhelm him that he decides to commit suicide. God intervenes with a still, small voice as the pastor is in the woods preparing to kill himself.

God sends an angel to Epenetus to tell the poor, discouraged pastor that God "saw with how much malice the grand enemy of souls desired thy ruin, and let him go on with hopes of overcoming thee, but still upheld thee by his secret power; through which, when Satan thought himself most sure, the snare is broken, and thou art escaped."[3]

The angel goes on to tell the pastor that he and the angel will take a journey together in a vision. The angel takes hold of Epenetus, and they see things Epenetus has never seen before. For example, the pastor asks the angel what a little spot far below them is. The angel says, "That little spot…that now looks so dark and contemptible, is that world of which you were so lately an inhabitant. Here you may see how little all that world appears, for a small part of which so many do unweariedly labour, and lay out all their strength and time to purchase it."[4]

Then the pastor and angel rise far above the world into the heavens beyond the sun and stars until they reach the third heaven (2 Cor. 12:2). They first make their way to the mansions of the blessed, where they stop to talk with the prophet Elijah. The pastor has many questions for the prophet, such as how heaven can be a place of perfect joy while its citizens are always experiencing new joys. Elijah explains that the blessed object of their happiness is the infinite and eternal God: "For the divine perfections being infinite, nothing less

---

2. George Offor, introduction to *The Whole Works of John Bunyan* (London: Blackie and Son, 1862), 1:cxxvi; John Brown, *John Bunyan: His Life, Times, and Work* (London: Hulbert Pub. Co., 1928), 434.

3. [George Larkin], "The World to Come," in *Bunyan's Grace Abounding to the Chief of Sinners; Heart's Ease in Heart Trouble; The World to Come, or Visions of Heaven and Hell; and the Barren Fig Tree* (London: J. F. Dove, 1827), 248.

4. Larkin, "The World to Come," 249.

than eternity can be sufficient to display their glory, which makes
our happiness eternally admit of new additions; and by a necessary
consequence our knowledge of it shall be eternally progressive too."[5]

Epenetus then notices that some saints seem to shine brighter than
others. He asks Elijah if there are different degrees of glory in heaven.
Elijah explains that the happiness and glory that the blessed enjoy in
heaven is a result of their salvation in Christ, their communion with
God, and their capacity for the love of God. "The ever-blessed God is
an unbounded ocean of light and life, and joy and happiness, still fill-
ing every vessel that is put therein, till it can hold no more; and though
the vessels are of several sizes, whilst each is filled there are none that
can complain."[6]

Next, Epenetus sees his mother. She "appeared extremely glorious, compassed round with rays of dazzling lustre." Epenetus can
scarcely bear to look upon her face because of its brightness. She gives
praise to God, saying, "For what I am, to Him that is on the throne,
and to the Lamb, be all the praise and glory; for He alone has made
me so. This robe of glory, which you see me wear, is only the reflection
of His own bright beams."[7] Epenetus says his mother speaks as one
filled with joy. She answers:

> You should not think this strange. The mighty wonders of
> Divine love and grace will be the subject of our song for ever.
> Nor should you call me mother here, although I once was so;
> for here all such relations cease, and are all swallowed up in
> God, who is alone the great Father of all this heavenly family:
> and I must tell you, Epenetus, you are far more dear to me, as
> you are one that loves and fears the Lord, and so, through faith,
> are his adopted son, than as you are the son born of my body.
> It is here our greatest mercy, that we have God the fountain of
> our happiness: and that all we enjoy is in and through Him,
> who is an object that is every way so adequate to all our most

---

5. Larkin, "The World to Come," 249.

6. Larkin, "The World to Come," 275.

7. Larkin, "The World to Come," 300–301.

enlarged capacities, that in enjoying Him, we enjoy all that we can ask or think.[8]

Such, and much more, are the glories that await us in eternity. Let us now leave Larkin's tour of heaven so we may travel with another seventeenth-century guide.

The Beautiful Picture

Our next guide is Samuel Rutherford, author of his famous *Letters*. A stalwart Covenanter, Rutherford is regarded as one of Scotland's greatest theologians. He lived in tumultuous times. He was appointed minister of the parish of Anwoth in 1627, but in 1630 was prosecuted for nonconformity. In 1638, he was deposed from office, barred from preaching, and imprisoned in Aberdeen. During his long life, Rutherford buried two wives and all his children. Through that suffering he found great comfort by contemplating the glories of Christ and heaven.

In 1630 Rutherford wrote to Lady Kenmure, Viscountess of Kenmure, who would lose her husband to an untimely death four years later. She would marry again, only to become a widow again after a short period of time. Her brother would be executed in 1661 for treason because of his Covenanter convictions.[9] Lady Kenmure needed an eternal perspective to prepare her for the years ahead. Rutherford wrote this letter to the Lady soon after the death of his first wife, who had suffered for many months. His thoughts are full of eternity:

> Madam, when you are come to the other side of the water, and have set down your foot on the shore of glorious eternity, and look back again to the waters and to your wearisome journey, and shall see in that clear glass of endless glory nearer to the bottom of God's wisdom, you shall then be forced to say, "If God had done otherwise with me than he hath done, I had never come to the enjoying of this crown of glory." It is your part now to believe, and suffer, and hope, and wait on: for I protest in the presence of that all-discerning eye who knoweth what I write

---

8. Larkin, "The World to Come," 302.

9. Rutherford himself was charged with treason in 1661, but died before his case could be tried.

and what I think, that I would not want the sweet experience of the consolations of God for all the bitterness of affliction: nay, whether God come to his children with a rod or a crown, if he come himself with it, it is well.[10]

Rutherford offered Lady Kenmure the same comfort that pastors today often give to believers who are perplexed by their suffering. Doubts and discouragements can also darken our minds as pastors when we minister to suffering parishioners in our congregations. The prospect of finally knowing God's purposes in our sufferings and how they were part of His wise and perfect plan will certainly be one of the great joys of eternity. To hear countless saints give praise and thanks because of God's grace in their lives will also be a tremendous blessing. It will be like walking through a vast art gallery to marvel at each beautiful portrait of God's grace, painted on the canvas with the dark strokes of suffering. As the late Corrie ten Boom often said, "God has a divine pattern for each of His children. Although the threads may seem knotted like embroidery…on the other side is a crown."[11]

Our tour guide isn't finished yet with what he wants us to know about heaven. In 1631 Rutherford wrote to Marion M'Naught about increasing persecution in the land. King James was attempting to compel the Scots to accept changes in public worship to bring the practice of the national church into conformity with the Church of England. Rutherford and many other ministers who opposed this conformity were ejected from their charges and prosecuted as criminals. In writing to M'Naught, Rutherford said that sixteen or seventeen pastors had already been "banished and silenced" in England. Rutherford reminded M'Naught that Christ, the heavenly husband and head of His earthly bride, the church, had also experienced many blows in "wooing his kirk" [church]. The bride should therefore not be surprised if she received similar treatment.

The devil would not succeed in destroying this marriage. But in the meantime, suffering Christians should keep in mind the consolation that awaits them in heaven. So Rutherford wrote: "When he

---

10. Rutherford, *Letters,* 19.

11. Corrie Ten Boom, *Tramp for the Lord* (Fort Washington, Pa.: Christian Literature Crusade, 1974), 104.

shall put his holy hand up to your face in heaven, and dry your face, and wipe the tears from your eyes, judge if you will not have cause then to rejoice."[12]

Glorified Minds and Bodies

Two more guides will lead us through the next part of the tour. Rutherford took us through God's art gallery of grace. Richard Baxter and Robert Bolton will now take us into the courts of heaven and through the restored lands of a new world. Baxter's qualification as a tour guide comes from his awareness of human mortality expressed in *The Saints' Everlasting Rest* (1649), written during a period of grave illness, and *Dying Thoughts* (1683), published not many years before his death in 1691.

Bolton wrote *The Four Last Things,* which contains the last series of sermons he preached to his congregation prior to his death in 1631. Bolton preached the first three topics, "Death, Judgment, and Hell," but became seriously ill on the weekend he had planned to preach on heaven. He died shortly after that, making clear what he had already written, "God then preparing him for the fruition of those inexplicable joys which he had provided for his people in contemplation."[13]

Baxter wrote in his books that what we will see and become in heaven is beyond our comprehension. But that should not stop us from looking into the things of heaven to contemplate their beauty. In *The Saints' Everlasting Rest*, he offers twelve reasons why our hearts ought to be fixed in heaven while we are still on earth. One of his reasons seems particularly apt for pastors: "Keeping your hearts in heaven will maintain the vigor of all your graces, and put life into all your duties."[14] Baxter also wrote about our curiosity about heaven and our insatiable need to have answers to many of life's perplexing questions. He then asked:

> If an angel from heaven came down on earth to tell us all of God
> that we would know, who would not turn his back on libraries

---

12. See Revelation 21:4. Rutherford, *Letters*, 24.

13. Bolton, *The Four Last Things,* iv.

14. Richard Baxter, *The Saints' Everlasting Rest* (New York: American Tract Society, n.d.), 287.

and universities, to go and discourse with such a messenger? For one hour's talk with him, what travel should I think too far, what cost too great? But here we must only have such intimations as will exercise faith, excite desire, and try us under the temptations of the world and the flesh. The light of glory is to reward the victory obtained by the conduct of the light of grace.[15]

He added these reasons for keeping our hearts in heaven:

- A heart set upon heaven is one of the most unquestionable evidences of your sincerity, and the mark of a work of grace in your life.

- A heart set upon heaven is the highest excellence of a truly Christian temper, or state of heart and mind.

- A heart set upon heaven is the nearest and truest way to enjoy the comfort we have in Christ.

- A heart set upon heaven will be a most excellent preservative against temptations and sin.

- A heart set upon heaven, with views of glory, will help us greatly in times of affliction.

- A heart set upon heaven will enable us to converse to others about heaven and be a blessing to them.

- A heart set upon heaven highly honors God as our Father in heaven.

- A heart set upon heaven obeys God and makes full use of wonderful discoveries that God's Word imparts concerning our future life of glory.

- A heart set upon heaven is a fitting response to the heart of God, which is so much set on us.

- A heart set upon heaven is a heart set on our greatest and most lasting interests in life as the children of a heavenly Father and heirs of an eternal kingdom.

---

15. Baxter, *Dying Thoughts* (Edinburgh: Banner of Truth, 2004), 67.

- A heart set upon heaven is wise, because there really is nothing but heaven worth setting our hearts upon. All we have and need comes from heaven; all that we hope and long for is waiting for us in heaven.

Bolton reminds us of the resurrected and glorified bodies that God's saints will have when Christ makes all things new. He said these bodies "shall last as long as God himself, and run parallel with the longest line of eternity."[16] He also said these bodies will be "utterly incapable of any corruptible quality, action, or alteration."[17]

They will be bodies with extraordinary power, too. Imagine, if you will, that our souls are made of the same substance and nature as the angels. Just one angel in a single night killed more than 185,000 men (2 Kings 19:35). Bolton went on to say,

> But then, when, to the soul's native strength, there is an addition of glorifying vigour, and God's mighty Spirit's more plentiful inhabitation; and it shall also put on a body, which brings with it, besides its own inherent power, an exact servicableness and sufficiency suited and apportioned to the soul's highest abilities and executions; how incredibly powerful and mighty may we suppose a saint in heaven shall be![18]

Consider too that our bodies will be spiritual and heavenly, not natural and earthy (1 Cor. 15:44, 47–49). We will no longer be encumbered with the weight of earth but will be swift in motion and never again weighed down with life's burdens. We will move so fast that "the body will presently be there where the soul would have it, of extraordinary speed, and incredibly short time."[19]

Baxter also reminds us that we will have glorified minds with which to contemplate all that God has done and to perfectly know ourselves and others. Imagine the joy of fellowship that never ends in parting. Baxter wrote:

---

16. Bolton, *The Four Last Things,* 107.
17. Bolton, *The Four Last Things,* 107.
18. Bolton, *The Four Last Things,* 108.
19. Bolton, *The Four Last Things,* 110.

I know that angels now love us, minister unto us, rejoice in our good, and are themselves far more holy and excellent creatures than we are; it is therefore my comfort to think that I shall better know them, and live in near and perpetual acquaintance and communion with them, and bear my part in the same choir in which they preside. And when I think how sweet one wise and holy companion has been to me here on earth, and how lovely his graces have appeared, O what a sight it will be when we shall see millions of the "spirits of just men made perfect" shining with Christ in perfect wisdom and holiness.[20]

It will be joyous to have all of eternity to investigate the work of God's hands in nature with eyes that are sharp and minds that never tire or forget. Baxter wrote in *Dying Thoughts:*

If indeed, we clearly saw the nature and connection of every creature in sea or land, what a connection of every spectacle would this spot of the creation be! How much more to see the whole creation! And I shall have as much of this as I shall be capable of; the wonders of God's works shall raise my soul in admiring, joyful praise forever.[21]

Robert Bolton said our minds "shall be extraordinarily and supernaturally enlarged and irradiated with the highest illuminations, largest comprehensions, and utmost extent of all possible comfortable knowledge of which such a creature is capable."[22] We will need these new minds so that we will "with wonderful ravishment of spirit, and spiritual joy, be admitted to the sight of those sacred secrets and glorious mysteries" which we cannot yet comprehend.[23]

Christ Our Glory
Even these glories dim beside the greatest hope of all for the Christian, which is to see Christ as He is and to be with Him forever. Fellow pastor, what hope can fill your heart more than the expectation of being with Christ? A few days before he died, Rutherford said, "I shall

20. Baxter, *Dying Thoughts*, 70.
21. Baxter, *Dying Thoughts*, 68.
22. Bolton, *The Four Last Things*, 113.
23. Bolton, *The Four Last Things*, 115.

shine, I shall see him as he is, I shall see him reign, and all his fair company with him…. My eyes shall see my Redeemer."[24] Richard Sibbes wrote,

> Heaven is not heaven without Christ. It is better to be in any place with Christ than to be in heaven itself without him. All delicacies without Christ are but as a funeral banquet. Where the master of the feast is away, there is nothing but solemnness. What is all without Christ? I say the joys of heaven are not the joys of heaven without Christ; he is the very heaven of heaven.[25]

Let us thus set our minds on heaven and our hearts on Christ. As Colossians 3:1–4 says, "If ye then be risen with Christ, seek those things which are above, where Christ sitteth on the right hand of God. Set your affection on things above, not on things on the earth. For ye are dead, and your life is hid with Christ in God. When Christ, who is our life, shall appear, then shall ye also appear with him in glory." Christopher Love asked, "Shall Christ our head be in heaven, and shall our hearts who are his members, lie groveling on the ground, and panting after the dust of the earth, making all our inquiry and labor after these?"[26] If we would be of any earthly good, we must first of all be heavenly minded.

To set your mind on heaven, fill yourself with thoughts of the most glorious Person ever to live. Thomas Goodwin said,

> Is Christ so glorious? What will heaven be, but the seeing of the glory of Christ? If God had created worlds of glorious creatures, they could have never expressed his glory as his Son; therefore heaven is thus expressed, John 17, "I will that they be with me, to behold my glory." Wherein lies therefore that great communion of glory that shall be in heaven? It is in seeing the glory of Christ, who is the image of the invisible God that is worshipped…. It is therefore the seeing of Christ that makes heaven; wherefore one

---

24. Samuel Rutherford, *Joshua Redivivus: or, Three Hundred and Fifty-two Religious Letters* (Glasgow: John Bryce, 1765), 522.

25. Richard Sibbes, "Christ is Best, Or St. Paul's Strait," in *Works*, 1:339.

26. Christopher Love, "Heaven's Glory, Hell's Terror," in *The Works of that Faithful Servant of Jesus Christ, Mr. Christopher Love* (Dalry: J. Gemmill, 1805), 1:8.

said, If I were cast into any hole, if I could have but a cranny to see Christ always, it would be heaven enough.[27]

Whatever discouragement you may face at present, whatever dark hole you may find yourself mired in, by the Spirit's gracious power, lift up your heart to God in heaven and contemplate the heavenly glory of Christ, seated at the right hand of power. That will be enough to raise your spirits, renew your sense of calling, and rekindle your love for God's Son, who first loved us.

27. Thomas Goodwin, "Three Sermons on Hebrews 1.1,2," in *Works*, 5:547–48.

Epilogue

The Puritan pastors of the seventeenth century constructed a vehicle to keep pastors moving forward in a Christ-centered and God-glorifying way. We hope you have found encouragement through their writings. Now that you have tasted some of their work, you might consider reading more.

However, their books and sermons will not bring you comfort, encouragement, and true zeal for ministry unless you have the keys to start the engine. One of those keys is beautifully illustrated in *Pilgrim's Progress* when Christian is imprisoned in Doubting Castle. Both Christian and Hopeful face the daily beatings and abuse of a giant named Despair. They didn't have to stay there, however, because Christian had the key called "Promise" all along. That key opened the doors of the dungeon in Doubting Castle. Likewise, discouraged pastors need not stay locked up in the dungeon of despair when there are so many wonderful promises already available to them in God's Word.

Richard Baxter tells us that there is another tyrant we must break free of to enjoy God's strength. To enjoy the freedom that Christ has already won for us, consider the tyrant described in a riddle in *The Reformed Pastor:*

> Yet it is so prevalent in some of us, that it inditeth [writes] our discourses, it chooseth our company, it formeth our countenances, it putteth the accent and emphasis upon our words.... It fills some men's minds with aspiring desires and designs; it possesseth them with envious and bitter thoughts against those

who stand in their light, or who, by any means, eclipse their glory, or hinder the progress of their reputation. O what a constant companion, what a tyrannical commander, what a sly and subtle insinuating enemy....

But alas, how frequently doth it go with us to our study, and there sit with us and do our work. How oft doth it choose our subject; and more frequently still, our words and ornaments. God biddeth us to be as plain as we can, for the informing of the ignorant; and as convincing and serious as we are able, for the melting and changing of unchanged hearts. But [it] stands by and contradicteth all, and produceth its toys and trifles, and polluteth rather than polisheth.[1]

This tyrannical enemy is *Pride*, which can be a terrible slave master for pastors. The apostle Peter says in 1 Peter 5:6–7 that the key to unlock the fetters of this giant is to "humble yourselves therefore under the mighty hand of God, that he may exalt you in due time: casting all your care upon him; for he careth for you." The key of humility unlocks the door and frees us from the giant Pride, and the key of promise frees us from the giant Despair through encouragement.

Christ is our ultimate encouragement. Dear pastor, your comfort and courage must be Christ, for in Him we find a glory that makes us press on to know Him better (Phil. 3:7–14). Pursue the Redeemer. William Bates (1625–1699) said God's glory shines in all His works, but "especially his glory is most resplendent in the work of redemption.... It is here that wisdom, goodness, justice, holiness, and power, are united in their highest degree and exaltation."[2]

When our souls are dry and our hearts are heavy, we need a glimpse of glory. John Owen said, "A continual contemplation of the glory of Christ, in his person, office, and grace...will carry us

---

1. Richard Baxter, *The Practical Works of the Rev. Richard Baxter, William Orme* (London: James Duncan, 1830), 14:154.

2. William Bates, "The Harmony of the Divine Attributes in the Contrivance and Accomplishment of Man's Redemption by the Lord Jesus Christ," in *The Whole Works of the Rev. W. Bates*, ed. W. Farmer (Harrisonburg, Va.: Sprinkle Publications, 1990), 236.

cheerfully, comfortably, and victoriously through life and death, and all that we have to conflict withal in either of them."[3]

Owen said, "Temptations, afflictions, changes, sorrows, dangers, fears, sickness, and pains do fill up no small part of [this present life]. And on the other hand, all our earthly relishes, refreshments, and comforts, are uncertain, transitory, and unsatisfactory; all things of each sort being embittered by the reminders of sin."[4]

However, "Our beholding by faith things that are not seen, things spiritual and eternal, will alleviate all our afflictions—make their burden light, and preserve our souls from fainting under them. Of these things the glory of Christ…is the principle, and in a due sense comprehensive of them all. For we behold the glory of God himself 'in the face of Jesus Christ' [2 Cor. 4:6]."[5]

So seek Christ, fellow pastors. Consider the counsels and suggestions of this book with the single-minded aim of knowing Christ better. Even if you walk in darkness and have no light, cling to Christ and do not let Him go.

Annie Hawks and Robert Lowry summarized these thoughts so well in the following verse: "I need Thee every hour, Most Holy One; O make me Thine indeed, Thou blessed Son! I need Thee, O I need Thee; every hour I need Thee! O bless me now, my Savior, I come to Thee."

---

3. John Owen, "The Glory of Christ," in *Works*, 1:277.
4. Owen, "The Glory of Christ," in *Works*, 1:278.
5. Owen, "The Glory of Christ," in *Works*, 1:278.